MarkMy Words

Instruction and Practice in Proofreading

Peggy Smith

Third Edition

EEI PRESS®

First edition 1987
Second edition 1993
Third edition 1997

Library of Congress Cataloging-in-Publication Data

Smith, Peggy, 1922–
    Mark my words : instruction & practice in proofreading /
Peggy Smith. — 3rd ed.
        p.   cm.
    Includes index.
    ISBN 0-935012-23-0
    1. Proofreading.   I. Title.
Z254.S653   1997
686.2'255—dc21   97-47038
                                                            CIP

EEI Press publishes other books on editorial topics and *The Editorial Eye*, a subscription newsletter focusing on standards and practices for excellence in publications. For a free catalog, call 800-683-8380, send e-mail to press@eeicom.com, or use the Web form at http://www.eeicom.com/press/.

EEI Press offers discounts for quantity orders from individuals, bookstores, corporations, nonprofit associations, and educational organizations. For more information, call or write to

EEI PRESS®
A Division of EEI Communications

66 Canal Center Plaza, Suite 200
Alexandria, VA 22314-5507
(703) 683-0683
Fax (703) 683-4915

"Proofreading," says James J. Kilpatrick,
"is like scrimshaw: It is getting to be a lost
art."

May this book help save the art and craft
of proofreading.

Contents

Chapter 6. Process, Procedures, and Tasks 84

Chapter 7. Queries and Corrections 98

Figures

Exercises

Answer Keys

Preface

Mark My Words is a manual for people who want to learn to proofread using the techniques that professional proofreaders have found most practical and effective.

This revision brings up to date the information proofreaders need in these times when fully electronic publishing is prevalent.

Throughout this book, the word *proofreader* refers to anyone who looks for errors in printed copy. A proofreader these days may well be someone who mostly does work other than proofreading—the operator of a word-processing program who keys a proposal from a writer's handwritten notes, the typographer who sets the type for a book, the editorial assistant who works in a newsletter publisher's office, the copy editor who prepares material for a scholarly journal, or the author who verifies the accuracy of the transcript that she dictated.

Whether you (or those you work for) think of the work as an expense or an investment, this book will start you on the way to a professional approach to proof-reading—working at the appropriate level with the techniques appropriate to your situation.

The exercises in this volume are designed for use in either a course of supervised instruction or a self-study program. Many of the exercises require comparison proofreading at a professional level with standard marks. The rationale is this: if you can read proof well by comparison, you can do any kind of proofreading; if you can meet high standards, you can adapt to lower.

The exercises also introduce you to some new tasks that proofreaders do—changes in traditional proofreading resulting from changes in technology. Good proofreaders, those who pay minute attention to detail, now do many kinds of checking, from verifying that a computer has sorted material properly to determining factual accuracy—of dates and quotations, for example.

1 The Principles of Proofreading

Read the following sentence slowly:

FROZEN FOODS ARE THE RESULT OF YEARS OF SCIENTIFIC STUDY AND THE DEVELOPMENT OF REFRIGERATION

Now count aloud the F's in that sentence. Count only once.

The average person finds four F's. Identifying all seven is unusual—an indication of a mind already attuned to letter-by-letter reading. Because the mind knows there is an F in the unimportant word "OF," it is difficult to recognize the letter when reading for sense as well as for F's.

—The Complete Guide to Editorial Freelancing
Carol L. O'Neill and Avima Ruder
Dodd, Mead & Company, 1974

What proofreading is

Most people think of proofreading as skimming a document critically to catch and mark errors. In this general sense, most people occasionally proofread, if only to check the personal letters they write.

Professional proofreading, however, has had a somewhat different meaning, especially in the printing and publishing industries, as the following paragraphs explain.

Comparison proofreading

Professional proofreading always used to, and often still does, involve *comparison*—the comparison of two versions of the same document—to catch errors and to mark them so the corrector understands the instruction.

In the past, a typesetter replicated an author's typewritten manuscript, and a proofreader verified the typesetter's accuracy. Proofreading then involved painstaking comparison of the author's and the typesetter's documents to be sure the *live copy* (the newly produced version) matched the *dead copy* (the author's original version) word for word and letter for letter.

Today, word-processed manuscripts are more common than typewritten, and a publisher can "preserve the keystrokes" and eliminate the need for rekeying the manuscript. If a manuscript is rekeyed, a proofreader can compare the dead copy with the live copy either on paper (*hard copy*) or on the screen of a computer monitor.

When the live copy is on paper, a proofreader writes instructions (with proofreading marks, the traditional shorthand) telling the person who will be making the corrections what to do about the problems.

When there is no live hard copy, a proofreader may be the one to make the corrections on the screen (this process is discussed in Chapter 5).

Noncomparison proofreading

Proofreading by comparison, however, is less and less the way professional proofreaders work. Comparison proofreading, in fact, may not be possible in fully electronic publishing. Here's an example of how that situation can occur:

Let's say the editor of a newsletter writes an article, "proofreads" it on his computer's screen, corrects misspellings and other errors, and then transmits the article by telecommunication from his office in Connecticut to the publisher's computer in Washington, D.C.

Only when the publisher's production editor prints out the article does she have live copy on paper—hard copy. And although that hard copy might be considered a *proof,* and it needs to be read, there is nothing to compare it with. So the proofreading cycle for that document will start with noncomparison or *dry reading.*

From now on in the publishing process, however, every proofreading stage—making sure that all marked corrections are made properly and that no new errors have been introduced—should be done by comparing the relevant parts of the marked copy (now dead) with the corrected copy (now live). This continual comparison of all changes constitutes an important aspect of quality control.

What a proofreader does

A proofreader works with language in type. (From a proofreader's point of view, *type* is broadly defined as a collection of characters put on paper or other material mechanically. Even typewriters and rubber stamps produce type on a page.)

In *comparison* reading, a proofreader is expected to mark the live copy where it differs from the dead, such as where letters, words, or lines are omitted or repeated.

In *any* proofreading, a proofreader is expected to spot the following problems in the use of type:

- Deviations from specifications (*specs*), including use of the wrong typeface—*roman* (standard upright type), for example, where *italic* (slanted type) is specified.
- Problems in technical quality, such as misalignment, defective characters, wrong end-of-line word division, or bad spacing.

And, depending on the situation, a proofreader must stay alert for problems in language and thought, such as these:

- Nonstandard grammar (She don't talk good)
- Incorrect or missing punctuation (do'nt, dont)
- Inconsistent editorial style (in compound words, capitalization, abbreviation, and so on; for example: *$10* Bargains at *Thousand-Dollar* Yard Sale)
- Incorrect arithmetic (Profits Fall 150%)
- Factual errors (Shakespeare's *You Can't Take It With You*)
- Inanities such as mixed metaphors or "Irish bulls" (If you're going to stand on this corner, you'll have to move on).

How much authority a proofreader has

Proofreaders must do one of three things to every error or problem they find: *ignore* it, *mark* it, or *query* it (ask a question about it). In comparison proofreading, a proofreader is expected to find and *mark* the live copy where it deviates from the dead copy; that's one of the main reasons the document is being proofread. But some problems originate in the dead copy. For these problems, the proofreader will have an assigned level of authority determining how much to ignore, mark, or query. The ability to stay within the authorized limit is a mark of the proofreader's competence.

Everyone for whom proofreaders work may have a different idea of how much needs to be done, and every job (or every step in the publishing process) may allow a different level. Proofreaders working beyond level 1 in the following classification must be sure they have the authority to do so.

1. *First level*

   - Mark only the following, nothing more:
     —Deviations from specifications, from appropriate typographic standards (such as page and column breaks), and from dead copy (if it exists)
     —Misspellings (that originated in the dead copy)
     —Wrong word divisions (line-end word breaks)
   - Query nothing.

2. *Second level*

   - Mark as in level 1.
   - Tactfully *query* glaring errors in language—the kind that would be noticed by anyone with a high school education who was good in English and that would embarrass the author or confuse the reader.

3. *High level*

   - Mark as in level 1.
   - Also *mark* glaring errors in language, the kind you queried at level 2.
   - Tactfully *query* moderate errors in language—those instantly conspicuous to a trained eye (such as that of a high school English teacher).

4. *Top proofreading level*

   - Mark any errors that might embarrass a *careful* writer or editor, irritate a knowledgeable reader, or confuse an inattentive reader.
   - Also, tactfully query any lesser errors.

5. *Minimum copy editing level* (proofreading plus light copy editing)

   - Mark as in level 4.
   - Go ahead and make the changes you would only have queried at lower levels.

Figure 1 summarizes the levels of authority.

At level 1, queries of even the most blatant and indefensible problems are useless and unwelcome. In jobs at this level, the deadlines or budgets are too tight for extra corrections or no one is available to answer queries.

Editorial proofreading (catching some of the errors a copy editor would) starts at level 2 with minimal querying on both comparison and noncomparison proofreading and progresses to level 5, which is equivalent to a light copy edit.

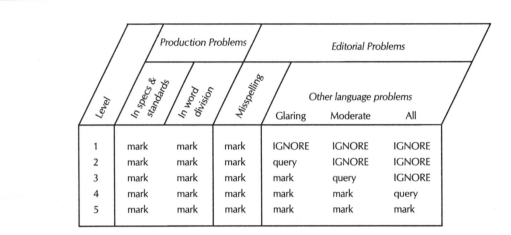

Level	Production Problems			Editorial Problems		
	In specs & standards	In word division	Misspelling	Other language problems		
				Glaring	Moderate	All
1	mark	mark	mark	IGNORE	IGNORE	IGNORE
2	mark	mark	mark	query	IGNORE	IGNORE
3	mark	mark	mark	mark	query	IGNORE
4	mark	mark	mark	mark	mark	query
5	mark	mark	mark	mark	mark	mark

Figure 1. Levels of authority for proofreaders

The level of authority may well be cut back at certain stages of production. Although today's desktop publishing (DTP) systems make corrections easier than ever before, corrections at late stages can still be costly; some are just too expensive for a proofreader to authorize.

How proofreading and copy editing differ

At level 5, the distinction between proofreading and copy editing blurs. But in traditional publishing, proofreaders seldom work at levels 3 to 5, partly because of publication deadlines, partly because of the cost of corrections. Generally, proofreading and copy editing differ in these ways:

- Copy editors correct an *author's* work and prepare the document for the next stage in the production process.
- Proofreaders come into the picture at a later stage; they correct a *keyboard operator's* or *typesetter's* work—and may query other problems.

What it takes to proofread well

In addition to broad general knowledge, to proofread well takes specialized knowledge, technical know-how, judgment, vigilance, and a "typographic eye."

The specialized *knowledge* needed is twofold—of type and of language.

To criticize type—what a document looks like—you must know how the type you're reading is produced, what the equipment's capabilities are, what the accepted typographic standards are for the kind of copy you are working on, and what can go wrong.

For example, although copy from a typewriter is all but gone from the proofreader's purview, typewriter typefaces are still available—on computers. The conventions of typewritten copy, however, work well only with these fonts; they are inappropriate in more sophisticated typography. One common mistake occurs because many word processing operators are former typists accustomed to using two hyphens to represent a common dash (--), a practice that is correct only with a typewriter font. A typeset (as opposed to typewritten) font provides a separate symbol for the hyphen and the common dash (-, —), and when such a font is used, copy that shows two hyphens instead of a proper dash lacks typographic nicety.

To criticize language—how a document says what it does—you must, above all, know the rules of spelling. (Take the spelling test on page 149 and read "Spelling" in Chapter 8.) For certain kinds of proofreading you should also know the rules for punctuation, grammar, usage, and editorial style, and, for some jobs, you must be able to detect illogical reasoning and inappropriate *tone* (attitude).

With the needed *technical know-how,* you can find errors quickly and efficiently and mark them so whoever makes the corrections understands what to do.

With *judgment,* you can work effectively at your level of authority. Nothing you do is wasted; everything you do matters.

Knowledge of type and language and technical know-how can be learned, and judgment comes with experience. But *vigilance*—unrelenting watchfulness—is a part of your character, your attitude, and your general state of physical and emotional health.

The *typographic eye* is a visual nitpicking ability. You must be able to spot evidence of poor workmanship, such as a capital *O* instead of a zero (O, 0), a letter *l* instead of the figure *1* (l, 1), or a backwards apostrophe (the '80s, the '80s). And you must be able to see minute misalignment of figures like that in the following column as well as small disparities in space like that shown in the parallel lines.

.05
.06
.07
.08
.09
.10

What the methods of comparison proofreading are

Solo proofreading is one-person proofreading. Team proofreading is two-person or partner proofreading.

In team proofreading, the *copyholder* reads aloud the dead copy to the *proofreader* (sometimes called the *first reader* or *copymarker*), who marks the live copy. Everything is read—punctuation, capitalization, changes in spacing or typeface, and so on. Equally qualified partners may sometimes switch roles.

Two other forms of proofreading use some of the techniques of team reading. In tape proofreading, a reader uses a tape recorder to record the dead copy. Later, a marker listens while following the live copy. The reader and marker may be the same person.

In electronic reading, a device that simulates the human voice reads the copy aloud to the proofreader-marker.

Chapter 5 presents the methods of proofreading in detail.

How to proofread

The following advice will help you get started on the way to a professional approach to solo proofreading. More detailed advice appears in later chapters. Assuming that you write directly on the live copy—

- Read and absorb the instructions and specifications.
- Know exactly what your authority is, what's expected of you, and what your deadline is.
- Be sure you have all the dead and live copy. Check the numbers on pages or galleys and make sure that none is missing or repeated. If pages or galleys aren't numbered, number them on their backs, or write the numbers very lightly and erase them later.
- Verify that the live copy follows the instructions and specs. For typeset copy, use a type gauge to measure the live copy's line width and depth (see Appendix D). As you read, check that the correct style of type has been used at every change, for example, in headings and footnotes.
- Put the dead copy (if you have it) and the live copy side by side on your workspace (if you're right-handed, the live copy will be on the right).
- Use a guide such as a ruler to keep your place in the dead copy, line by line. Use the eraser end of your pencil to follow the live copy letter by letter. Turn your pencil over when you need to mark corrections or write queries.
- Compare the two versions minutely. Read a few words of the dead copy and then the same words in the live, verifying that every letter, every punctuation mark, every number, and every symbol are the same.
- Experiment to find out how much dead copy you can accurately remember at one time to compare with the live copy: in some jobs, or in some parts of jobs, you'll be able to read whole sentences; in others, just a few characters.
- Watch the live copy for typographic errors (*typos*).
- Watch the live copy for typographic faults such as uneven margins, broken letters, and characters that lack sharpness.
- Watch also for misspellings and errors in language—errors that appear in the dead copy and have been faithfully duplicated.
- If you have the authority to query, do so tactfully; if you have the authority to make corrections, keep them to a reasonable minimum.
- Be sure you can back up every kind of correction or query that you make with a rule or model from a recognized reference work.
- Use a standard dictionary to verify spelling. You don't have to be a spelling-bee winner to be a good proofreader, but you *must* know which words give you trouble, and you must take the time to look them up.
- Use a dictionary or a word division guide to verify end-of-line word breaks.
- Have on hand a standard dictionary, an almanac, an atlas, and whatever other reference books the job you're proofreading requires. But don't check anything except spelling unless you're sure you're expected to do more.
- Prefer standard proofreading marks—modified, if necessary, to suit the copy and the correction process. Standard marks and modified marks are both presented in this book.
- After your comparison reading, read the live copy by itself—from beginning to end—to catch anything you may have missed and to be sure it all makes sense. Stay vigilant. If you find something dubious, check the dead copy.

- If you need to, and if you have time, go over the live copy again as often as necessary to recheck what you know you tend to miss when you try to do everything at once. For example, you may need to check word breaks or the sequence of numbers in footnotes or the pairing of quotation marks and of parentheses. Some experienced proofreaders make three separate passes, each with a different objective. Chapter 6 goes into this kind of rechecking in more detail.

Why standard marks are best

The marking system used by professional proofreaders has proved its efficiency and effectiveness over the centuries. Without the shorthand of proofreading marks, specific instructions to correct the errors in the following sentence take more words than the sentence itself:

Add t to Thirty   Thiry days hath SEptember   *Lowercase E*

With standard proofreading marks, the instructions are clear and specific:

t   Thiry days hath S*E*ptember   *lc*

Standard marks and marking techniques are practical for several other reasons:

- They are widely understood.
- They ensure that a job divided among proofreaders will be marked uniformly.
- In the evolution of printing and typesetting, they are examples of the survival of the fittest—designs achieving maximum accuracy, speed, and clarity for those who write them and those who read them.
- They are basic to traditional forms of typesetting and printing. Slightly modified, they work with any form. A proofreader who knows them well can easily adapt them to different kinds of jobs and employers.

When to use standard marks

Use standard marks and marking techniques as described in Chapters 2 and 3 when *all* the following conditions are met:

- You know that the corrector understands standard marks or is willing to improve speed, accuracy, and clarity by learning them.
- The copy won't be harmed by the marks. Any kind of duplicate, such as a copy from a copying machine, or any kind of preliminary printout, such as a page from a computer, is a candidate for standard marks. When in doubt, make copies on a copying machine and mark the copies. Or use a marking system that won't harm the copy, as shown later in the book.
- The copy has too little room between lines for you to write there easily. Typeset pages like this one have too little room for writing between lines; so do single-spaced typewritten pages. When you use standard proofreading marks properly, you never write between lines; the only thing that goes inside the text is a locator mark.

A full list of standard proofreading marks is found at the end of Chapter 3.

How to mark for correction

Chapters 2 and 3 discuss standard marks in detail, and Chapter 4 discusses the ways standard marks may be modified to suit different kinds of copy.

If you need to get started quickly, Appendix A provides a "cheat sheet"—an introductory marking system that will be understood by any corrector who knows standard marks.

What you need to know

If you proofread only once in a while, or if you mark and correct your own work, you may need to learn no more than the cheat sheet teaches. But if you want or need to be fully informed, you will read Chapters 2, 3, and 4. And if you want to be fully professional, you will begin by working your way through this entire book.

2 Standard Proofmarks

Rules for using standard marks

1. *Mark an error twice—first in the text, then in the margin.*

The in-text and the marginal marks are almost always different. In-text marks show *where* to make a correction; marginal marks show *what* correction to make.

Marginal marks also keep the corrector from having to search for in-text marks.

2. *Separate marks in the margin with slashes.*

Slashes in the margin serve three purposes:

A. To call attention to an inconspicuous mark; for example, add a slash after the colon to be inserted here:

          :/   Proofreading your quality control

B. To separate multiple marks for errors found in the same line; for example, add a slash between the *r* and the *i* to be inserted here:

          r/i   Poofreading: your qualty control

C. To show how many times in succession the same correction is needed; for example, add two slashes after the two consecutive insertions of *r* here:

          r //   Poofreading: your quality contol

The same set of slashes can both count and separate. In the following example, the two slashes mean, "insert *o* twice in succession," and the same slashes separate the *o* from the next mark:

          o // i   Profreading: yur qualty control

You may use a slash after any mark, but it saves time and effort (and makes for a cleaner margin) to reserve slashes for the three purposes described.

3. *Mark in both margins, using the margin nearer the error.*

To prevent overcrowded margins, use an imaginary line to divide the type area into right and left halves. Where you find errors in the left half, put the marginal marks in the left margin; where you find errors in the right half, put the marginal marks in the right margin:

          n/i   Commend me to your proofreaders. Thy are soul ad prosperty of a printing office.   *e/the*

                                            —Crapelet

4. *Mark from left to right.*

As the example for Rule 3 shows, mark from left to right where more than one error occurs in a line.

5. *Ring instructions and explanations.*

A ring means that the message in the ring isn't to be set or typed. The following example shows a ringed instruction:

> Oh, that they who set the types and they who read the proofs would free their texts from error.
>
> -|Schoeffler   (set em dash)

Cautions

- Don't confuse in-text and marginal marks. No characters or words belong between lines; only proofreading marks go there. In-text marks show where to make a correction; marginal marks show what correction to make. Here are examples of right and wrong ways to mark:

	Wrong		Right	
i	in-text and marginal marks		in-text and marginal marks	i

- Ordinarily, don't try to mark to adjust the spacing after a correction that changes the number of characters in a line. Correctors—or their equipment—will do it automatically.

For example, if you mark to insert a letter between words, don't mark for the space that must be added:

	Proofmark	Corrected copy
y	qualit control	quality control

If you mark to delete a word, don't mark for the adjustment needed in spacing. For example, if you mark to delete "reading" in the following example, don't try to explain what to do after the deletion is made—how to fill the blank space by moving the next three words to the left margin and then how to fill the line by moving a word up from the next line. Just mark for the deletion, as shown:

	Proofmark	Corrected copy
𝒮	Expert proofreading ~~reading~~ assures you of quality.	Expert proofreading assures you of quality.

- Cross out characters carefully and clearly, including punctuation; the corrector must be unable to mistake what you want:

	Acceptable in-text mark	Unacceptable mark	
𝒮	Proofreading. ~~ing.~~	Proofreading. ~~ing.~~	𝒮

- Cross out characters lightly; the corrector must be able to read what you have crossed out:

Acceptable in-text mark	Unacceptable mark
ſ Proofreading. ~~ing.~~	Proofreading. ~~ing.~~ ſ

Five classes of correction

The five classes of correction are these:

- Deletion
- Insertion
- Replacement, including transposition
- Typographic changes
- Moving type and space.

This chapter introduces standard proofmarks for the first four classes. The next chapter completes the study of standard marks.

Names of proofmarks

Some marks have names:

caret (insertion mark): ∧ or ⋋

> or <

⊰ or ⊱

cancel, slash: /

dele (rhymes with steely), delete sign, take-out sign: ſ

octothorp, space sign, grating: #

paragraph sign, pilcrow: ¶

close-up mark, tie, liaison, bump sign: ◡

Note that the cancel or slash has many names—shilling (or shill), virgule, slant bar, oblique, stroke, solidus, separatrix, and diagonal.

Note that the dele has many variations. (Some are shown in Chapter 4 under "Alternative marks.") This book uses a simple, quickly written dele.

The basic marks

Deletion

Mark for deletion surplus characters or words, including *doublets* (mistakenly repeated characters, words, or lines, also called *dupes,* short for duplicates) and *repeaters* (longer mistaken repetitions).

Simple deletion takes out characters and leaves space. Deletion with the close-up mark takes out characters and closes up space.

Simple deletion

To mark for simple deletion—

- In the margin, use the dele: ꝑ
- In the text
  —For a single character, use a slash: /
  —For two characters next to each other, use two slashes: //
  or a crossbar: —
  —For three consecutive characters or more, up to a line, use a crossbar: —

Figure 2 shows examples.

Note that every in-text mark needs a corresponding marginal mark. In (b) of Figure 2, for example, the two in-text slashes are matched with the equivalent of two marginal deles—a dele and two counting slashes.

(a) A single character	Every girl should have a formal photograph taken when she is 180 years old, because she will never be prettier.
	In printer's jargon, a *monk* is a smudge or blotch of unwanted pink, and a *friar* is a blank area where an inked image should be.
(b) Two adjacent characters	Accuracy is no rnomore important than truth.
	(or)
	Accuracy is no nomore important than truth.
(c) Three consecutive characters	The child knows how to tie a boweww now.
(d) A word	Doublets can occur at the the end of one line and the beginning of the next.
(e) A partial line, a full line, and another partial line of consecutive text	Particularly susceptible to typographic error are words that become other words with a one-letter addition or omission and words that be- one letter addition or omission and words that come become other words with a transposition of two letters. A list of these terrible twins would include *angel/angle, bride/bridge, county/country, death/dearth, marital/martial, nuclear/unclear, scared/sacred, trial/trail,* and *widow/window.*

Figure 2. Simple deletion

Delete several lines or whole passages with a box, a big X, and a dele, like this:

Delete multiple lines or whole passages with a box, a big *X*, and a dele, like this: Delete multiple lines or whole passages with a box, a big *X*, and a dele.

Where doublets appear within one line or where each constitutes an entire line, it makes no difference which one you delete. But where both appear as parts of different lines, you, the proofreader, must decide which deletion will cause fewer problems for the corrector. In the following example, it's best to delete the second *the,* as shown, because the deletion will affect only one line (it won't hurt for the last line of the quotation to end short of the margin). Deleting the first *the* would be less desirable because the deletion would affect two lines.

> A word . . . is the skin of a living thought and may
> vary greatly in color and context according to the
> the circumstances and the time in which it is used.
> —Oliver Wendell Holmes

> For practice in marking for simple deletion,
> turn to Exercise 1.

Deletion with the close-up mark

The *close-up mark* or *tie* deletes space and joins characters. It looks like this:

proofreading

Combined with the dele, a close-up mark means, "delete and then close up what's left; leave no extra space."

Deletion with the close-up mark, or *tied deletion,* applies only *within* a word or group of characters.

To mark for deletion with the close-up mark—

- In the margin, use the closed-up dele:
- In the text
  —For a single character, use a closed-up slash:
  —For two characters, use either closed-up slashes:
    or a closed-up crossbar:
  —For three or more characters, use a closed-up crossbar:

Figure 3 shows examples.

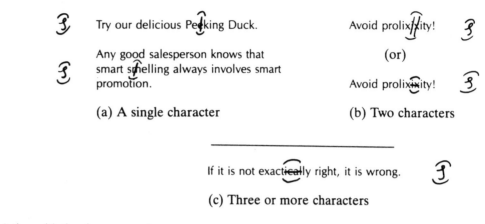

(a) A single character

(b) Two characters

(c) Three or more characters

Figure 3. Deletion with the close-up mark

For practice in marking for deletion with the close-up mark,
turn to Exercise 2.

Distinguishing simple deletion
from deletion with the close-up mark

You must distinguish between simple deletion and deletion with the close-up mark, and you must make the two marks accurately.

- Use simple deletion for characters that have space on one or both sides, including the following:
  —Characters at either end of a word:

  characters at either ₹endɖ of a word

- —A whole word:

  a whole ~~whole~~ word

- —A whole group, including punctuation:

  a whole group, including punctuation: ~~punctuation.~~

- Use deletion with the close-up mark for characters that have other characters on both sides, including the following:
  —Characters in the middle of a word:

  characters in the midddle of a word

  characters in the middiddle of a word

- —Characters in the middle of a group, including punctuation:

  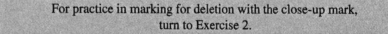
  characters in the middle of a group, including punctuation: :

> For practice in marking simple deletion and deletion
> with the close-up mark, turn to Exercise 3.

Insertion

Mark *outs* (omissions, anything left out) for insertion. You will need to distinguish between short outs and long outs and between simple outs and closed-up outs.

Short outs

A short out is one that can be written neatly in the margin of the live copy—from one character up to about seven words, or one line.

To mark a short out:

- In the text, place a caret.
- In the margin, write what needs to be inserted.

Figure 4 shows examples.

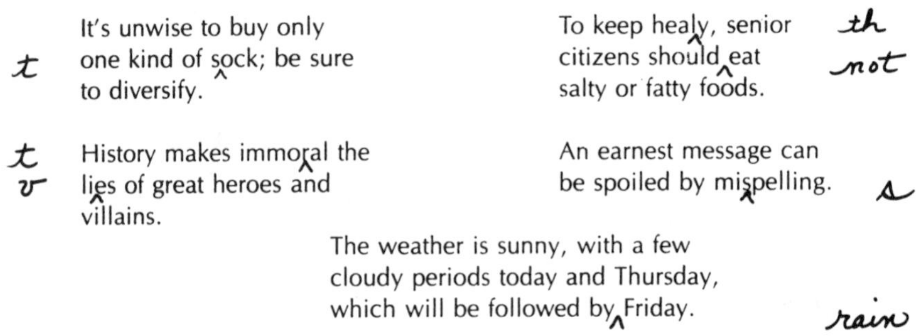

It's unwise to buy only
one kind of sock; be sure
to diversify.

History makes immoral the
lies of great heroes and
villains.

To keep healy, senior
citizens should eat
salty or fatty foods.

An earnest message can
be spoiled by mispelling.

The weather is sunny, with a few
cloudy periods today and Thursday,
which will be followed by Friday.

Figure 4. Insertion

One insertion, no matter how long it is, is considered one marginal mark and needs only one in-text caret.

A caret must point up from the bottom of a line to the exact spot the out begins. Where you need more precision, extend one leg of the caret to pinpoint the spot:

proofreading

In the margin, take great care to write legibly. Write horizontally, never vertically. If your handwriting is bad, print, but not in block letters because you must distinguish carefully between lowercase and capital letters. (See the print-script example under "Handwriting" in Chapter 8.) Be sure to group together characters that form words and to leave space between words. Use the proper signs for punctuation marks.

is that plain words

If the side margins lack room, write the insertion in the top or bottom margin and run a guideline to the caret:

The first rule of construction should
be taken to mean what they say.

For practice in marking for simple insertion,
turn to Exercise 4.

Always put a close-up mark (a tie) on the mark in the margin if an insertion is supposed to connect to a group of characters. Put the close-up mark at the left of the marginal mark if the insertion belongs with the character on its left, at the right if the insertion belongs with the character on its right. Here's how:

⊃e   mark to ti an insertion   ⊃
          at either end of a word

Without the close-up marks, the corrector may misunderstand and make a simple insertion or hook the insertion to the wrong group:

Wrong mark	Wrong "correction"
He had cute appendicitis	He had a cute appendicitis
	(or)
	He hada cute appendicitis

a

You needn't close up insertions that go in the middle of words. And normally, you needn't mark for any spacing changes that insertion will cause.

For practice in marking for insertion with the close-up mark,
turn to Exercise 5.

Long outs

A long out consists of more copy than can be written comfortably in the margin—usually longer than seven words or longer than about one line of the live copy. How you treat a long out in the live copy depends on whether the corrector will be able to refer to the dead copy.

If you're sure the corrector will be able to see the dead copy—

1. Mark the caret in the text.
2. In the margin, write "Out, see copy p. x," giving the page number where the out can be found in the dead copy. Remember to put a ring around the entire instruction.
3. Mark the passage in the dead copy with brackets as shown in Figure 5. Write "set" near the opening bracket. Put a ring around "set."

4. Flag the page in the dead copy. You can use a small, gummed self-stick note, a paper clip, a plastic or metal signal of the type sold in office supply stores, or an improvised flag of colored paper.

Figure 5 shows an example of the way to mark a long out (without the flag).

Dead Copy

```
When in the Course of human Events,
it becomes necessary for one People
to dissolve the Political Bonds which
[have connected them with another, and
to assume among the Powers of the Earth,
the separate and equal station to which]
the Laws of Nature and of Nature's God
entitle them, a decent Respect to the
Opinions of Mankind requires that they
```

(set)

Live Copy

When in the Course of human Events, it becomes necessary for one People to dissolve the Political Bonds which the Laws of Nature and of Nature's God entitle them, a decent Respect to the Opinions of Mankind requires that they

Figure 5. Typical long out

If you're not sure that the corrector will have access to the dead copy—

1. Mark the caret in the text.
2. Make a photocopy of the dead page that contains the out.
3. In the margin of the live copy, in a ring, write "Out, see attached."
4. On the photocopy, in a ring, write "Insert for p. x," giving the page or galley number of the live copy.
5. On the photocopy, mark with brackets the passage to be inserted.
6. Attach the photocopy, face up, to the top of the live copy, using removable tape, such as drafting tape.

Never write a long insertion by hand. If you can't get a photocopy, type the insertion on a separate sheet of paper. Be careful to introduce no errors. Prepare your typed sheet as described for a photocopy.

If several long outs occur on a page, key them "A," "B," and so forth, both in the margin and on the insert.

> For practice in marking long and short outs,
> turn to Exercise 6.

Insertion of space

To insert space, use the space sign (#), for example:

Proofreading‸Manual   #

Remember that the close-up mark serves an opposite purpose—to delete space and join characters:

‿/   roofreading Manual

Note, however, that marks for insertion or deletion of space are often more complicated, as explained in the next chapter.

> For practice in inserting and deleting space,
> turn to Exercise 7.
>
> For practice in marking for deletion and insertion,
> turn to Exercise 8.

Replacement

Mark wrong characters, words, or passages to be replaced with correct ones. To mark for replacement—

- In the text, use slashes or crossbars the same way you do for simple deletion.
- In the margin, write the correct characters or words the same way you do for simple insertion.

Think of replacement as a separate operation. Don't confuse the corrector by marking an error first for deletion and then for insertion. Use just one mark in the text and one in the margin. Only in the text is replacement marked like deletion; only in the margin is replacement marked like insertion.

Figure 6 shows examples of replacements.

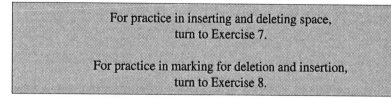

(a) One letter	Inferior decoration	*t*
	Methuselah lived to be 969 years odd.	*l*
(b) Two adjacent letters	a worthy principil	*l/e*
	(or)	
	a worthy principal	*le*
(c) One word	Call us for help in finding the right doctor for Family Practice, OB/Gyn, Pediatrics, and most specialities, including sorcery.	*surgery*
(d) Several words	Water, water everywhere and not a drop to drink	*nor any*

Figure 6. Replacement

Make in-text marks one for one with marginal marks; that is, match the number of in-text marks you make with the number of marginal marks you make. But note that one mark can encompass a group of characters, and that the number of characters or words you mark in the text won't necessarily match the number of characters or words in the margin. Here, for example, you see two marks in the text and two marks, one with two characters, one with four, in the margin:

abcdefgkjklmxrstuvwxyz   *hi / nopq*

Here is an example of the one-for-one principle:

Two in-text marks, two deles in the margin	The speech was *ff*relevant.	*ʒ ll*
One in-text mark, one dele in the margin	The speech was ~~ir~~relevant.	*ʒ*

To demonstrate this one-for-one principle further, part (b) of Figure 6 shows a two-letter replacement marked two different ways. First, it shows two marks (slashes) in the text and two separate marks (of one character each) in the margin. Second, it shows one mark (a crossbar) in the text and one mark (a group of characters) in the margin. Either of the two ways is acceptable.

Don't bother adding a close-up mark to a mark for replacement where no change in spacing is involved at the end (or beginning) of a word. To mark economically, reserve the close-up mark for an *insertion* at either end of a word. It's not that it's wrong to close up a replacement (or an insertion in the middle of a word); it's just that it's almost always needless. Here's an example showing an insertion that requires a close-up mark and a replacement that doesn't:

Insertion	Replacement	
C ly practical‸perfect proofreading	practical~~ness~~ perfect proofreading	*ly*

For efficient, effective proofreading, learn to think in terms of replacement and mark for the single operation of replacement instead of marking first for deletion and next for insertion.

Replacement: the better way	Deletion plus insertion: not recommended	
proficient ~~porcifeint~~ proofreading	~~porcifeint~~‸proofreading	*ʒ/ proficient*

- Marking for replacement is often the best way to handle a problem.

Where a single word has several errors, mark the whole word to be replaced:

proofreading   ~~pooffreeding~~

- Where a line has many errors, mark the whole line (or the part containing the errors) for replacement rather than write each correction separately.

- To delete a character and replace it with space, slash the character and make the space sign in the margin:

Love/thy proofreader.

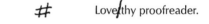

For practice in marking for replacement,
turn to Exercise 9.

Transposition

To mark in the traditional way for the transposition (exchange) of adjacent characters or words—

- In the text, use a double loop: N
- In the margin, write "tr" in a ring: (tr)

Figure 7 shows how.

(tr)   Keep the home files
        burning.

(tr)   Unfiled we stand,
        divided we fall.

At first I didn't succeed, so
I tried again. And this time I
succeeded, as just the time-worn   (tr)
advice to try, try again implied   (tr)
I would.

In spring!   (tr)

Figure 7. Transposition

Some styles reserve the double loop for transposed words and require transposed letters to be marked as simple replacements:

r/o   pofofreading

If you have no special instructions, prefer the double loop for marking a pair of transposed letters.

But to keep marks easy to interpret, avoid the double loop for groups of letters within a word.

Mark like this: ~~preadroofing~~   *proofreading*

Not like this: preadroofing

And always mark transposed words that aren't next to each other for simple replacement:

Proofreading: ~~control~~ quality ~~your~~   *your*/*control*

For practice in marking for transposition,
turn to Exercise 10.

The symbol "tr" also stands for "transfer." Rules for transferring copy to another spot are discussed in the next chapter under "Moving type and space."

Special replacement marks

Mark a defective character—broken, dirty, too light, too dark, or otherwise inconsistent with the quality of the rest—with a ring around the character and a ringed *x* in the margin:

proofreading   Ⓧ

Use this mark cautiously: a machine copy or a poor printout can make good type look poor, and some proofs don't come near to representing the quality of the final product. Also, if the same defect occurs repeatedly, the problem probably has a single solution so repeated marks are needless. Where you see recurrent defective characters, write a general comment:

Oh, that they who set the types and they who read the proofs would free their texts from error.

ck crowded th throughout

—Schoeffler

Replace an abbreviation, numeral, or symbol with its spelled-out form by ringing it and writing "sp" with a ring around it in the margin:

Instruction to spell out		Corrected copy
ⓈⓅ	Ⓐ 3 in.	three inches
ⓈⓅ	5%	5 percent
ⓈⓅ	Pa.	Pennsylvania

Mark for replacement where there's any possibility of misunderstanding what the abbreviation stands for:

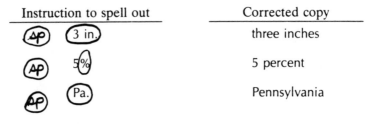

circa   ~~ca.~~   m² square meters

avoirdupois ~~avdp~~   ~~USA~~ U. S. Army

Use ordinary replacement where you want the shorter form to replace a spelled-out word. Write the abbreviation, numeral, or symbol in the margin:

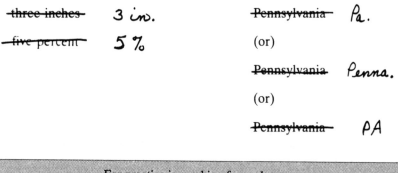

For practice in marking for replacement,
including the use of special replacement marks,
turn to Exercise 11.

Correcting wrong proofreading marks

You can restore material marked incorrectly by stetting it. *Stet* means "let it stand" or "ignore the mark." In the margin, cross out the incorrect mark and write "stet" (in a ring); then put dots or short dashes under the in-text mark, as in this example:

I've never met a proofreader I didn't like, but then, the ~~only~~ proofreader I've ever known is my mother.

For practice in using the marks you have learned so far,
turn to Exercise 12.

Standard marginal marks for punctuation and symbols

When you insert or replace punctuation marks, write them in the margin.

Circle all periods:

period

Mark colons and semicolons with a slash to make them more conspicuous:

colon :/

semicolon ;/

Use V's and upside-down V's to distinguish the marginal marks for commas from those for apostrophes and quotation marks (quotes). Think of the V's as pointing to the baseline of the type:

baseline XxYyZzz   apostrophe
                       comma

Put an upside-down V over a comma:

comma ⋀

Put an upright V under an apostrophe:

apostrophe ⌄

Put upright V's under quotes:

open single quote ⌄

closed single quote ⌄

open double quote ⌄

closed double quote ⌄

(Think of open quotes as little sixes; closed quotes, as little nines: [6]quote unquote[9].)

Use V's pointing up or down to the baseline of the type also to distinguish *subscript* (inferior, low-set) characters from *superscript* (superior, high-set) characters:

baseline XxYyZz   superscript⌄

subscript⋀

Here are examples of marks for subscript and superscript:

	Proofreading mark		Corrected copy
	In the text	In the margin	
Replacement			
Subscript	H₂O		H_2O
Superscript	e = mc²		$e = mc^2$
Insertion			
Subscript	H O		H_2O
Superscript	e = mc		$e = mc^2$

The marks for subscript and superscript can be used together; for example, to insert a comma between superscript footnote references 2 and 3:

Footnotes[2,3]

Marks for subscript and superscript are often combined in mathematical copy; for example, to indicate that superscript 2 has the subscript a:

Mark	Corrected Copy
x2	x^{2a}

Hyphens, dashes, and minus signs

Figure 8 summarizes the differences between a font that follows typewriter conventions and a font that produces higher quality typography with desktop publishing (DTP) or typesetting equipment.

	Typewriter font		DTP or typeset font	
	Symbol	Example of use	Symbol	Example of use
Hyphen	hyphen:-	great-uncle	hyphen:-	great-uncle
Minus sign	hyphen:-	4 - 2 = 2	minus sign:–	4 – 2 = 2
Short dash	hyphen:-	pp. 6-9	en dash:–	pp. 6–9
Long dash	2 hyphens:--	yes--or no	em dash:—	yes—or no
Extra-long dash	4 hyphens:----	But d---- it all	2-em dash:——	But d—— it all
	6 hyphens:------	Poe, "Lenore" ------, "Shadow"	3-em dash:———	Poe, "Lenore" ———, "Shadow"

Figure 8. Hyphens and dashes

As shown in Figure 8, the symbols for typeset dashes are measured in *ems* and *ens*.

An em is a unit of measure relative to type size originally named for the size of a capital M. An *em dash* (or long dash) is the common dash of punctuation; its mark looks like this: $\frac{|}{M}$

An en is a unit of measure relative to type size originally named for the size of a capital N. An *en dash* (or short dash) has special uses; its mark looks like this: $\not{N}$

These are the main rules for the use of hyphens and dashes:

- Use the hyphen for these purposes:
  - —To divide words at the ends of lines (divide words)
  - —To form permanent compounds (words that are always hyphened) according to your dictionary (great-uncle, self-confident, twenty-one)
  - —To form temporary compounds to help the reader; for example, as a *unit modifier,* which is an adjectival unit preceding a noun (small-business owner, six-year-old child, three-inch nails).

Note that a *suspensive hyphen* has no connection at its right (five- and six-year-old children, two- or three-inch nails).

- Use the short dash (en dash) for these purposes:
  —To indicate continuing or inclusive numbers (pp. 2–10, 1889–1903)
  —To act as a break between figures and letters (B–17, Section II–B–4–c).
- Use the long dash (em dash) for this purpose:
  —To mark a pause for a sudden change of thought or a further explanation (The galleys—where are they?).
- Use the extra-long dash (2-em dash) for this purpose:
  —To indicate an omission (To h—— with it).

Here are examples of hyphens used for dividing and for compounding and of short and long dashes:

> You can join—right now—the fa-
> mous typos-of-the-month club and
> receive 24–60 clippings a year.

You must mark hyphens and dashes correctly. It is an indefensible error, for example, to mark for an en dash to divide a word at the end of a line; a hyphen is required. If you have the smallest doubt about how to use these punctuation marks, read more about them in a style guide, such as *Words into Type,* the *U.S. Government Printing Office Style Manual, The Chicago Manual of Style,* or *Webster's Standard American Style Manual.* (Newspaper style guides and most books on punctuation or grammar don't cover the topic.)

Here are the proofreading marks for the dash group of symbols. Note that a slash follows some of these marks to prevent their being overlooked.

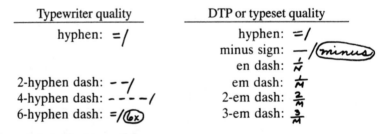

Typewriter quality	DTP or typeset quality
hyphen: =/	hyphen: =/
	minus sign: —/ (minus)
	en dash: ⅟N
2-hyphen dash: - -/	em dash: ⅟M
4-hyphen dash: - - - -/	2-em dash: 2/M
6-hyphen dash: =/ (6x)	3-em dash: 3/M

Parentheses, brackets, and braces

These are several kinds of enclosure (fences):

parentheses: ( )
square brackets: [ ]
braces (curly brackets): { }
angle brackets: ‹ ›
elbow brackets: < >

When you mark for a parenthesis, add a short horizontal line through the sign to help identify it:

where (and why⌃   )⃗

where ˰and why)   (⃗

Label square brackets, elbow brackets (representing in mathematics *greater than* and *less than*; in etymology, *derived from* and *whence derived*), and braces:

[where (and why)ʌ   **]**   *(sq bracket)*

orange ʌ *naranja*   **>**   *(elbow bracket)*

2 }
4 }
6 }   }   *(set 3-line brace as shown)*

Other punctuation

Distinguish the question mark in a query from the instruction to set a question mark, as shown:

Set a question mark:

Whoʌ   *(set)* ?

Answer the query:

Who   *whom /(?)*

(See Chapter 7 for more on queries.)

Give an exclamation point the same treatment, with the ringed word "set":

Ohʌ   *(set) !*

The traditional mark for a virgule (slash) is "shill"—the abbreviation for shilling. If you use this arcane mark, be sure the corrector understands what it means. You may prefer the nonstandard, but more commonly understood, mark:

andʌor   / *(slash)*

(or)

andʌor   / *(shill)*

For practice in marking for punctuation,
turn to Exercise 13.

Put diacritical marks in the margin with the letter they go with, not alone. If it is possible that the corrector is unfamiliar with diacritical marks, add the name of the mark (ringed).

garçon ç (cedilla)   entrée é (acute)
señor ñ (tilde)   Schönberg ö (umlaut)

Type marks

Traditionally, underscores in a manuscript specify the type style to be set: One underscore means "set in italic"; two underscores mean "set in small capitals"; three underscores mean "set in full capitals"; and a wavy underscore means "set in boldface." Figure 9 shows how these marks look and how to mark for combinations such as caps and small caps (C+sc) and caps and lowercase (Clc).

Marginal mark	In-text mark	Corrected copy
(ital)	Set in italic	*Set in italic*
(sc)	Set in small caps	SET IN SMALL CAPS
(caps)	Set in capitals	SET IN CAPITALS
(bf)	Set in boldface	**Set in boldface**
(bf ital)	Set in boldface italic	***Set in boldface italic***
(bf caps)	Set in boldface caps	**SET IN BOLDFACE CAPS**
(C + sc)	Set in caps and small caps	SET IN CAPS AND SMALL CAPS
(Clc)	Set in caps and lowercase	Set in Caps and Lowercase
(Clc)	SET IN CAPS AND LOWERCASE	Set in Caps and Lowercase

Figure 9. Type marks

In typewriter-quality copy, an underscore is used the same way as italic is used in higher quality copy—to emphasize or set something off. To delete, insert, or extend an underscore or part of an underscore, mark like this:

ʃ (score)   Romeo and Juliet by William Shakespeare

ʃ (score)   Romeo and Juliet by William Shakespeare

(add score)   Romeo and Juliet by William Shakespeare

(extend score)   Romeo and Juliet by William Shakespeare

In the traditional vocabulary of typesetting, a straight line is called a *rule.* Vertical rules are *down rules* and horizontal rules are *cross rules.* Rules under type, equivalent to underscores, are *baseline rules,* which are rarely used in typeset copy. Rules that cross over more than one column under a heading in a table are *straddle rules.*

To change italic to roman, ring the italic type and write "rom" (in a ring) in the margin:

Romeo and Juliet by William Shakespeare

To change boldface to lightface (in many fonts, called "regular" or "book"), ring the boldface and write "lf" (in a ring) in the margin:

Romeo and Juliet by **William Shakespeare**

"Wrong font" means that a different typeface or type size from the one specified has been set. Where you recognize wrong font, ring it in the text and write "wf" (in a ring) in the margin:

Romeo and Juliet by William Shakespeare

To lowercase one or two letters, slash them in the text and write "lc" (in a ring) in the margin. To lowercase more than two letters, slash the first, overscore the rest, and write "lc" (in a ring) in the margin:

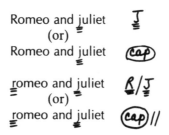

To capitalize single letters, underscore them three times. Then, in the margin, write the correct letter with three underscores or write "cap" (in a ring):

In type with too little room for three underscores, treat the problem like a replacement and slash or cross through the in-text letters.

For practice in marking punctuation, capitals, and lowercase,
turn to Exercise 14.

For proofreading practice,
turn to Exercise 15.

3 Standard Proofmarks, Continued

Moving type and space

The following discussion of spacing and positioning is divided into these categories:

- Placement
- Alignment
- Contour
- Line, word, and letter spacing
- Breaks, including those for sense, for consistent format, and for good appearance, as well as word breaks at the ends of lines.

Placement

Wrongly placed lines or passages need to be transferred to where they belong.

To transfer a whole line or more to another position on the same page, bracket it and mark it like this:

> The difference between a word that is right
> ference between the lightning and the light-
> and a word that is almost right is the dif-
> ning bug.
>
> —Mark Twain

To transfer part of a line or a passage including part of a line to another position on the same page, bracket it or box it so there's no doubt where it begins and ends:

> To enjoy good houses and good books seems
> to me to be the pleasurable end in self
> respect and decent comfort towards which
> all societies of human beings ought now
> to struggle.
>
> —William Morris

To transfer a passage to a different page or galley, mark as shown in the following illustrations:

- Bracket or box the passage and write "tr to p. x" (in a ring) in the margin.

- On the page of destination, mark a caret in the text and write "tr fr p. x" (in a ring) in the margin. Add a guideline from the caret to the marginal mark if it makes the instruction clearer.

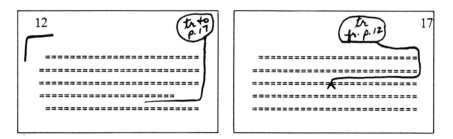

Alignment

Letters in a word should have a common baseline; lines, paragraphs, and margins should be straight. But the live copy you see may not represent the final alignment of type; for example, proofs that were photocopied crooked weren't necessarily set crooked.

Crooked type is seldom found in electronic *composition* (typesetting) but it sometimes occurs when corrections are pasted up, and it may occur in pasted-up graphics or in rub-on materials.

Underscore and overscore a horizontal misalignment—a crooked word, line, or block of type—and write "straighten" (in a ring) in the margin, as shown in these examples:

Mark a vertical misalignment—a margin or a column in a table—like this:

A proofreader should scrupulously avoid giving himself over to choler, to love, to sadness, or indeed yielding to any of the lively emotions. . . especially should he shun drunkenness.

—Jerome Hornschuch (1608)

For some misalignments, it's helpful to mark brackets to show the direction matter should be moved. An in-text bracket should "push" or "pull" the misaligned matter approximately to the right position—up or down, roughly to the horizontal line; right or left, roughly to the vertical line.

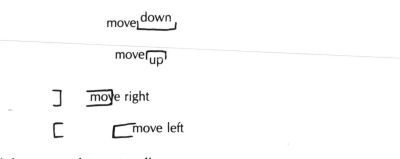

And here is how you mark to center a line:

 ☐ move to the center ☐

These move-up and move-down brackets are used mostly for misalignment within a line; the move-right, move-left, and move-to-the-center marks are used mostly for whole lines or passages.

Contour

Justified copy has even left- and right-hand margins. *Ragged right* copy has lines of varying width, making an uneven right margin, as you see in most type-written copy. *Flush* means vertically aligned. Justified copy is flush both right and left; ragged right copy is flush left only.

Figure 10 illustrates justified, ragged, and flush margins.

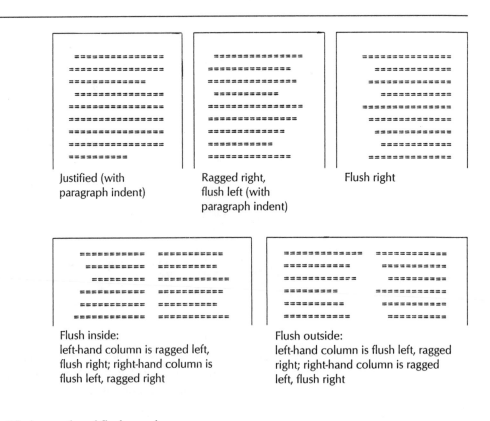

Figure 10. Justified, ragged, and flush margins

Ragged right copy should have no discernible shape, that is, the line endings should not form the silhouette of an object. Also undesirable are *hangers* (long lines that protrude between short lines) and *holes* (noticeably short lines), especially when a *tight rag* (all lines ending close to the margin) is specified. To correct a bad rag, you may mark to shorten a line by bringing a short word or part of a word down to the next line; or you may mark to fill a short line by bringing a short word or part of a word up to the previous line, as shown in the following example.

ragged right copy set with
a hanger—a line protruding between   *(run over)*
short lines.

ragged right copy set
with a hole—an
~~unnecessarily~~ short line   *un-nec-es-sar-i-ly*

Keep in mind that such a correction will change the position of words on the following lines; don't call for a change that causes further problems. In fact, a rule of thumb for ragged right copy is this: Mark bad rags only when they are obvious and easily changed; forget the rest.

Line, word, and letter spacing

Line spacing or *leading* (rhymes with sledding), a term many people still use, refers to the space between lines. (The word *leading* comes from the kind of composition that prevailed for more than four centuries, in which metal characters were hand-set one by one and lines of type were separated by strips of metal called *leads.*)

Line spacing and *word spacing* (the space between words) may need correcting to make them consistent with the rest of the type, with typographic standards, or with the specifications.

The general marks are these: the space sign (#) to add space; the close-up mark or tie (⌒) to delete *all* extra space; and either "less #" or "*ʃ* #" to delete *some* space.

The in-text mark for most errors in line spacing is a long sideways caret (>——— or ———<); for errors in word spacing, an upright caret. Figure 11 illustrates these marks.

If any man were to ask me ʌ what I would suppose   *(less #)*
to be a perfect style of language, I would answer,
that in which a man speaking to a hundred people,

ʃ # >———

of all common and various capacities, idiots or
lunatics excepted, should be understood by them
> all, and in the same sense which the speaker in-
tended to be understood. ʌ

—Defoe

Figure 11. Errors in line and word spacing

In justified typeset copy, word spacing will vary slightly from line to line but must appear to be equal within any one line. Where word spacing is unequal, use checkmarks to show where the problem is and, in a ring, mark "eq #"—for equal space—in the margin:

Proofreading is alive and well in Alexandria, Virginia. *eq #*

The equal space mark can also be used for line spacing:

eq # Proofreading is alive and well in Alexandria, Chicago, Dubuque, Los Angeles, Montreal, Paris,

London, New York City, Rome, St. Louis, Toronto, Washington, D.C., and everywhere people care about accuracy and quality in the printed word.

Sometimes you may see the need for a hair space—a very thin space:

 n'est-ce pas? *hr #*

In justified copy, wide word spacing can result in *rivers of white*—long, uneven vertical areas of white space—or in *lakes*—open areas of white space within the text. Rivers and lakes are rare, but when they occur, they need to be marked as shown in Figure 12.

—The Crime Control Act of 1973 (Public Law 93-83). This Act further refined L.F.A.A.'s administrative structure, revised block and discretionary funding requirements, expanded the role of the National Institute of Law Enforcement and Criminal Justice, and added security and privacy guidelines to safeguard criminal history information.

River of white

The commission, an independent agency of 12 members of Congress and three executive branch officials who evaluate and encourage compliance with the 1975 agreement signed by 35 nations, held hearings Wednesday and yesterday on the human rights guarantees of individual "freedom to practice and profess... religion or belief" and "of equality before the law" for minorities.

Lakes

Figure 12. Rivers and lakes

Letter spacing means adding extra space between letters. The letter spacing of lowercase characters used to be considered unacceptable in high-quality work. (Goudy, a famous designer, said, "Anyone who would letter space lowercase would steal a sheep.") But lowercase letter spacing is often seen in the justified columns of newspapers and periodicals, and more and more often in book work.

An entire letter-spaced line is less objectionable than one letter-spaced word within a line (see (a) and (b) in Figure 13).

Conspicuous lowercase letter spacing may be acceptable in a narrow, justified column, as shown in part (c) of Figure 13.

In high-quality work, wide word spacing is usually preferred to letter spacing. But specs may require you to follow a different standard by marking for lowercase letter spacing in preference to wide word spacing, as shown in part (d) of Figure 13.

Volunteers from the Nursing Program at Northern Virginia Community College will be testing patients' hearing, vision, b l o o d pressure and blood chemistry. Tests for oral temperature

(a) One letter-spaced word

Sort of surprised me, too. To be offering a kit for d e c o r a t i n g jeans. But it's in and I wanted you to be sure that t h e o n e y o u s p e n t y o u r m o n e y o n w o r k e d and s t a y e d o n in m a c h i n e wash- ings.

(c) Narrow justified column

"The couples there who expressed problems in working as equals seemed to be the ones who were very caught up in conventional role-playing."

(b) An entire letter-spaced line

Proofreading   excellence   comes through knowledge, technical know-how, judgment, and vigilance. Training can only make a start toward excellence.

(d) Letter spacing needed

Figure 13. Lowercase letter spacing

The letter spacing of capitals may mean the insertion of equal amounts of extra space between letters or it may mean "optical" or "visual" letter spacing. Optical letter spacing is a refinement in high-quality work that involves varying the amount of space between capital letters to make the letters appear equally spaced, like this:

letter-spaced: CAPITALS

not letter-spaced: CAPITALS

While proofreading high-quality typography, you will see kerned letters and ligatures. *Kerning* involves *negative* letter spacing—reducing the space between certain pairs of letters so they fit together better. The following sentence includes three kerning pairs—roman Ya and Va, italic *Wh:*

kerns: Yawning Valleys of *White* space Vanish

no kerns: Y awning V alleys of *White* space V anish

Which pairs of letters are automatically kerned varies from one font to another and from one program or kind of equipment to another. An operator can set a font to kern other pairs and also can kern letter by letter. An automatic kerning program may affect as many as a hundred character pairs. Here are a few pairs shown kerned and not kerned:

Kerned	Not kerned
Y. Ya YO yo	Y. Ya YO yo
WA Wa We we Wo	WA Wa We we Wo
T. TA Ta Te To Tr Tu Tw Ty	T. TA Ta Te To Tr Tu Tw Ty
P. PA "A A" "V V"	P. PA "A A" "V V"

A *ligature* is a unit formed of two or more letters linked together. These are the common *f*-ligatures:

Ligature	No Ligature
ff, fi, fl, ffi, ffl	ff, fi, fl, ffi, ffl

These diphthongs are also considered ligatures, but they are seldom specified:

$$Æ \quad æ \quad Œ \quad œ$$

The following example is set with ligatures for *fi* and *fl*. Here's how to call for the others—*ffi, ffl,* and *ff:*

His rifled office files baffled the sheriff.　ffi/ ffl/ ff　(3 ligs)

> For practice in marking changes in space,
> turn to Exercise 16.

Breaks

Familiarize yourself with the rules for word breaks; correcting wrong end-of-line hyphens is always a proofreader's responsibility.

A common way to mark word division for correction is to combine insertion, deletion (simple and tied), and replacement:

Insertion + simple deletion

.... inco-
/rect word break

Deletion with close-up mark + insertion:

........incorf-
ect word break

Replacement + deletion:

........incorre/
et-word break

In the last example, note that *replacement* (of the hyphen) is the efficient way to mark the problem. Also note that an insertion at the beginning of a line is closed up, but a replacement at the end of a line isn't.

> For practice in marking word division with combination marks,
> turn to Exercise 17.

Mark a ring around unacceptably long *ladders* of consecutive line-end hyphens and write "break up" (in a ring) in the margin. A ladder of more than three word-break hyphens is usually unacceptable (high standards allow no more than two hyphens). Be sure you know how many hyphens constitute an unacceptable ladder for each job you proofread. Here's how to mark:

> Long *ladders* (stacks of line-end hyphens) and *knotholes* (identi-
> cal characters stacked up on consecutive lines) are never desir-
> able. How many stacked hyphens are acceptable varies among pub-
> lishers and type shops and depends on the width of the line mea-
> sure.

Mark a ring around unsightly blocks (*knotholes*) of stacked characters, and write "break up" (in a ring) in the margin:

> Standards for blocks vary with the number of characters and lines
> involved. They also vary with the typographic factors such as line
> width and line spacing and are often a matter of judgment rather
> than of rule.

Mark to insert a paragraph break with a caret in the text and a paragraph sign (⁊) in the margin.

> *The riddle:* The land was white, the seed was black. It
> will take a good scholar to riddle me that. *The answer:*   ⁊
> A book.

Note that in many books the paragraphs immediately following headings and subheadings are set flush left; the reasoning is that indention isn't needed where other elements make it clear that new paragraphs begin.

Where paragraphs aren't involved but type needs to be moved to the line above or below—for example, in a heading, to "break for sense"—show which words and characters should be moved back to the previous line or carried over to the next line. The traditional marks, "run back" and "run over," shown below, derive from old ways of typesetting, as does much typographic terminology. You may prefer to use "run up" and "run down," which some operators find clearer. Use the marks that work best in your situation.

Proofreading mark	Corrected copy
ANOTHER DAY, ANOTHER DOLLAR—ANOTHER DEADLINE	ANOTHER DAY, ANOTHER DOLLAR— ANOTHER DEADLINE

Proofreading mark	Corrected copy
PROOFREADER HANGED BY DANGLING PARTICLE	PROOFREADER HANGED BY DANGLING PARTICLE

If you prefer the traditional terms, here's a way to help you remember them:

run <u>back</u> means "Back ↑ up a line."

run <u>over</u> means "Put ↓ down a line."

Another in-text break mark is a big, block-letter Z. It can be used for a sense break instead of the run-over mark, or it can be used to mark for consistent style, as shown in the list below:

Aquarium, Department of Commerce Building,
14th St. between Constitution Ave. and E St., N.W.

 Botanic Garden, 1st St. and Maryland Ave., S.W.

Dumbarton Oaks,
1703 32nd St., N.W.

National Arboretum,
Bladensburg Rd. and R St., N.E.

Where a paragraph begins mistakenly, draw a connecting line in the text from the break to the start of the next line, and write " no ¶ " (in a ring) in the margin.

Where no break is wanted but " no ¶ " doesn't apply, draw a connecting line from the break to the start of the next line and write "run on" or "run in" (they mean the same thing). The following list shows how this mark can be used to call for consistent style:

Chicago, Illinois. Population: 3 million (city); 7.1 million (metropolitan area). Area: 200 square miles on Lake Michigan.

Los Angeles, California. Population: 3 million (city); 7.5 million (metropolitan area). Area: 463.7 square miles on the Pacific Ocean.

 New York City, New York. Population: 7 million (city); 13.6 million (consolidated area). Area: 300 square miles at the mouth of the Hudson River.

A *widow* is a short line of a few characters or words at the beginning or end of a page or the end of a paragraph. Standards defining acceptable widows vary. The following list is a general guide to what you should catch, presented in the order these widows are usually objected to (the first is the worst) by designers and publishers:

- A heading appears at the bottom of a page with fewer than a specified number of text lines (2–6) following the heading. The example shows one line of text following a heading:

```
============
=========
   HEADING
============
```

- The last line of a paragraph is the top line of a page or column and takes up less than one-third of the specified line width:

```
=====
===========
===========
===========
```

- The entire last line of a paragraph is the end of a broken word or of a compound expression that should not be broken (for example, *Los Angeles, 6:00 PM, page 207*):

```
=============
=============
=========bro-
ken
```

- The last line of a page or column is the first line of a paragraph. (Some people call this fault an *orphan.*)

```
=============
=============
=========
===========
```

- The last line of a paragraph is less than a specified limit, for example, one-third the line width or a specified number of characters (usually 2–6):

```
=============
=============
=============
=
```

Usually you should simply point out widow lines that aren't acceptable and not try to figure out how to fix them; that's usually up to the typesetter or the editor:

The rest is up to the typesetter or ed-
[itor.

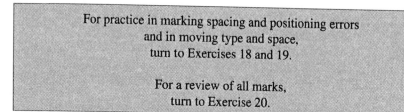

For practice in marking spacing and positioning errors
and in moving type and space,
turn to Exercises 18 and 19.

For a review of all marks,
turn to Exercise 20.

Written-out instructions

Write out the instruction for symbols that have no special mark, for example:

Greek characters: β *(lc Grk beta)*

reference marks: † *(dagger)*

mathematical, scientific, or technical symbols: ± *(plus or minus)*

ampersand: & *(ampersand)*

bullet: • *(bullet)* (or) • *(bold ctr dot)*

Write out the instruction if the designated character is the same as a proofreading mark:

#4 and ‸5   # *(number sign)*
either‸or   / *(slash)*
2 + 2‸4   =/ *(equal sign)*

Write out the instruction where a mark might be confused with another character, for example, zero with letter *o* or lowercase el with numeral one:

20,600   o *(zero)*
All   *(reset as letter "els")*

Write out the instruction wherever you can't use standard marks:

(Ctr hed on 2 cols) center heading over two columns
(P U art)   pick up (and insert) artwork

> For practice in proofreading,
> turn to Exercise 21.

Measuring type and space

To detect deviations from specifications, you need to understand the capabilities of the equipment that produced the type you're proofreading.

Capabilities vary greatly, not only from desktop publishing equipment to traditional typesetting equipment, but also within each of these categories. Furthermore, the categories overlap. The following descriptions are broad generalities.

Typewriter quality

Although most word-processing programs can provide fonts of the higher quality we usually see in desktop publishing and typesetting, typewriter-quality fonts may be preferred for certain documents, for example, for business letters and for direct-mail solicitation. The theory seems to be that documents that appear to be typewritten are more personal, more informal—friendlier.

Character width

Typewriter-quality type is uniformly spaced; that is, every character is the same width as every other; a period takes the same amount of horizontal space as a zero; and nine lowercase *i*'s take the same space as nine capital *M*'s:

```
MMMMMMMMM
iiiiiiiii
```

Word spacing

On a typewriter, one stroke of the space bar leaves blank the same amount of space that one character takes. Most typewriter copy follows the convention of one blank space between words and two blank spaces after a sentence. (Typeset copy and other proportionally spaced copy almost always is set with just one word space after a sentence, as described in the next section.)

Justifying uniformly spaced type, which increases the space between words, usually results in uneven word spacing and inevitably creates rivers and lakes.

Indention

In typewriter quality, paragraph indention is specified by the number of spaces to be left blank. Where the common five-space paragraph indent is specified, typing starts on the sixth space. *Block indention* may be specified for extracts (quotations that are set off). Here is how you can mark for correct indention:

```
→ 5   Where a five-space indent is specified,
      typing starts on the sixth space.

→ 5   Block indention--usually at the same space
      as paragraph indention--may be specified
      for quoted extracts.
```

Type size

The standard sizes of uniformly spaced type are *elite* and *pica*. Elite prints out at 12 characters per linear inch and is specified as 12 *pitch* or 12 *cpi* (characters per inch); pica prints out at 10 pitch (or 10 cpi). (Don't confuse this pica with the typesetter's unit of measure, which is discussed later.) Fifteen-pitch type or smaller may also be available.

Line spacing

Typewriter fonts can print out in *single space* ("SS") and in multiples of single space, such as *double space* ("DS"), *space and a half* (½#), and *triple space* ("TS").

Type quality from different kinds of equipment

Figure 14 presents examples of the kinds of type quality discussed in this section.

Most high-quality type used for desktop publishing and computerized typesetting is designed on the basis of dots per inch (*dpi*). Beginning at 300 dpi, desktop publishing systems with laser printers produce "near-typeset-quality" type. Advanced laser printers can produce much greater resolution; at 2,000 dpi or

ABCDEFGHIJKLMNOPQRSTUVWXYZ1234
abcdefghijklmnopqrstuvwxyz
"I am the Roman emperor and am
above grammar."   --Sigismund

(a) Dot matrix printer

ABCDEFGHIJKLMNOPQRSTUVWXYZ1234
abcdefghijklmnopqrstuvwxyz
"I am the Roman emperor and am
above grammar."   --Sigismund

(b) Typewriter quality

ABCDEFGHIJKLMNOPQRSTUVWXYZ1234
abcdefghijklmnopqrstuvwxyz
"I am the Roman emperor and am
above grammar."   —Sigismund

(c) Laser printer, 300 dpi

ABCDEFGHIJKLMNOPQRSTUVWXYZ1234
abcdefghijklmnopqrstuvwxyz
"I am the Roman emperor and am
above grammar."   —Sigismund

(d) Laser printer, 1200 dpi

ABCDEFGHIJKLMNOPQRSTUVWXYZ1234
abcdefghijklmnopqrstuvwxyz
"I am the Roman emperor and am
above grammar."   —Sigismund

(e) Imagesetter, 2540 dpi

Figure 14. Type produced by different equipment

more, type is considered true typeset quality. For most proofreaders, however, at about 600 dpi the distinction between near-typeset quality and true typeset quality blurs.

Desktop publishing and typeset quality

The standard fonts for typesetting, including desktop publishing, are designed with *proportional spacing*; that is, different characters occupy different amounts of horizontal space. For example, 9 *M*'s may take up the same space as thirty-six *i*'s:

MMMMMMMMM

iiiiiiiiiiiiiiiiiiiiiiiiiiiiiiiiiiii

There are many other variables and refinements. Depending on the equipment, thousands of typefaces are available and dozens (perhaps hundreds) of extra characters within a typeface—dashes of various lengths; small caps; ligatures; kerning pairs; symbols of all kinds; and minute variations in letter, word, and line spacing. An operator can easily change typeface, type size, and spacing with a few keystrokes; for example, italic can be set for emphasis or a different type size can be set for a heading.

Absolute measurements: Points and picas

Every proofreader of typeset or near-typeset copy should memorize the following table:

    12 points = 1 pica
     6 picas   = 1 inch
    72 points = 1 inch

In fonts based on traditional printers' measure, 6 picas or 72 points equal a fraction less than an inch, and an inch ruler is inaccurate beyond 3 or 4 picas. In some desktop publishing fonts, however, the pica-to-inch correlation is exact.

Type size is measured in points. Type up to 14 points in size is usually used for *text* or *body type*. Larger type is usually used for *display,* as in headings. In Figure 15, which illustrates some type sizes, the heavy vertical line shows the true size; the white space above and below each capital H represents the space needed to accommodate *ascenders* (such as the ascending stroke in a lowercase *b*) and *descenders* (as in a *p*).

In some word-processing programs, line spacing is specified in the typewriter convention as single space, space and a half, double space, etc.; in some, it is specified in decimal fractions of inches (e.g., 0.5, 1, 1.5, etc.); and in some, in printers' measure (points).

In true typesetting, type size is specified in points, usually in combination with line spacing.

Type size along with line spacing is usually specified as if it were a fraction; for example, 9-point type set with 1 point of extra space between lines makes a line depth of 10 points and is marked 9/10; 10-point type on a 12-point line is marked 10/12.

Line width, also called *column width, line measure,* or just *measure,* is usually specified in picas. Here are examples of specifications for type, including typeface, type size, line spacing, and column width.

Times Roman bold 9/10 × 22

Century Expanded 10/12 × 18

The first example, "9 on 10 times 22," signifies 9-point Times Roman boldface set with 1 point of line spacing at a 22-pica line measure. The second, "10 on 12 times 18," signifies 10-point Century Expanded set with 2 points of line spacing at an 18-pica measure.

To verify the line depth (type size plus leading), line width, page depth, and indention, you need a line gauge like one of those pictured in Appendix D.

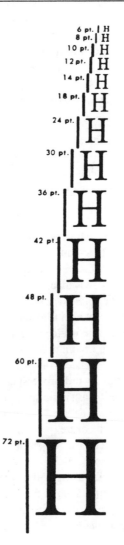

Figure 15. Type size

To measure type size, however, a line gauge is not the best tool, because different faces of the same size fill different amounts of vertical space. Compare the two faces shown below, both in 36-point type:

abcde   abcde

Cheltenham   Times
                  New Roman

To verify type size, a common tool is a transparent overlay on which characters of the type face in use are printed in various sizes. But if such a tool isn't available, you can usually make do by using a line gauge to measure the line depth from baseline to baseline, a measurement that includes type size.

To verify the width of a straight rule (hairline, half point, or other size), it's better to compare with a sample produced on the equipment you are reading instead of using a line gauge.

Fixed spaces: Ems and fractions of ems

An *em space* (also called *em quad, mutton quad,* or *molly quad*) is a blank square the size of the type being used; in 10-point type, an em space is 10 points wide and 10 points deep.

An *en space* (also called *en quad, nut quad,* or *nellie quad*) is a blank rectangle half the width of an em; in 10-point type, an en space is 5 points wide and 10 points deep.

Em spaces are commonly specified for paragraph indents. En spaces may be specified for the sides of columns in a table.

Ems measure type as well as space. Typographers may charge customers by the number of ems set. Proofreading may be related to the number of ems read; for example, accuracy may be rated by the number of errors per 10,000 ems.

To mark to correct indention or to insert specific quantities of space (as between columns), use carets in text and the following marks in the margin:

1 en	*en* #	3 ems	3
1 em	□	4 ems	4
2 ems	⊏⊐		

A *figure space* is the width of any single-digit figure—from 0 to 9—and of a dollar sign; in some systems, a figure space is the same as an en space. A *thin space* (thin #) is the width of a punctuation mark such as a period or comma. Among the uses of figure spaces and thin spaces is the alignment of columns of figures.

Variable spacing

Picas and points are absolute measurements; em, en, figure, and thin spaces are fixed spaces relative to the type size; but word spaces vary minutely from line to line to achieve justification. A variable word space may be called a *space band*, a term left over from typesetting equipment such as the Linotype.

In most copy, the space after a sentence is the same variable space as that between words; DTP operators and typesetters press the space bar only once.

Letter spacing is sometimes set to be variable. And leading, when it isn't *modular* (invariable), may vary slightly on facing pages where, between aligned top and bottom lines, one page has more lines than the other.

Recommendations for useful marking

- The most important things in proofreading are, first, catching the errors and, second, marking so the corrector understands your instructions. Marking so the corrector understands is the main reason to use standard marks. It may also be the reason to use nonstandard marks when it's practical: some organizations have developed their own marking systems. Common sense should tell you whether to choose to do what works or to seek to persuade people to change.
- Many standard proofreading marks are self-explanatory; however, if you are proofreading typeset copy and the corrector is an operator recently converted to typesetting, some of the marks—in fact, some of the concepts, such as that of the en dash—will be mystifying. You may want to use the proofmarks listed in whatever dictionary the corrector has, or you may want to provide a copy of the list of standard marks at the end of this chapter.
- Within the system of standard marks, many errors can be marked in more than one way. Here are examples of alternative marks, any of which will do the job; the last is the simplest and most efficient:

Be sure of it; give me ~~proof~~/ocular/the/   *ʃ/(tr)/ proof ⊙*

Be sure of it; give me/proof/ocular/~~the~~.   *the /(tr)/ ʃ*

Be sure of it; give me ~~proof~~ ocular ~~the~~.   *the / proof*

- Never invent a mark on the spur of the moment; it's better to be thought an amateur than to be misunderstood. Write out the instruction when you forget how to mark or can't quickly figure it out. Also write out the instruction whenever you find deviations from specs that can't be marked with standard proofmarks:

(reset in Baskerville)   change typeface to Baskerville

(reset 9/10)   change to 9-point type with 1 point between lines

(reset × 30)   change column width to 30 picas

> For practice in checking specifications,
> turn to Exercise 22.

List of standard proofmarks

GENERAL RULES

- Mark every error both in text and margin.
- Use left and right margins, according if which is closer to the error.
- Mark from left to right, and use slashes in the margin
- —to separate multiple marks, and
- —to call attention to inconspicuous marks.

OPERATIONS
(delete, insert, replace, transpose)

- delete one character
- delete more than one character
- delete and close up space
- inset one character or more—up to seven words
- insert more than seven words
- insert and close up at left
- insert and close up at right
- replace one character
- replace more one character
- transpose (words)(adjacent)
- transpose adjacent letters
- (or) replace transposed letters

SPECIAL MARKS

- don't set ringed explanation in type
- ignore marked correction
- defective character
- query at author (if answer likely)
- query at author (if answer uncertain)
- make some correction consecutively as many times as slashes
- spell out (abbrev.) numeral, or symbol)

SPACE AND POSITION

- close up space; make one word
- insert space; make two words
- less space between words
- equalize space between words
- insert line space
- take out line space
- move right
- move down
- move left
- move up
- center
- align horizontally
- align vertically

LINE BREAKS

- no new line
- break Begin new line
- carry over to next line
- carry back to previous line
- start new paragraph. Here
- no new paragraph. Here
- correct word division as shown
- correct word division as shown
- divide words to fill out short line at appropriate point

TYPESET COPY ONLY

- en dash
- em dash
- two-em dash
- indent 1 em or insert 1-em space
- indent 2 ems or insert 2-em space
- indent or insert number of ems shown

TYPED OR WORD-PROCESSED COPY ONLY

- indent five spaces; type on sixth
- indent five spaces
- either hyphen or en dash; type closed up
- two hyphens; type closed up (equivalent to typeset em dash)

TYPE STYLE

- italic
- small caps
- full caps
- boldface
- caps and small caps
- lowercase
- single-letter caps
- caps and lowercase
- CAPS AND LOWERCASE
- wrong font
- ligature (as in off)
- kern (as in Won)

PUNCTUATION AND SYMBOLS

- inferior, subscript
- superior, superscript
- apostrophe
- comma
- colon
- exclamation point
- hyphen
- parentheses
- period
- question mark
- quotation marks: double, single
- semicolon
- virgule (slash, shilling)

4 More on Marks

Alternative marks

You may see coworkers using different marks from the ones in this book. You may need to change your marks to please a corrector, a supervisor, or an employer.

Book system vs. guideline system

What you have been learning here is the *book system* of proofmarks. Another standard is the *guideline (kitestring)* system in which guidelines connect the in-text mark with the marginal mark, like this:

The guideline system is another standard.

Guidelines are neither so neat as the unconnected marks of the book system nor, for practiced proofreaders and correctors, so quick to mark or so easy to follow on one-column text. Some organizations insist on guidelines, however, and some kinds of proof can be more clearly marked with guidelines.

If you have a choice, use the book system as much as you can, but use guidelines where they are more practical, for example, in dense tables with many errors.

Recognizable variations

Many marks are recognizable variations of those on the list of standard proofmarks; for example, the sign for an em dash may be written in one of these ways:

Abbreviations may differ, as in "S.O." for "spell out" or "W.O." for "write out." Instead of the abbreviation for "center," the marginal mark may repeat the in-text mark:

]PROOFREADING: A GUIDE[   ][

The dele, which derives from the lowercase Greek delta (δ), is especially variable. All variations have kept the loop, and most have kept the tail, but few look like a delta otherwise. Many editors like to use a simple loop, but this version is a poor choice for proofreaders because it could be read as a lowercase *e*. (If you use a loop, put a tail on it, or turn it upside down.)

Editor's loop (not recommended):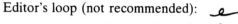

Loop with a tail:

Upside-down loop:

Other forms of the dele include those shown in Figure 16.

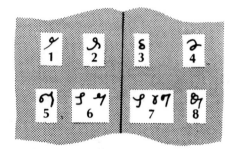

PAGES FROM THE DELE FAMILY ALBUM

Except for a loop—the one trait all have in common—deles (delete signs) may not look much alike. Many, however, have a strong family resemblance to each other. Reading from left to right across both pages of the "family album," the samples shown are found in the following:

1. *Words into Type,* Prentice-Hall; also *Pocket Pal,* International Paper Company.
2. *The Chicago Manual of Style.*
3. The Greek alphabet. The lowercase delta is the great-grandfather of all deles.
4. *Copy Preparation for Printing,* Cabibi; McGraw-Hill.
5. *Copy Editing,* Judith Butcher; Cambridge University Press.
6. (two deles) *Government Printing Office Style Manual.*
7. (three deles) *Webster's New Collegiate Dictionary,* Merriam.
8. *General Printing,* Cleeton, Pitkin, and Cornwell; McKnight & McKnight.

Figure 16. The dele family album

Bad breaks

Some typographers prefer that bad word breaks be marked to show every place a hyphen is correct, so the corrector can choose the break that best fits the line:

```
. . . . . . . . .inco
rrect word break
```

Less space

Some editors and typographers mark either the bottom half or the top half of a close-up mark to call for less space in a line:

less⌒space

(or)

less⌣space

Some distinguish "close up all space" from "reduce space" with one or the other half of the close-up mark; you have to figure out which symbol means what:

less ‿ space   less ⌒ space
           (or)
cloͦse up all space   cloͮse up all space

Line spacing

Instead of space marks for errors in the line spacing of typeset copy, some people use the marks "ld" and "𝄐 ld," meaning "add leading," and "delete leading." Some just mark "wr ld," meaning "wrong leading." And some mark excess line spacing with a vertical close-up mark.

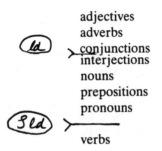

adjectives   adjectives
adverbs   adverbs
conjunctions   conjunctions
interjections   interjections
nouns   nouns
prepositions   prepositions
pronouns   pronouns

verbs   verbs

Uncommon marks

Some lists of marks include a few holdovers from old forms of composition. Here are a couple of these marks:

push down: ⏝
invert: ❾

In metal type, the *push-down* mark represented a finger pushing down spacing material that worked up too high, picked up ink, and printed. Here's an example:

mainly⬛on diesel

In photocomposition, the push-down mark signals a *density* problem; that is, words or lines that are conspicuously darker than others and that need "pushing down" in *color* (blackness). (Density can, of course, also be too light.) Here's an example of a density problem:

Words like glass **darken whatever**
they do not help us see.
—Joubert

In metal type, the *invert* mark represented a finger describing a clockwise motion and showing that an upside-down character needed to be turned upright.

Today, the invert mark represents upside-down material (produced, for example, in careless paste-up of corrections or graphics). Here's an example of an inversion problem:

> Where are the proofreaders of yesterday who knew
> at a glance what ⟨IΛXXXꞀWϽW⟩ stood for?   ℧

Some lists of marks include one for centering a character vertically; for example:

Marked for center dot	Corrected
⚇ 2x ⌣ 13x	2x · 13x

Use these marks only if you know the corrector understands them. Writing out "density problem" or "turn over" or "center vertically" takes a bit longer but may be surer.

Understanding editing marks

To read manuscript against live copy, you must be able to interpret an author's or an editor's marks. You may also have to use editing marks yourself.

Editing marks are not the same as proofmarks. Many of the symbols are the same, but they are usually used differently for these reasons:

1. Editing marks are usually used on copy that will be rekeyed; proofmarks are usually used on copy that's already been keyed and needs only correction.

2. Editing marks are usually used on copy that has plenty of space to write between lines; proofmarks are usually used on copy with too little space to write between lines.

Editing marks go right in the text where their instructions can readily be followed while the entire text is being rekeyed. At this stage, marginal marks are unnecessary and confusing. Editing marks look like this:

```
The (combinations) possible) from the 26 letters of

the alpẖabet, if each is used only once, number

620,448,‿401,733,239,439,360⊙
```

Proofmarks go both in the text and in the margin. The in-text marks are specific locator marks; the marginal marks not only describe the corrections needed, but they also flag the line containing the error so that the person making the corrections need not search the entire text for occasional marks. Proofmarks look like this:

```
The (combinations) possible) from the 26 letters of    (ΔP)
the alpₐabet, if each is used only once, number
620,448,‿401,733,239,439,360
                                    ⊙
```

Editors working with single-spaced typewritten or word-processed copy may resort to proofmarks or to a combination of proofmarks and editing marks.

Proofreaders working with copy that has generous extra space between the lines may be told to use no proofmarks but to use editing marks in the text and checkmarks in the margin, as explained later in this chapter under "Modified marking techniques."

Standard editing marks are shown in the following list. A well-marked edited page appears in Figure 17.

STANDARD EDITING MARKS
(Marks not listed are the same symbols as proofmarks but they are used in the text only.)

BASIC MARKS
deleteg character
delete ~~delete~~ word
delete and closḙe up
close up entirely;
   change to one worᵈd
close up part way
   use less ⌢ space
insert word or cᴬaracter
connect insertion to the
character at its left:
   sing low (for sings low)
connect insertion to the
character at its right:
   sing low (for sing slow)
replace a character or ~~characters~~ *word*
transpose order change

SPACING AND POSITIONING
insert#space
(or) insert#space
xxx. Begin paragraph
(or) xxx. Begin paragraph...

xxxxxxxxxxxxxxxxxxxx.
⌐xxxxx. run on same line

⌋center⌐

⌐move left

⌋move right

PUNCTUATION AND SYMBOLS
comma ⌄
period ⊙
change comma to period⊙
change period to comma⌄
hyphen =
apostrophe ⌄
inferior ⌃
superior ⌄

TYPE MARKS
/lowercase character
/LOWERCASE word
c̲ap character
c̲a̲p̲ word
set in italic
set in boldface
set in caps and small caps

SPECIAL MARKS
retain hyphen, as in bell-
   like (used at ends of lines)
delete hy-
   phen and close up
   (used at ends of lines)
spell out ringed matter
   (change 3 oz. to three ounces)
use figure, symbol, or abbreviation for
   ringed matter (change three ounces
   to 3 oz.
     end (or) **30** (or) **#** (end of copy)

Note: Appendix E, Editing Marks and Proofmarks Compared, presents a chart of the two kinds of marks side by side.

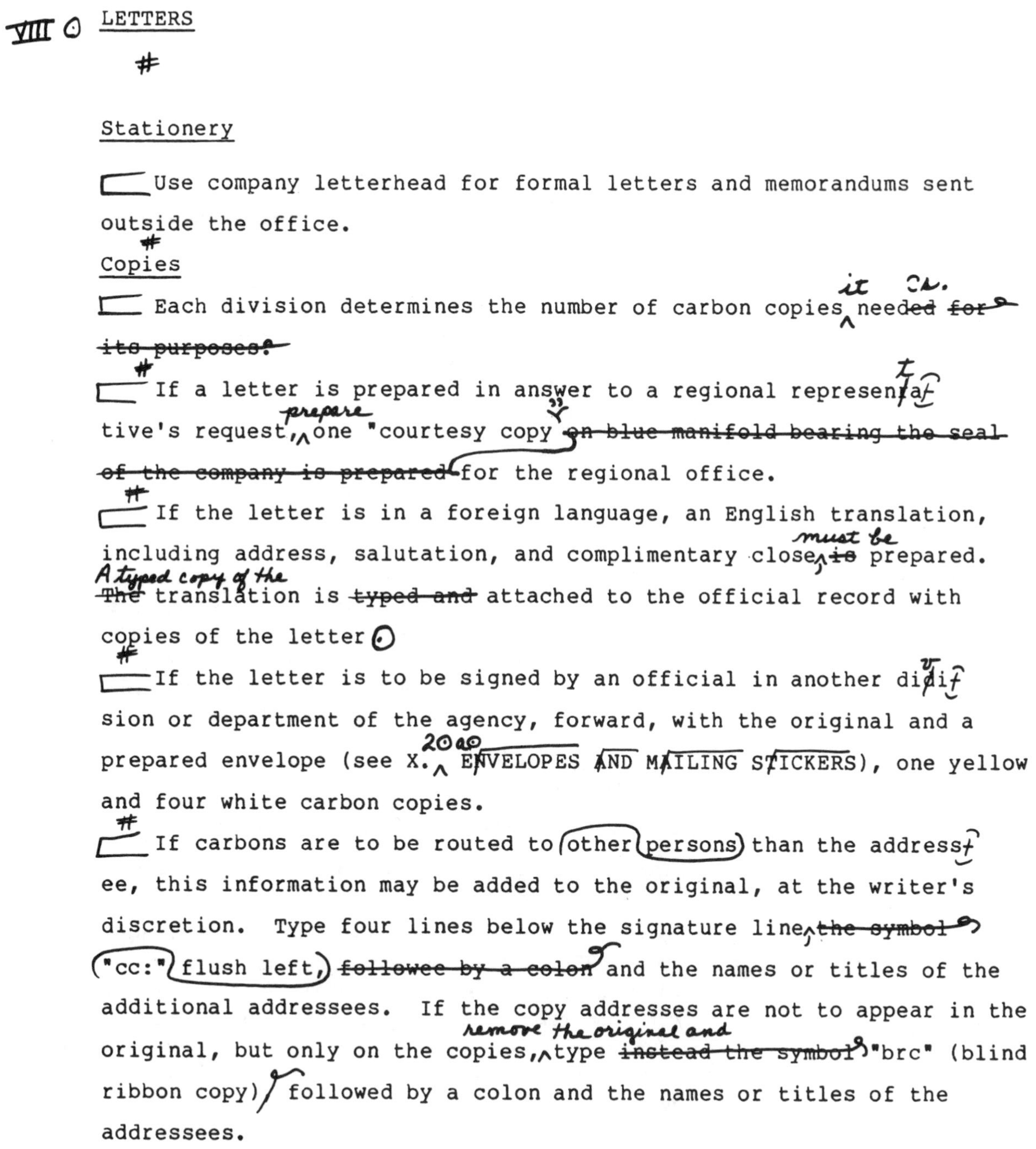

VIII ○ LETTERS
#

Stationery

Use company letterhead for formal letters and memorandums sent outside the office.

Copies

Each division determines the number of carbon copies needed for its purposes.

If a letter is prepared in answer to a regional representative's request, one "courtesy copy on blue manifold bearing the seal of the company is prepared for the regional office.

If the letter is in a foreign language, an English translation, including address, salutation, and complimentary close, is prepared. The translation is typed and attached to the official record with copies of the letter.

If the letter is to be signed by an official in another division or department of the agency, forward, with the original and a prepared envelope (see X. ENVELOPES AND MAILING STICKERS), one yellow and four white carbon copies.

If carbons are to be routed to other persons than the addressee, this information may be added to the original, at the writer's discretion. Type four lines below the signature line, the symbol "cc:" flush left, followed by a colon and the names or titles of the additional addressees. If the copy addresses are not to appear in the original, but only on the copies, type instead the symbol "brc" (blind ribbon copy) followed by a colon and the names or titles of the addressees.

Figure 17. A well-marked edited page

Interpreting editing marks may be easy or challenging. You may see recognizable variations of standard marks, but then again you may see proofmarks used incorrectly or even marks that are personal inventions.

Marks that have different meanings to different markers pose the biggest difficulty. You have to figure out which interpretation is sensible. Here are two examples:

xx⌢xx This mark can mean "less space" or "close up" or "set ligature."

∟ This mark can mean "new paragraph" or "move left."

A careful editor may mark unusual usage or spelling to prevent mistaken "correction" or needless querying in one of the following ways:

```
William Shakespere   (Folo copy)
                (stet)
"Hello!  How it goes?" he asked.

MariAnn

pom-(pon) girls.
                        (C.Q.)
The medium is the massage.
```

"Copy" in "Folo copy" means the dead copy. "Stet," of course, means "Let it stand." A checkmark means "I have checked this." The box means "It's correct as written." And "CQ," originally the code used by telegraphers to start a transmission, means, "Pay attention to the unusual—but correct—way it's written."

Newspaper copy editors and people who have taken journalism courses may underscore a handwritten lowercase *u* and overscore an *n:*

Some journalists underscore a u and overscore an n.

Some people also underscore *w* and *a* and overscore *m* and *o.*

Some people underscore a, u, and w and overscore m, n, and o.

You may see a zero marked with a diagonal line through it to distinguish it from letter *o.* The slashed zero appears as a character in certain technical material and on some computer screens and printouts. You may see letter Z crossed through to distinguish it from figure 2; you may see figure 7 crossed through in the European manner; and you may see figure 1 with a beak or with a beak and a base; and you may see the notation "el" to distinguish the lowercase letter from the numeral:

letter o:	O	figure 7:	7̶
zero:	∅	figure 1:	1 (or) 1
letter Z:	Z̶	lowercase l:	(el)
figure 2:	2		

For practice in proofreading edited copy,
turn to Exercise 23.

Modified marking techniques

You may need to adapt standard marking techniques to the preferences or
needs of an employer or customer, a typist or typesetter, or the particular form of
copy.

(*Caution to novices.* Read this section on modified techniques as background
information but, to avoid confusion, don't work the exercises. When you need to
use one of these techniques, reread the part of this book that applies, and do the
accompanying exercise as a starting point.)

Some of the exercises have already introduced you to one modified marking
technique—marking in one margin only. Other modified techniques include the
following:

- Writing out instructions instead of using proofmarks. This technique is
  used for correctors who don't know proofmarks and are unwilling to learn
  them. Here's an example:

take out and   *change o to p*   The art of art, the glory expression and
and the sunshine of the light of letters
is simplicity.

—Whitman

add of

cap W

- Marking in the margins only. This is one of the techniques used for *camera-ready copy* (final pages ready to be printed):

and the   *simplicity*   The art of art, the glory expression and
and the sunshine of the light of letters
is simolicity.

—whitman

glory of

whitman

- Proofreading without marking copy: writing a correction list by hand. This
  is another technique for camera-ready copy. Include page, paragraph, and
  line numbers for both dead and live copy. (See Figure 18.)

Figure 18. Handwritten correction list

- Proofreading without marking copy: typing a correction list. Include page, paragraph, and line numbers for both dead and live copy. (See Figure 19.)

```
          Correction list for Whitman quotation

Dead copy         Live copy       Corrected       Correction
p   para line     p   para line   error           to make

                            1      glory of        add "of"
                            2      and the         delete extra
                                                     "and"
                            3      simplicity      change o to p
                            4      Whitman         cap W
```

Figure 19. Typed correction list

- Proofreading without marking copy: using self-adhesive notes. In the form shown previously for "Marking in the margins only," write a correction or query on a self-adhesive slip when you find an error or problem, and affix the slip to the margin next to the line in question.

Copy. . .   Added
                                             . . .margin

- Proofreading without marking copy: using an overlay of tracing paper. Attach the see-through paper firmly; read the copy through the tracing paper; and mark on the overlay, being careful to use a light hand so your marks don't gouge the proof.

Tracing paper · : · · · · · · · · · · · · · · · · · · Tape

                                          · · · · · · · · · Back of copy

- Making corrections directly in the text. This technique is used for copy that will be rekeyed or corrected and reprinted. Write over the copy where you can do it neatly.

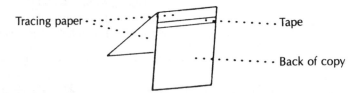

```
                              of
The art of art, the glory expression and
and the sunshine of the light of letters
is simplicity.
                              --Whitman
```

- Using editing marks with checkmarks in the margin. The checkmarks help the corrector find the in-text marks. You must have plenty of space between lines:

```
The art of art, the glory expression and       ✓

and the sunshine of the light of letters        ✓

is simplicity.                                   ✓

                              --whitman  ✓
```

- Using standard editing marks. This technique is used for copy that has extra room between lines.

```
The art of art, the glory expression and

and the sunshine of the light of letters

is simplicity.

                              --whitman
```

> For practice in any of the modified techniques,
> turn to Exercise 24.

5 Methods of Proofreading

The three main methods

There are three basic ways to proofread. In any of the three methods a proofreader may be instructed to do *editorial proofreading*, that is, to mark queries or corrections or both, working at level 2 or above as shown in Figure 1, Chapter 1 (page 17).

The traditional method is called *comparison proofreading* and involves directly comparing dead copy with live copy.

The second, today the increasingly common method, has several names, including *dry reading, cold proofreading,* and *noncomparison proofreading.* This method is used when there is no true dead copy because the document has lived in an electronic file from the author's earliest draft; what is proofread is the latest—and presumably final—version.

The third method involves making corrections directly on a computer, perhaps using a program for spellchecking or finding editing problems, perhaps comparing the keystrokes in two files and reconciling the discrepancies. Each method is discussed in the sections that follow.

Comparison proofreading

Two main methods of comparison proofreading

In comparing the two main methods, keep in mind that a proofreader adept in one method may not adjust readily to another and that competent workers may have strong preferences for the method they're used to.

Solo proofreading

Sometimes called *single proofreading* or *horsing,* solo proofreading is done by one person who places the dead copy and the live copy side by side and compares them. This method is the slowest (in terms of elapsed time), the least expensive, and the most common. For nonprofessionals, it's undoubtedly the least accurate method: the greatest danger is that omissions and repetitions are likely to be missed. A good professional solo proofreader, however, can do a remarkably accurate job; and, for certain material, such as for the short takes in advertising copy or for mathematical expressions that must be compared character by character, solo proofreading is usually the preferred method.

Appendix B is a job description for a professional solo proofreader. Appendix C discusses speed and accuracy standards for solo proofreading. Much of the content of these appendixes applies also to other methods of proofreading.

Team proofreading

Team proofreading, sometimes called *double proofreading* or *partner proofreading,* was the common method for many years, but is now likely to be used only for training proofreaders who will eventually work solo.

Team reading is the fastest (in terms of elapsed time) and the most expensive method. For nonprofessionals, it's the only method likely to produce acceptable results. Its supporters consider it the most accurate method for tables, long lists of numbers, and hard-to-read or hard-to-handle dead copy (such as handwritten manuscript or index cards).

Solo or team: Which is better?

Opinions conflict on the comparative value of team or solo proofreading. Assuming straightforward, easy-to-read dead and live copy, here are some of the arguments for and against team proofreading.

Pro. Properly done, team proofreading is much faster.

Con. Not that much faster. A fast team can cut a fast solo proofreader's speed by only about one-third. If each team worker is paid the same as a solo worker, the team costs one-third more.

Pro. A second person improves quality by adding the sense of hearing to the sense of sight. Experiments show that reading aloud activates more areas of the brain than reading silently.

Con. A second person's voice interferes with concentration. Besides, solo proofreaders can always read difficult copy aloud to themselves.

Pro. Constantly shifting the eyes from dead to live copy, as a solo worker does, breaks the flow, tires the eyes, and leads to missed errors.

Con. Experience accustoms the eyes to shifting and teaches solo proofreaders to watch for the most likely misses—omissions and repetitions. In a team, a copyholder often breaks the flow by reading too fast or enunciating unclearly so that the copy marker must stop and ask questions.

Pro. A second person's input increases the validity of queries.

Con. A second person's input slows queries.

Pro. Interaction with a second person is stimulating and keeps a team alert.

Con. Interaction with a second person is irritating. Working alone establishes the most effective pace.

Pro. Solo proofreading depends on short-term memory, but most people can hold only seven to nine words or numerals in short-term memory. Because a team proofreads as the words are spoken, it doesn't depend on short-term memory in the same way a solo proofreader has to; team members use short-term memory only to remember the sense of a sentence until it ends.

Con. Experienced solo proofreaders can hold up to two short sentences in short-term memory, and the effort takes more intense concentration and results in greater alertness.

Two less common methods

Tape proofreading

In the first step of tape proofreading, the *recorder* reads the dead copy aloud into a tape recorder's microphone. In the second step, the *marker* plays back the tape while following and marking the live copy. Tape proofreading works best when the dead copy is again available in the second step to check doubtful or misread parts.

For maximum speed and efficiency, the recorder and the marker are the same person. Next best is for the marker to be someone familiar with the material, such as the copy editor.

For this method, dictating equipment is ideal, but an inexpensive cassette recorder will work, too, if it has a pause switch to start and stop instantly.

The advantages of tape proofreading are these:

- Both dead and live copy need not be available for the first step (a photo-copy of the dead copy can be read into the tape recorder while the live copy is being keyboarded).
- Some of the advantages of team proofreading apply; however, two proof-readers needn't be available at the same time.

Tape proofreading comes midway between solo and team proofreading in cost and speed. If it's not done with care, however, tape proofreading is less accurate and less economical than team proofreading.

Much of the section on methods of team reading, particularly the verbal short-cuts and codes, applies also to tape reading.

Electronic-partner proofreading

The improvement in voice output terminals (VOTs), which can read aloud from type or electronic input in a choice of pleasant voices, has moved some people to a new kind of team proofreading—with a computer as partner. Unlike the usual human team, where one partner reads the dead copy aloud, the electronic partner reads the *live* copy aloud.

VOTs can read more than 90 percent of words correctly, can spell out the others, and can be set to read punctuation and capitals. And their speed, unlike the speed of a human partner, is precisely adjustable.

Although a VOT can't use the verbal shortcuts and codes that human partners use, electronic proofreading can match the accuracy of team reading and the speed of solo proofreading.

Proofreading speeds

Figure 20 compares the time needed to proofread 25,000 words by the four methods.

	Solo	Tape	Team	Electronic partner
Total work hours	10.0	6.0 recording 6.5 marking	5.0	10.0
Elapsed hours	10.0	12.5	7.5	10.0

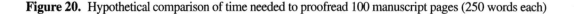

Figure 20. Hypothetical comparison of time needed to proofread 100 manuscript pages (250 words each)

Techniques of solo proofreading

Tools

For solo proofreading, working on a *bank* (a surface with a slanted top) is less fatiguing than on a flat surface, but banks are seldom provided outside professional proofrooms. Ideally, on a flat surface you'll have enough room for four stacks of paper (the dead and the live copy you're working on and the dead and the live copy you're done with) as well as enough room to move the two stacks you're working on back and forth, keeping the words you're reading approximately aligned.

As a beginner, you want to learn to keep your place in both dead and live copy and to concentrate on no more than one line at a time. To help block out the distraction of lines above and below the one you're reading, use masked rulers on both dead and live copy to cover all but the line you're working on. Particularly useful are straightedges designed for reading computer copy; a good one is made of transparent blue plastic and has one clear line. Or you can make masked guides: take two transparent rulers and, on each, tape over all but one line's width and depth in the middle. A one-pica (12-point) line depth is the most useful.

You may find a magnifying ruler (opticians sell them) useful to isolate long lines of small type. And a T-square is handy to follow line by line on a stack of the fanfold copy that's used for continuous computer printouts.

When you're more experienced, you may graduate from masked rulers to plain straightedges, perhaps rulers of different colors, perhaps index cards. And when you're proficient, you may use a straightedge for the dead copy and, for the live copy, the nonwriting end of your pen or pencil (choose a pencil without an eraser that might catch on the paper).

How much to read

The size of the unit you read will vary. With straightforward text and clean dead copy, you may read 10 to 20 words, perhaps two short sentences, at a time. With unfamiliar technical language or heavily edited dead copy—or when you are expected to do meticulous typographic proofreading (checking, for example, kerns, rags, rules, word spacing, and letter spacing)—you may read only one or two words at a time.

If you are missing typos, you are going too fast or reading too many words at a time.

Spend at least twice as much time with the live copy as the dead. Be especially alert for omissions and repetitions. Be sure each page or galley reads properly into the next.

It may help to read difficult copy aloud to yourself. (Some proofreaders read everything aloud, as explained in the following paragraphs.)

Reading aloud

Some solo proofreaders follow an audiovisual approach: using voice, ears, and eyes together, they believe, increases their concentration and helps them do a better job. This is what they recommend: Read aloud, at a whisper if need be; or, if you must be silent, sound out what you're reading in your mind. (But don't be embarrassed to read aloud—or at least to move your lips. Aristotle always read aloud, as did his pupil, Alexander the Great. In fact, everybody did until the fifth century A.D. when Christian monks made the great discovery of silent reading.)

Later in this chapter, "Vocalization" and "What to read aloud" explains the technique of reading aloud, and "Shortcuts" lists many refinements. These methods are easily adaptable to solo proofreading.

Separate steps

To read text in an uninterrupted flow, you may prefer to perform some tasks as separate steps; for example, you may first check the ends of lines for bad word division and then read the *running heads* (the repeated heads at the tops of pages that usually give the title of the document).

Review

After comparison proofreading, some solo proofreaders review their work: they may skim the live copy or they may scrutinize it; they may even use a technique that forces them to look at individual words and characters rather than reading for sense. These techniques aim to avoid the pitfalls of "seeing" what *should* be there instead of recognizing the typos and misspellings that *are* there. One way to avoid reading for sense is to read backward, one word at a time. Another way is to scan every line first from its middle to its end, then from its beginning to its middle.

Professional proofreaders use techniques like these only for review. Their first proofreading requires understanding the sense of sentences to catch such errors as misspelled homophones (*there* for *their*), typos that make words (*every* for *very*), and slips in grammar and usage (*whom goes there?*).

Techniques of team proofreading

General description

The traditional proofreading team consists of a senior member, called the *copy marker* (or *proofreader* or *copy reader* or *first reader*) and another person called a *copyholder* (or *second reader*). The copyholder reads aloud to the copy marker from the dead copy. The copy marker follows the live copy while listening to the dead and does all the marking and querying. The copyholder must be keenly aware of the copy marker's need for an adjustment of speed or a pause to write a mark.

In some teams, the copy marker keeps the live copy and does all the reading aloud, marking, and querying. By this method, the copy marker can regulate speed and occasionally make an intentional error to be certain the copyholder is paying attention.

Another kind of team consists of two qualified proofreaders who share responsibility equally, who alternate reading aloud, and who may alternate every few hours as *holder* (of the dead copy) and *marker* (of the live copy). If the dead copy is handwritten, extensively edited, or in any way hard to read, the holder should read aloud to the marker. If the dead copy is clean, whatever works to produce fast, accurate proofreading is acceptable.

In this kind of proofreading, the partner who reads faster may do most of the reading aloud, or partners may switch reading aloud every chapter or every hour. (Don't switch dead and live copy as you switch reading aloud; for greatest efficiency, one partner must act as holder and the other as marker for at least a couple of hours.) When copy permits it, some proofreaders even like to alternate reading paragraphs aloud, because this keeps them alert and eliminates the need to identify a new paragraph verbally.

Speed

The team member who reads aloud should strive for optimum (not maximum) speed, a rate that depends on how clean the copy is, how skillful the team members are, and how many errors must be marked.

A somewhat slower, steadier pace can be as productive as a rapid, uneven pace in which the marker often has to stop the reader to verify syllables and words that have been imprecisely enunciated.

Agreement between partners

Partners working together for the first time must take the trouble to agree on signals and shortcuts and to find the highest rate of speed comfortable to both. When the person reading aloud isn't marking, speed and pauses must be adjusted to the marker's needs. For example, partners may work side by side or directly across from each other so that the copyholder can take the movement of the copy marker's pencil as the signal to stop reading aloud. In some teams, the copy marker signals the copyholder by repeating the word where the reading should stop and, when ready to resume, repeats the word again.

Vocalization

Although reading must be done intelligently, never automatically, the normal, social speech pattern, with pauses for clarity and with emphasis for meaning, is far removed from a proofreader's read-aloud technique. In reading proof, vocalization is a rapid, steady, clearly enunciated near-monotone.

If you are not normally soft-spoken, try to become so when you proofread. The reduction in volume decreases fatigue and may well increase fluency and speed. Be aware that vowel sounds are those that most exercise (and tire) your jaw muscles; in American speech, they are the sounds that slow you down, and they are not always important to clear enunciation (compare the British pronunciation of *secretary* to the American). On the other hand, crisp consonant sounds make for precise speech. When consonants aren't stressed, rapid reading aloud may become slurred and indistinct, especially in final consonants such as the *s* in plurals and the *ed* in past participles.

What to read aloud

Read aloud words, punctuation marks, and all typographical descriptions such as changes in typeface, underscores, and capital letters. Read aloud all changes in spacing or indention—in heads, paragraphs, lists, and anywhere else. Spell out or otherwise identify the correct spelling of proper names when there is the slightest possibility of error. Read figures character by character: 365 as "three six five."

You can use certain shortcuts, code words, and signals to increase speed. Some of these are listed later in this chapter. Many are one-syllable abbreviations of the words for punctuation marks or typographical changes, like "com" for comma.

The following example demonstrates how a quotation from Milton would be read with one-syllable shortcuts (shown in parentheses) for punctuation marks and capital letters.

Copy (dead and live):

> "As good almost kill a man as kill a good book:
> Who kills a man kills a reasonable creature,
> God's image; but he who destroys a good book
> kills reason itself."
>
> —Milton

Reader:

> (flush left quo cap) as good almost kill a man as kill a good book
> (cole cap) who kills a man kills a reasonable creature (com cap)
> God (pos s) image (sem) but he who destroys a good book kills
> reason itself (point close quo) (flush right dash cap) m i l t o n

Experienced proofreaders may omit some of the particulars; for example: the cap in standard proper nouns such as God, Milton, Chicago, or Mr. Jones; or the "point cap" at the end and beginning of sentences (when partners agree that a drop in voice or a pause gives the same information).

An unusual usage repeated many times needn't be signaled in full after partners learn it firmly; for example, after reading the abbreviation "UHF all caps, bumped" several times, partners may assume that when "UHF" is read it should be all caps and *bumped* (closed up, with no space or punctuation).

When partners understand each other perfectly, any reasonable shortcut, code, or signal that increases speed is acceptable. Some things are so often set or typed incorrectly, however, that they must never be omitted from reading aloud. Always read possessive apostrophes, capital letters in Clc (caps and lowercase) headings, and specifications for different levels of headings.

Useful shortcuts

Shortcuts such as the codes and signals in the following list can be used by all proofreaders—team, tape, or solo—who read aloud or sound out what they are reading in their minds.

Punctuation and type style

Code	Meaning
pos	apostrophe
brack ... close brack	bracket ... closing bracket
spot, bull	bullet
cap, up, nonverbal signal (e.g., tap table)	single capital letter
caps	all capitals
three up	three words with initial capitals
nish	initial capital
click, cluck, c-l-c	capitals and lowercase
caps bumped	capital letters, no space or punctuation, as in USA
cen	centered
dit	ditto mark or same characters repeated on following line

Code	Meaning
cole	colon
com	comma
three dots, dot dot dot	three ellipsis points (...)
bang, 'sclam, shout	exclamation point
hy, hook	hyphen
hyph	hyphen, in a word with "high" as a syllable, as high-income
two hooks	two hyphens, as in day-to-day
tal ... rome	italic ... back to roman type
indent, dent, in	indention
dent three, dent all, in all	long indention, as in a set-off extract
dent three, in three	indented three spaces or three ems
elsie (l-c), down, small	lowercase
elsie (l-c) bumped	lowercase with no space or punctuation, as in rpm
pups	pp. (pages)
graph, pare, nonverbal signal (e.g., partners may switch reading aloud)	paragraph
pren, curve	parenthesis
pren ... close pren	open parenthesis ... closing parenthesis
prens	parentheses
in the hole	single word or character in parentheses
dot, stop, point	period, decimal point
(vocal inflection: slight pause, dip in pitch)	period at end of sentence, cap at start of new sentence
kwes, hay, huh, query	question mark
quo ... close quo	open quotation marks ... closing quotation marks
sem	semicolon
sing quo ... close sing quo	single quote ... closing single quote
sco ... end sco	underscore ... end of underscore

Numbers

Note: When mathematicians speak of a number, they use the word "and" only between a whole number and a fraction ($100 \, 5/16$ is expressed as "one hundred and five sixteenths"; $105/16$ is "one hundred five sixteenths"; 100.023 is "one hundred and twenty-three thousandths"; .123 is "one hundred twenty-three thousandths"). In reading proof aloud, identifying the fraction as a "frac," $100 \, 5/16$ becomes "one oh oh frac five slash one six," and $105/16$ becomes "frac one oh five slash one six"; $100 \, \frac{5}{16}$ becomes "one oh oh frac five over sixteen," and so on.

Code	Meaning
noom three, fig three	3 (numeral)
spell three	three (spelled out)
three five	35 (numerals)
thirty hyph five	thirty-five (spelled out)
thou	three zeros, or the word "thousand"
spell five thou	five thousand (spelled out)

Code	Meaning
noom five com thou	5,000 (numerals)
hun	two zeros or the word "hundred"
mil	six zeros or the word "million"
ciph (for cipher), nought, oh (where no confusion possible with letter *o*)	0 (zero)
frac	fraction
super, soup	superscript, superior character
sub	subscript, inferior character

Symbols and diacritical marks

Code	Meaning
cute *e* (or other letter)	acute accent: é
short and, et, amp	ampersand: &
angle ... end angle	angle brackets, arrow brackets, greater than, lesser than: ‹ ›
elbow ... end elbow	elbow brackets: < >
astrik, star	asterisk: *
back slash	back slash: \
short *a* (or other letter)	breve: ă
cut *c*	cents sign: ¢
soft *c*	cedilla: ç
flex, doghouse	circumflex: ô
dag	dagger, obelisk: †
double dag	double dagger: ‡
ball	degree sign: °
doll, buck	dollar sign: $
di, umlaut *o* (or other letter)	diaeresis, umlaut: ö
div	division sign: ÷
grahv *e* (or other letter)	grave accent: è
French quotes	guillemets: « »
wing, wedge, swing a	hacek: ǎ
fist	index, fist: ☞
long a (or other letter)	macron: ā
times, mult	multiplication sign: × or •
num sign	octothorp: #
pare sign, pilcrow	paragraph sign: ¶
balls	percent sign: %
squiggle, sec	section sign: §
uh	schwa: ə
snake	swung dash: ~
snake *n* (or other letter)	tilde: ñ
Swede *a*	volle, Swedish *a*: å

Noncomparison proofreading

Proofreading with little attention to dead copy

More and more publishers and typographers are adopting the practice of non-comparison proofreading sometimes called *railroading:* both dead and live copy are available, but only the live copy is read word for word; the dead copy is referred to only when the reader sees something puzzling or needs to check figures or the spelling of people's names.

Studies seem to show that the decreased accuracy associated with this method isn't significant enough to outweigh its increased speed and decreased cost. The danger, of course, is that a proofreader may not recognize a mistake because the text seems to make sense. Outs—a missing *not* (as in "guilty" instead of "not guilty") or omissions of several lines (not an uncommon fault)—can be disastrous. For this kind of proofreading to be safe for legal, scientific, or technical material, the proofreader must be an expert in the subject matter; some organizations, therefore, add noncomparison proofreading to the tasks of the copy editor.

This method of proofreading is the practice for many scholarly journals; the final responsibility for accurate live copy rests with the author. If you're an author who's expected to proofread your own work, find a partner who will mark the live copy (pick a good speller) while you read aloud from the dead copy. Next, do a solo reading; last, read the live copy only.

Proofreading with no dead copy

When no dead copy is available, you are doing neither true proofreading in the classic sense nor true copy editing, but something in between, often called *dry reading,* or *cold proofreading.* This technique is fast becoming the norm as authors and editors work directly on computers to revise and correct. At or near the final point in the production process, a proofreader is asked to carefully read the latest version of the document word for word to catch any remaining problems.

Dry reading is done at different levels, depending on the stage of the job and the degree of authority you've been given. The levels of authority for general proofreading, described in Chapter 1, Figure 1, (page 17) correspond with the levels of authority for dry reading. If you are asked to proofread with no dead copy, you should find out which kinds of errors you will be expected to correct or query before you begin.

At all levels, typographic proofreading is in order: Mark deviations from specifications and from appropriate typographic standards (such as page and column breaks) and wrong word divisions (line-end word breaks).

At all levels, you are also expected to catch misspellings.

Beyond catching misspellings, however, finding the right level of editorial proofreading at which to work can be tricky; you need a lot of good judgment.

The following cautions apply to any level:

- Don't change the meaning.
- Don't make needless changes.
- Don't query or correct the grammar unless you can back up your corrections with rules from an established authority.
- Don't try to rewrite a whole sentence. It's not your place, for example, to change passive voice to active nor to break a long sentence into smaller sentences; you're not an editor.

You will probably be wise to ignore many minor faults; for example, don't change a pompous expression (*hebdomadal* to *weekly,* or even *necessity* to *need*), as you would if you were an editor.

Each of you will have your own idea of what constitutes glaring, moderate, and nitpicking errors. Here are the general guidelines, restated from Chapter 1:

Glaring errors are the kind that would be noticed by a high school graduate who was good in English and that would embarrass the author.

Moderate errors are instantly conspicuous to a trained eye, such as that of a good high school English teacher.

Small, nitpicking errors in language would embarrass a *careful* writer or editor or confuse a knowledgeable (or inattentive) reader.

For a list of typographic and editorial problems to catch, see "Summary of errors and problems to mark or query (or ignore)" in Chapter 7.

For practice in dry reading,
turn to Exercise 25.

Proofreading with computers

Scamping

Word processing and computer composition reintroduce *scamping,* an old way to check hurried, cheap typesetting. In the days of handset type, one person could read aloud from the manuscript while a typesetter compared what was being read aloud with the metal type itself and corrected errors right in the metal.

One person today can read aloud from the manuscript while a keyboard operator compares what is being read aloud with the screen display and corrects errors right on the screen.

This method saves time and reduces cost, but it's imperfect because the operator is sure to miss some errors and to introduce new ones. The next section describes some ways to keep records so corrections can be checked.

Direct correcting

In a word-processing program, corrections of many kinds are easily made. For example, a wrong character might be corrected just by moving the electronic cursor to the character on the screen and striking the key for the right character. Because it may take only a few minutes to learn to make simple corrections, proofreaders may be expected to correct errors as they find them when comparing the dead copy with the display on the screen.

But few proofreaders enjoy working that way. For one thing, it requires some typing skill—at least a minimal familiarity with a keyboard. For another, it's physically uncomfortable to compare a piece of paper (the dead copy) with a computer screen (the live copy). If you must work at a screen, try scamping (with another person reading aloud to you) or tape proofreading.

No direct correcting is reliable unless the corrections are checked against some kind of record, and some kinds of software make a record for you. With a file-comparison program, you work on a copy of the original electronic document (say, on a floppy disk). The program then compares the document you've worked on with the original document and puts a marker wherever there's a difference.

One kind of comparison, which is found on some word-processing programs, will put a *change bar* in the margin at every line containing a change.

Another kind of software *redlines* (displays) changes. Different software programs redline differently: on a screen, changes may flash or show in reverse type; on a screen or a printout, changes may appear in a different color, in a different typeface, with a box around them, or with a special symbol identifying them. Some programs will print out a list of changes.

Without a file-comparison or redlining program, you may have to make the record while you work. You needn't record exactly what was done, only that a correction was made at that point. One way to make a record is to type an x on the screen in the margin at the line where a correction is made and to mark the dead copy with a caret or an underscore, as shown in Figure 21. You can then use the word-processor's search facility to find the x's and delete them as you check the corrections.

Live copy		Marks on dead copy	
Error found on screen	*Corrected screen display or printout*	*Text*	*Margin*
poofreading	proofreading	proofreading	✓
prooofreading	proofreading	proofreading	✓
pro ofreading	proofreading	proofreading	✓

Figure 21. Examples of recorded corrections

Dual keyboarding

Dual keyboarding can greatly simplify proofreading. In one form, two operators key the same copy, the computer (with a file-comparison program) kicks out the differences, and the proofreader chooses the correct version. In another form, no proofreader is involved: one operator keys the copy; then another operator keys the same copy and, when the computer indicates that the input is different, decides what's correct. The second form is widely used by typesetters who don't know English.

Spellcheck programs

Most word-processing programs include spellchecking. A good spellcheck program can catch many typos and misspellings and either correct them at your command or allow you to correct them.

Some programs will catch not only single-word misspellings (mispellings) but split-word errors (can not, be cause). Some will also flag certain similar-word spellings ("form March to April" for "from March to April"). And some will flag homophones (to/too/two), and ask you if you're sure you want that spelling—a check that can slow you down significantly.

But even when you use all these aids, there remain many typos to catch—typos that make words, whether it's a word needing a deletion (*A Table of Two Cities*), an addition (*War and Pace*), a substitution (*The Count of Monte Crisco*), or a transposition (*Ode on a Grecian Run*).

Most spelling programs are based on a dictionary; some, on a dictionary plus algorithms involving roots, prefixes, and suffixes. A large dictionary is desirable, although on some equipment it slows production too much to be useful. But a small dictionary will slow you down, too, because it will display all the perfectly good words that it doesn't have in its lexicon. Most programs will allow users to add words, which is practical for jobs using a special vocabulary.

> For practice in catching errors that methods
> other than word-by-word proofreading
> would probably miss, turn to Exercise 26.

Editing programs

A typical editing program provides spellchecking and some useful proofreading capabilities. Such a program flags deviations from its rules, describes a problem, and presents advice on how to correct it.

It can also find errors like these: repeated words (such as "of of"); paired punctuation with half the pair missing (such as a lonely parenthesis); doubled punctuation (such as two consecutive commas); and some incorrect punctuation (such as a period placed outside closing quotes). In the following examples, the "at" sign (@) marks errors.

```
repeated words @words, paired punctua-
tion with half the pair missing
@(such as a lonely parenthesis, dou-
bled punctuation,,@ and some incor-
rect punctuation, such as a period
placed outside closing quotes—"clos-
ing quotes".@
```

With each signal, such a program gives an error message, for example:

@eXample:

> @mixed capital and lowercase letters

An editing program can also flag other problems, suggest a change, and let the operator decide what to do. The problems include certain grammatical errors, commonly confused words, incomplete and long sentences, passive voice, and wordy or otherwise undesirable expressions.

An experienced copy editor may accept many of the suggestions. Except for some of the so-called grammatical errors, however, most of the suggested changes are beyond a proofreader's authority.

Here are a few examples of undesirable expressions:

Signaled expression	Suggested change
make out a list of	list
consensus of opinion	consensus
due to the fact that	because
different than	different from
the reason is because	the reason is that
conflagration	fire

An editing program may calculate the *readability* level of a document. Most readability scores are based on word and sentence length and indicate whether text is harder to read than the level of the intended audience. For example, in the *Gunning Fog Index,* a score greater than 12 needs further editing to make it accessible to a high school (12th grade) graduate. The process of reducing readability levels is likely to be entrusted only to an editor.

For more practice, turn to Exercise 27.

6 Process, Procedures, and Tasks

The role of proofreading in production

A document or publication goes through the hands of a proofreader several times as production progresses. At each stage, as new live copy is produced, the live copy from the previous stage becomes the dead copy. In the last few years, advances in technology and changes in production values have changed the process drastically, and it continues to change rapidly.

It's crucial that you know the purpose of the document you are reading, the way it was produced, how it will be corrected at the stage of production you are seeing, and what the next stage is. These are the reasons you need all that information:

First, standards vary. Typographic excellence may not be a major consideration in publications and documents produced under tight deadlines or budgets. And many refinements are impossible to achieve with lower-end equipment. For example, conspicuously wide word spacing in a line can be lessened in several ways: (1) by rewriting; (2) by running over a word or syllable from the line above and the line above that and so on for several lines; (3) by subtly adjusting letter space or compressing the type to make room for a short word or syllable run back from the line below; or (4) by inconspicuously expanding the letter spacing in the faulty line. Not all production schedules allow for these solutions, however, and not all equipment can do what's needed.

Second, for certain kinds of work and at certain stages of production, some of the usual proofreading tasks are needless and unwelcome. For example, if the copy you see is only for the preparation of a *rough* (a preliminary proof, a draft), you should skip the usual inspection for kerning, rivers, word division, widows, and so on—typographic details that will not be relevant until a later stage.

Third, corrections and changes almost always become more costly as production progresses. A heading slightly off center, for example, may not be important enough to mark for correction at a near-final stage.

Several proofreading passes

Some experts advise comparison proofreaders to make at least three systematic passes at the original material. A first pass may be a scan of the typography—format, alignment, indention; the second, a word-for-word comparison reading; the third, a quick reading of the live copy only, seeking editorial problems such as style inconsistencies.

For solo proofreaders, a first pass may be a scan of the typography, the second a careful reading, and the third a quick reading or checking step.

Some proofreaders like to make half a dozen or so quick passes for certain tasks, and some teams work more effectively when only one member performs such tasks, which can include the following:

- Measuring type and space
- Verifying type style
- Verifying *folio* (page number) sequence, style, placement, and *register* (exact positioning from page to page)
- Verifying the sequence of references and their callouts
- Checking heads, including running heads
- Checking pages for general appearance, including alignment and equal spacing
- Typing query lists (see Chapter 7)
- Detecting widows
- Initialing and dating proofs or administrative forms.

However many passes you make, the following paragraphs give detailed instructions for careful proofreading.

Preparatory steps

Collect the tools you will need. Typically, you'll keep handy a straightedge, a dictionary, a style guide, an erasable red pencil (for marking on proofs that will later be discarded, such as photocopies), a *nonphoto-blue* pen or pencil (for marking on camera-ready copy in a color that won't reproduce), a pad of self-stick notes and a black pen (for queries), and measuring tools (discussed later in this chapter).

Before you begin to read, find out exactly what you have in hand to work on and what you're supposed to do with it.

Determine at what stage the live copy is.

If you are reading by comparison, make sure you have matching sets of dead and live copy and that every page or galley is numbered and in order.

Carefully read your specifications or other instructions. The type specs including head levels may be on a job order, composition order, customer's work order, machine ticket, layout, dummy, sample pages, or checklist. Editorial style specs may refer to a style manual, word division manual, or dictionary, or all three. Administrative forms may include workflow charts or sheets and production sheets; you may be responsible for filling out these forms to move the job on to the next step.

Scan the live copy; check tops of pages, corners, and margins for attached notes or additional specifications. If you have a dummy or a layout, make the same kind of preliminary check.

Be sure you understand all the specs and all your responsibilities. Ask questions if necessary. Be sure you understand priorities and deadlines. Be sure you understand your level of authority (see Figure 1, Chapter 1) and what level of effort is expected. The deadline, the nature of the job, the stage of the job, and the practices of the employer all determine the level of effort. (See Figures 22A and 22B.)

1. *Railroading*	One person reads and marks the proof, referring to the manuscript only when something is suspect or names and numbers must be verified.
2. *Solo proofreading*	One person reads and marks the proof, comparing the proof with the manuscript word for word and, where necessary for accuracy, character for character.
3. *Team proofreading*	The copyholder reads aloud every word, punctuation mark, and typographical description in the manuscript while the copy marker marks the proof.
4. *Reader's review*	After earlier levels, the solo proofreader or copy marker reviews the proof, spot-checking it.
5. *Second readthrough*	After earlier levels, the reader *rereads* the entire proof as in level 1.
6. *Checker's review*	After earlier levels, someone highly experienced but not the original proofreader spot-checks the work as the proofreader did in level 4 and, if poor quality proofreading is found, rereads the proof as the proofreader did in level 5.
7. *Re-proofreading*	Different proofreaders repeat any level from 1 to 6.

Figure 22A. Levels of effort in comparison proofreading

1. *Readthrough*	One person reads and marks the proof at the appropriate level of authority.
2. *Reader's review*	A reader reviews the proof, spot-checking it.
3. *Second readthrough*	The reader *rereads* the entire proof as in level 1.
4. *Checker's review*	Someone highly experienced but not the original proofreader spot-checks the work as the proofreader did in level 2 and, if poor quality proofreading is found, rereads the proof as the proofreader did in level 3.
5. *Re-proofreading*	Different proofreaders repeat any level from 1 to 4.

Figure 22B. Levels of effort in noncomparison proofreading

Steps with first proofs

1. *Verify that typographic specs have been followed.*

Mark deviations for correction. Don't rely on your eyes; use the appropriate tools to measure type and space.

Check *body copy* (the main text) as follows:

- Typefaces. If possible, use a specimen sheet from the same equipment that produced the proof to check that the typefaces are those specified.
- Type sizes. Use a type sizer (preferably a transparent overlay with printed examples of different sizes in the appropriate type style) to measure type size.
- Line spaces and line lengths. If measurements are specified in picas and points, use a pica rule (see Appendix D) to measure the following:
  —Line depth (type size plus line spacing) from baseline to baseline
  —Line width of body copy and of indented matter
  —Short lines of ragged-right type, if necessary (for example, if a minimum line width is specified)
- Positioning. Check for faults in indention, knotholes, failure to *clear for 10* (aligning right-hand digits in numbered lists of more than nine items), centering, and horizontal and vertical alignment.

Check *display type,* including the following elements, for deviations from type style, type size, line spaces, and positioning:

  —Captions
  —Extracts
  —*Epigraphs* (quotations at the start of a chapter)
  —Folios
  —Illustrations: charts, graphs, photos, drawings, etc.
  —Legends
  —Lists
  —Notes: *footnotes* (at the bottoms of pages), *end notes* (at the ends of sections or documents)
  —Tables
  —Titles and headings at all levels, including *running heads* (those at the top of every page) or *footers* or *running feet* (those at the bottom of every page)

2. *If you have dead and live copy, compare them; mark deviations.*

If the work requires close comparison, compare the live copy with the dead copy word for word and, where necessary (for example, where unfamiliar words or numbers are involved), character for character. Mark the live copy for the correction of errors resulting from the keyboarder's deviations from the dead copy.

3. *Mark deviations from typographic standards.*

The details of typographic standards as they relate to individual jobs and to stages of production would fill another book. Here are a few considerations:

- What dictionary or guide are you using for word division? Authorities differ, for example, as to *mea-sure* or *meas-ure, stand-ard* or *stan-dard.*
- How many consecutive end-of-line hyphens are allowed—two, three, four?
- Should punctuation in multi-line headings *hang,* that is, go into the left margin?

Hanging punctuation	Flush-left punctuation
'Proofreaders Infuriating,'	'Proofreaders Infuriating,'
Say Authors and Typesetters,	Say Authors and Typesetters,
'But Lovable Underneath'	'But Lovable Underneath'

- Is a footnote continuation allowed? If so, what are the rules? Must two full lines be left behind? carried over? If the break doesn't come in the middle of a sentence, must the footnote be labeled "continued" at both the break and the carryover?

4. *Ignore, query, or mark deviations from language standards.*

According to your knowledge of the required language standards and your level of authority on the job, mark or query as you proofread, following the instructions for the job or those in Chapter 7.

5. *Perform routine tasks.*

Here's a list of some routine tasks:

- Look at each page or galley as a whole (the forest, as opposed to the trees) to catch anomalies such as rivers of white or vertical misalignment.
- Verify the sequence of any notation in numerical or alphabetical order, including folios, list items, and *callouts* (references to subsequent material).
- Verify that references match what they refer to—that callouts match the material called out, including footnotes, bibliographic references, tables, figures, and other illustrations, and that captions and titles are accurate descriptions.
- Verify that alphabetical order is correct. Be sure you understand the difference between the letter-by-letter system (used in dictionaries) and the word-by-word system (used in telephone books). The letter-by-letter system alphabetizes up to the first punctuation mark, disregarding space and hyphens. The word-by-word system alphabetizes up to the first solid word and follows a "nothing-before-something" logic in which a space precedes a punctuation mark. Here are examples:

Letter by letter	Word by word
Southbridge	South Fork
South-brook Meadow	South Port
Southern Pines	South River
South Fork	South Tunnel
Southport	Southbridge
South Port	South-brook Meadow
South River	Southern Pines
South Tunnel	Southport

It's useful to know the editorial style standards for the alphabetization of personal and geographic names; some style guides (such as *The Chicago Manual of Style*) give details.

- If it's expected at your level of authority, check all simple arithmetic—addition (such as the totals in tables), subtraction, and percentages. Watch for incorrect or impossible percentages, fractions, and decimal figures. Use a calculator. Be sure graphics such as pie charts and bar graphs match their description and represent the figures given in the text.

- If you have galleys, you may be expected to mark them for page *make-up* (the assembly and positioning of text and display to fit the specified space). When you have the specs, mark for spacing; for example, to indicate a new page or a new right-hand page, like this:

 **CHAPTER TWO**

(*Sink* means to leave a top margin of the indicated depth.)
- When matter such as a footnote or a table is set separately and doesn't yet appear in its proper place in the proofs, or where a blank is to be filled in later, show where the future work must be done:
—Point out footnote callouts (reference marks or superscript numbers):

Jones's theory contradicts Anderson's.[*] ✿

This problem is discussed in Brooke's treatise.[1] (fn 1)

—Point out table callouts (first references):

Table A-1 lists our recommendations. (Table A·1)

—Point out callouts for artwork; include the size if it's specified (PU means "pick up"):

Figure 9 demonstrates this procedure. (Fig. 9)

The following graph shows the downward trend. (PU art)

—Point out cross-references left to be filled in. (In some jobs, you will see x's or blanks, in others, black squares where folios are to be added later.)

The principles discussed earlier (see p. xx) apply. (p. xx)

(or)

The principles discussed earlier (see p.) apply. (p. no)

Page proofs, repros, and other camera-ready copy

When you see copy in its final form, do these quality control steps.

- Verify that each page and each column reads properly into the next.
- Be sure that all elements of each page (such as captions, footnotes, and headings) are properly placed.
- Check for the appearance of equal, consistent spacing on facing pages. Keep in mind that the space around artwork, heads, and any other displayed

matter can be adjusted so the material will fit properly on a page or so facing pages will *balance* (top and bottom lines will line up evenly).

- Check for the uniform placement of running heads and folios on each page; they should be in exact register.
- Check the accuracy of folios in cross references and in *jump lines* (lines reading "continued on page x").
- Check the table of contents against the text for the accuracy of folio listings and for the same words and style (especially style for hyphens and commas).

Review

After the first reading, review your work as described in the following paragraphs. (Partners in a team may divide the tasks.) Review should take one-tenth to one-third the time of the full proofreading.

- Review your marks and queries for appropriateness, clarity, and correct placement.
- Reread any line where you marked an error as well as two or three lines before and after the marked error, looking for other errors. (Errors often occur in groups, and it's not unusual for a proofreader to catch one and overlook others nearby.)
- Read the first and the last line of each page or galley to be sure each reads properly into the next.
- Review all headings, including running heads.
- Review all boldface, italic, and all-cap portions and all other material set in type different from the body type.
- Reread the first galley or the first page or two. Then read the first paragraph a third time. (Proofreaders tend to miss errors at the beginning of jobs.)
- Check the ends of lines for wrong word division you might have missed.

Initials and mark-off

For certain jobs these steps may be required; for others, or for certain stages of a job, they are unacceptable. Read your instructions *carefully*.

- Initial each page or galley of live copy as you finish proofreading it. If no marks are allowed on the front of the copy, initial the back. Both members of a team may need to initial the live copy (the initials of the person who marked the copy go first), or the partner who read aloud may need to initial the dead copy.
- At the bottom of each galley or page, write the page numbers of the corresponding dead copy.
- If the instructions call for *mark-off,* mark the dead copy where the last word of every page or galley falls and write two numbers, that of the corresponding page or galley ending there and that of the one starting there:

```
a galley's final word⌐first word of next galley
```

- Mark each sheet of dead copy as you finish it with a diagonal line from the lower left corner to the upper right corner.

Finishing touches

- Fill out any required administrative forms.
- Label proofs as required. A common system uses these categories for page proofs: OK, OK a/c (OK as corrected), OK w/c (OK with corrections), or "Show revised proofs." Another system uses labels supplied by the typographer; a typical label is shown in Figure 23.

PROOF   JOB _____

Please check carefully, especially for names, addresses and numbers, with your original copy, marking all corrections on the proof. Return the proof, with your original copy, and check the appropriate box below. We cannot be held responsible for errors if the work is printed per your OK. Revisions or alterations to original copy will require an additional charge.

☐ Approved as is.
☐ Approved with noted changes.
☐ Approved with additional new copy.
☐ Request a second proof after changes have been made.

SIGNATURE   DATE

Figure 23. Label for proofs ready to be returned to a typographer

Revising

Revising (checking revisions) doesn't normally involve re-proofreading (although some publishers may use this step for another proofreading). This stage generally involves nothing more than ascertaining that all marked corrections have been made and that no new errors have been introduced during the correction process. (It's astonishing how often a keyboarder introduces new errors—or misses clearly marked corrections altogether.)

To verify corrections, put dead and live copy side by side. Compare the corrections made in the live copy against the marks in the dead copy. Be sure every correction has been made properly and that no new errors appear. Read one or two lines above and below every line containing a correction to be sure the corrected line is in its proper place.

Even a small addition or deletion can move words from one line to another and sometimes from one page or galley to another. You can look for changes or check the sequence of lines by *slugging*: fold the dead copy's left margin under and hold the folded edge against the live copy to see whether the first word on every line is the same. (Don't fold the live copy!) When you find changes, take these steps:

- Check all new word, line, and page breaks; watch for widows.
- Double-check that no lines have been dropped and that each galley or page reads properly into the next.
- Where changes have moved material to another page, do this:
  —Check that footnotes are still in sequence and still begin on the same page as their callouts.
  —Check that tables and artwork are still in proper position and that each still follows its first callout.
  —Check facing pages for balance.
  —Check the accuracy of the table of contents.
  —If indexing has begun, tell your supervisor about the page changes so the indexer can be notified to make the appropriate adjustments.

Re-proofreading

Re-proofreading (proofreading more than once, each time preferably with a different reader or team), sometimes half a dozen times or more, may be called for, especially for critical copy (such as expensive advertisements or legal or technical material). The same techniques and procedures are followed, but pencils of different colors may be used to distinguish one person's work from another's when each proofreader uses the same live copy.

Special treatment

References

Footnotes and endnotes

Proofread a footnote or endnote immediately after its callout in text. Be sure the typographic style is consistent: superscripts or reference marks (such as asterisks) may be bumped to or spaced from the first word of the footnote. If footnotes are separated from the text by a *cut-off rule* (a short rule), measure to be sure all such rules are the same width and depth. Be sure to verify the sequence of notes and their text callouts.

Be sure that there's a callout for every note and a note for every callout. Be sure that the callouts' and the notes' numbers, letters, or reference marks correspond, and be sure the 1-2-3 or a-b-c sequence is correct—nothing missing, nothing added. If you are required to, watch for inconsistencies in editorial style.

Descriptions of displayed material

Be sure that descriptions in text, captions, or legends match the tables or illustrations being described. Check graphs against their descriptions or data.

Galleys or preliminary page proofs

In the margin, mark callouts for the footnotes that need to be put in place (not, of course, for endnotes). Also, if the typesetter or paste-up artist hasn't done it already, mark copy for the insertion of tables, graphs, illustrations, page references, or any material needing to be filled in.

Pages

Unless material is grouped (as, for example, photographs might be in the center pages of a biography), be sure that what is called out follows the callout as soon as possible.

Footnotes should begin on the same page and column as their callouts; tables and illustrations should begin as soon as there is enough space—on the same page as the callout if possible.

Where space has been left for artwork, measure to be sure it's right. Check the sequence of the typesetter's numbering system for artwork to be inserted later.

Author-date citations

Learned journals and technical publications may use the author-date reference style. Check to be certain that the names and dates appearing in parentheses in the text agree with those in the reference list that follows the chapter or appears in the back of the book.

Source notes

If the publication uses source notes, a numbered reference list appears at the end of an article or document, and its numbers are called out in brackets or parentheses in the text. The numbers of the source notes may follow citation order (number 1, the first cited) or they may follow the list's alphabetical order. The first callout for each source note may appear with the author's name. Check to be certain callouts agree with source notes both in notation and in the way the author's name is treated.

Acronyms

For some jobs, you may be asked to query unfamiliar acronyms that aren't explained at their first occurrence.

Day and date

For some jobs, you may be required to check a perpetual calendar to be sure the day of the week corresponds with the date of the month when the two are mentioned in the text.

Bibliographic references

Be sure an author's name is treated the same way every time it appears—same spelling, same use of initials. Be sure the names of organizations are correct and consistent; for example, in publishers' names, check the use of hyphens (McGraw-Hill, Prentice-Hall, Houghton Mifflin), capitals (Macmillan), and commas (Van Nostrand Reinhold Co., Harcourt, Brace & Co.).

If required, watch for any inconsistencies in capitalization, punctuation, spelling, and sequence of data. But take care in what you query or correct; bibliographic data are complex.

Two different styles (codified in *The Chicago Manual of Style*) for an entry in a bibliography are shown in Figure 24. Chicago Press style is widely used. Other common styles, different still, include those of McGraw-Hill and the Modern Language Association.

Style A (literature, history, the arts)
Davidson, Roger H. *The Role of the Congressman.* Studies in Contemporary American Politics Series, no. 3. New York: Pegasus, 1969.

Style B (natural and social sciences)
Davidson, R.H. 1969. *The Role of the Congressman.* New York: Pegasus. *Studies in Contemporary American Politics.*

Figure 24. Two styles for bibliographies

Tables

When you proofread a table, in addition to checking everything you do in running text, check the following with special care:

Spacing and alignment. Columns should be aligned according to their content, which may mean aligning at the left or at the right or may mean centering each entry, aligning on decimal points or en dashes, or clearing for 10 (for example, aligning the number 1 with the zero in the number 10). (See "Alignment" in Chapter 8.)

Proper use of rules. Vertical rules are usually omitted; proper spacing clearly separates columns. Mark for *straddle rules* (rules under a head that crosses more than one column) or for total-line rules where they're needed for clarity.

Arithmetic. Verify calculations as required at your level of authority. Be sure to check headings, dollar signs, commas that separate figures, and single and double total lines. In comparison proofreading, watch especially for these two kinds of errors:

- Transposition.
  Note: If you can determine the amount of an error in addition or subtraction and can divide that amount by 9, the error is likely to be caused by transposition, as in this example:

Total Revenues	$569,200
Total Operating Expenses	325,049
Net Income	$244,511

  (The correct figure is $244,151—an error of $360, which is divisible by 9, and is indeed caused by the transposition of 151 to 511.)
- Slide errors, named after the way a trombone slides, occur when numerals are mistakenly omitted or added, changing the length of a string; for example, when an extra zero lengthens $10,000.00 to $100,000.00.

Consistency in editorial style, including the use of caps, punctuation (especially terminal periods), abbreviations, dashes, zeros, and blank cells.

Footnotes. Callouts for footnotes in tables go across the page from left to right and then from top to bottom.

Parallel construction of all analogous items.

In revising tables, watch for misplaced items. Check the figures above, below, and at the sides of corrections.

Look ahead before you mark a string of errors in a row or column; the problem may be solvable by marking a block of type instead of each item:

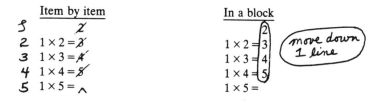

For practice in proofreading special kinds of material,
turn to Exercises 28 through 33.

Special tasks

You may be asked to perform tasks that are variations or extensions of proof-reading—using a computer's spelling checker, for example, or confirming that quotations from published material are exact.

Meticulous attention to detail is the requirement for most of the work proof-readers are asked to do. Discussion of one such task and of some problem tasks follows.

Sorted material

You may need to proofread live copy against dead copy that's not in the same sequence—a bibliography, for example, with dead copy arranged by author and live copy sorted by subject. Such a task takes an extra step as you seek the matching reference. Be sure to keep track of what you have compared: in both dead and live copy, put a checkmark as you finish each item (the marks on live copy may need to be in nonphoto-blue).

Sorting by computer is seldom as simple as a-b-c, 1-2-3. For example, to sort in correct numerical sequence, some computer programs need the same number of digits in every figure: a three-digit *111* will precede a two-digit *11*; you need a *011* to precede a *111*.

You may need to figure out some of the other options programmed into a particular sorting system, for example, the order in an alphabetical list in which punctuation, capitals, leading blanks, or figures appear.

For practice in proofreading sorted material,
turn to Exercise 34.

Problem tasks

You may be given a printout of copy that was edited on a word processor to proofread against the previous, unedited version. (Not everyone understands how computers work or what constitutes true dead and live copy.) "Proofreading" here involves only judicious comparison (perhaps for the spelling of proper names) and a good deal of guesswork.

You may be given proofs along with a printout of the word-processed copy that was converted to the typeset proofs—two versions identical in wording. Proofreading here involves minimal comparison, such as checking that lines have not been dropped, looking for incorrect or visible typesetting codes, and minimal dry reading (mostly for misspelling).

New problems to solve

In desktop publishing you will see some familiar problems and some new ones.

Electronic interference can cause computer problems. Data can be lost or altered (the word *data,* say, changed to *date* or garbled (like this: ////&*# 543 21rra sjvm,roo). Unskilled operators can cause unexpected errors (such as a paragraph moved to the wrong place). *Documentation* (instructions) for software can be ambiguous. Human beings can blunder.

Among the sad stories: thousands of address labels printed with the same address; every minus sign erased from a financial report; and two disks mixed up so the uncorrected disk was copied for safekeeping and the corrected disk (a day's work) was erased.

Here are some of the sources of problems:

The operator doesn't know the capabilities of the software. For example, he or she continues to follow typewriter conventions, such as setting double hyphens for em dashes or underscores for italic, or enters a single quote instead of an apostrophe preceding a contraction (wrong: 'Twas in '92; right: 'Twas in '92). (See "Electronic copy problems" in Chapter 8.) Or the operator learns a few tasks but not all those that would speed the work; for example, the person is not aware of the search-and-replace feature and painstakingly reads through the copy when the same change is needed repeatedly (as when roman numerals must be changed to arabic).

The operator doesn't know the limitations of the software. For example, the operator trusts the automatic hyphenation and turns out copy with word-division errors (ban-dleader, co-pied), or trusts the spellcheck program and doesn't catch the typos that make words (foe example, the types that make wards). Or the operator uses the search-and-replace feature globally instead of instance by instance (intending to change roman numerals to arabic, he changes every *x* to a *10* in a document about taxes, and the word *tax* then appears every time as ta10).

The user doesn't know the hazards associated with the equipment. Thousands of pages can be put at risk when backups aren't faithfully done. The security of proprietary information is at risk when the information is not protected.

A proofreading step is missed. For example, the operator is a writer who fails to reread the copy after every change. In such a case, you may see a new kind of doublet consisting of the writer's original expression in addition to a changed expression, like this:

> In desktop publishing you will see some old errors familiar problems.

Be suspicious of any new printout that's presumably unchanged. Look especially for spacing changes and typographic changes. For example, if a printer isn't set for an extra-wide margin, an oversized spreadsheet's right-hand margin won't print out; or if a change has been made from one kind of software, computer, or printer to another, formatting may be lost and such problems as misaligned columns in a table may appear. Read—or at least scan—every new version.

The equipment itself is faulty. Hardware and software can be defective. Computers have been known to produce garble, random characters, and intermittently dropped characters. Problems can be caused by *bugs* (errors in a program) or *viruses* (small, malicious programs hiding in larger, benign-appearing programs that are transmitted through a network or disk, replicated on your software, and when triggered cause mischief or real damage). And defective printing equipment, paper, film, and printing plates do turn up.

The proofreader fails to adapt to new technology. As an experienced professional proofreader once wrote—

> There's nothing static about proofreading. You have to adapt continually to new processes and new machines, and with every new one there's a period of chaos. Once the typesetters learn what they're doing with new equipment, we proofreaders can begin to learn what we're telling the typesetters to do to make corrections. In a couple of years, we're all comfortable (we get so we can even tell who set a take by the kinds of typos we find). Then they put in new equipment and the cycle starts again: we see a lot of errors, including kinds we've never seen before and we begin to learn our job all over again.

If you fail to learn how the copy you read is produced and corrected, you will mark ineffectively. And during the "period of chaos" resulting from new equipment, you may have to lower your expectations. For example, in current publications you will notice the prevalence of "buffoon typography" from untrained designers; in an extreme case you may see a new typeface for every new thought. Stay calm; deal with the problems within your province and ignore the rest. You will be busy enough meeting the never-ending challenge of keeping up with the job.

7 Queries and Corrections

Queries

How corrections and queries differ

Normally, when you proofread by comparison, the assumption is that you work with error-free dead copy and clear, detailed instructions. You're employed to be sure the typesetter or typist has faithfully reproduced the author's or editor's draft, according to the job specifications and good typing or typesetting practice. When the live copy doesn't follow the dead copy or doesn't meet the specs or standards, you mark the errors for correction.

But you may sometimes be expected to catch errors in the author's or editor's draft, for example, factual errors, dubious grammar, obvious discrepancies, or inconsistencies in editorial style. Usually you won't have the authority to mark such matters for correction; you can only *query* them—or ignore them.

Often you must ignore these problems. Querying is useless when no one is available or willing to answer the queries or when the deadline or the budget won't permit the extra time and money that querying takes. Querying may be unwelcome for reasons you don't know; for example, when copy editing or a technical review is planned for a later step.

When querying is welcome, few jobs require you to query anything other than blatant—indefensible—errors. A minimum querying standard requires you to call attention to questions written in the margins of the dead copy that apparently went unanswered before the live copy was prepared. When you see an unanswered query, either write something like this: "See Q in draft, p. x" or quote the unanswered query like this: "Q in draft, p. x: Is 'Jonson' sp right?"

Marks for correction are directed to keyboard operators, and usually only errors for which they are responsible are marked. Marks for correction are instructions that must be followed. Queries are directed to authors and editors, who may accept or reject them; if a query is accepted, it becomes a mark for correction.

Why query?

Proofreaders sometimes have difficulty understanding their limited authority in work for which they must query—not correct—editorial errors, even when something is obviously very wrong. There are several good reasons for this restriction:

- Proofreaders are seldom experts in the subjects they deal with. Many a beginner has "corrected" something erroneously: *diplomate* has been changed to *diplomat, corrasion* to *corrosion, adsorption* to *absorption, wove* (in reference to paper manufacturing) to *woven.* The exponent has been deleted from 10^3 *gallons* (because "there was no footnote 3," said the proofreader); and *feet per second per second,* the unit for measuring acceleration, has been mistaken for a doublet.

If you make such an error, you are responsible for harming the copy. But if you only query, no harm is done. Or if you make a valid query and it's discarded, the error isn't yours.

- Authors and editors have a right to decide if any detail of their work should be changed. By querying, you give an author or editor a fair opportunity to correct the oversights you've found (and, perhaps, to learn to be more careful).
- Proofreaders can't authorize the money or time needed for extra corrections. A change of one word—even of one character—can cause a complete line to be reset; if the line then overruns to another line, the whole paragraph is involved; and if the paragraph overruns to another page, an entire page must be reset; and so on. Even when the resetting is not done manually but by a computer such corrections can be costly.

Take warning! No matter how blatant an error is, don't correct it without explicit authority to do so.

- Marking for unauthorized corrections is unprofessional. On the other hand, proper querying is entirely professional. In fact, the ability to refrain from querying when it's unwelcome or ineffective but to write brief, specific queries when they're tolerated and needed is a major characteristic of a first-class proofreader.

What to query

You must always catch a misspelling and, if you're not authorized to correct it, query it (unless you know queries to be useless). But watch for the *diplomat-diplomate* kind of problem; look up the word in the specified dictionary if you have the slightest doubt about your knowledge.

When queries are tolerated, you must always query errors that would seriously embarrass the author or confuse the reader, as would blatantly bad grammar or obviously incorrect arithmetic.

Different levels of querying may be required for different jobs. Figure 25 shows the deepest level; included are queries of fact, grammar, inconsistency, and unintentional ambiguity.

REPORT OF NOVEMBER MEETING OF AXCI
The Board of Directors of the Association for Cross-Cultural Interchanges (AXCI) met at a working lunch at 12:00 p.m. on November 9. Only five of the 8 directors were present. Vice President George Stephaney distributed the results of the poll that each of the Board members having authority over specific committee were asked in October to administer. A total of 36 of the 700 members—more than half—responded. Dr. Stephany arranged the results in table form showing AXCI membership broken down by age and sex.

noon/(?)

was/(?)
each ... was
Stephaney/(?)
(see line 5)

5/eight/(?)
see line 1
a/(?)
36 0/(?)

categorized/(?)

Figure 25. Querying directly on live copy

Why these queries? Let's take them one by one:

- noon? 12 p.m. and 12 a.m. can be misunderstood. Better to say "noon" or "midnight."
- 5? eight? The number style is inconsistent. Consistent style would call for either "5 ... 8" or "five ... eight."
- *D*? The cap style is inconsistent; Directors is capped on line 1.
- a? The indefinite article seems to be missing.
- each ... was? "each ... were" incorrectly puts a singular noun with a plural verb.
- 360? 36 isn't "more than half" of 700, but 360 is.
- Stephaney? The name is spelled with a second *e* on line 3.
- categorized? "Broken down by age and sex" is unintentionally comic.

Forms of queries

You should find out whether queries are to be written directly on the live copy, on query slips, or in a comprehensive separate list.

Queries written on live copy

On galleys, page proofs, or photocopies, queries are sometimes written in the margin, usually in a different color from marks for correction; checkmarks, underscores, or carets go in the text, as Figure 25 shows.

Many organizations expect proofreaders to enclose a query in a ring. Indeed, a ring warns the typesetter or typist not to set or type the correction suggested in an unanswered query. If, however, a proofreader knows that a checker or editor or author will review the work carefully, rings around queries are undesirable. This is the problem: if the answer to a query is yes, the ring has to be canceled; the result looks like this:

Text	Margin
12:00 p.m.	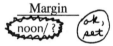

To avoid the problem, put a ring around the question mark only. Then if the answer to the query is yes, only the question mark need be crossed out, although sometimes the in-text mark needs to be changed, as shown here:

Text	Margin
12:00 ~~p.m.~~	noon/⊗

Be sure you know your employer's policy with regard to rings. And always use an enclosing ring when you're unsure whether someone will answer queries.

You may want (or be required) to label every query with a "Q" (or a "Qu" or "Qy") like this:

Query slips

Camera-ready copy requires separate query slips or lists; you mustn't mark the original.

The preferred medium is a self-stick note, such as a Post-it Note, because it adheres securely yet removes easily, leaving no mark, when a query is answered.

If a query takes more than one or two lines, it's best to type it; otherwise, use a dark-colored pen or pencil (no nonphoto-blue, please; it's too hard to read) and write as legibly as possible. Always, on every slip, list the live copy's page number (in case the slip falls off the page).

Never make a mark for a query in the text on camera-ready copy. Either locate the problem you're querying by writing a "Q" or a ringed question mark in nonphoto-blue *in the margin* or cite on the query slip the live copy's paragraph and line number along with the page number.

Count a line number as a subdivision of the paragraph; every paragraph begins with line 1. Where queries pertain to something in the bottom half of a long paragraph, start the line count at the last line; for example, "line last," "line 2 up," or "line 3 up."

Cite the dead copy's page, paragraph, and line number only when it's necessary to refer to the dead copy to answer the query; for example:

p 7, para 3, line 14 — 8 or 3 /ⓠ
(draft p 4, para 2, line 12 illegible)

Quote a key word or two. The following shows a good way and a bad way to query the same problem:

Text	Query slip	Comment
Wynken Blynken and Nod	Blynken⁁/ ⓠ	good
	commas / ⓠ	too unspecific

Query lists

Some people prefer query lists to query slips, perhaps because they want to keep a more convenient record of the work. Perhaps they've had bad luck with lost query slips. Or perhaps they've found that a list saves a little time because they can answer some of the queries without flipping the pages of the live copy and because they can discard a repeated query once instead of on every page the problem appears.

A query list should almost always be typewritten; before you submit a handwritten list, be sure it will be acceptable. Label your submission "Query List" and give the name of the job and the date. Organize the list into columns for section, page, paragraph, and line numbers. Figure 26 shows an example of a typed query list for the same problems as shown in Figure 25, which has queries written directly on live copy. Because queries on a list aren't immediately adjacent to the text, they must be more explicit than queries written directly on live copy.

The person who will answer queries is likely to prefer a typed list simply because typing is easier to read than most people's handwriting. The proofreader is likely to prefer to write a list by hand, however, because it saves a little time and can include proofreading marks. Figure 27 shows how proofmarks can help explain a query when a handwritten list is acceptable.

```
QUERY LIST
Report of November Meeting of AXCI

Draft          Final proof
p. par. line   p. par. line   Text              Query

not applicable          2     12:00 p.m.        noon? p.m. often
                                                considered midnight

                        2     five...8          5? or eight?
                                                for consistency

                        2     directors         Directors? cap as
                                                in line 1

                        4     over specific     over a specific?

                  3 up         each...were       each...was?  n.
                                                and v. disagree

                  3 up         36                360? over half of
                                                700

                  2 up         Stephany          spelling OK?  See
                                                "Stephaney" line 3

                  last         broken down       categorized?  Or
                                                seems like
                                                "shattered" by age
                                                etc.
```

Figure 26. Typed query list

Content of queries

Whenever you can, express a query as a question. Phrase the question so that if the answer is no, the entire query can be crossed out, but if the answer is yes, the question mark can be crossed out and the keyboarder can read what remains as an instruction; for example:

Text	Margin
Manufacturers is	are /?

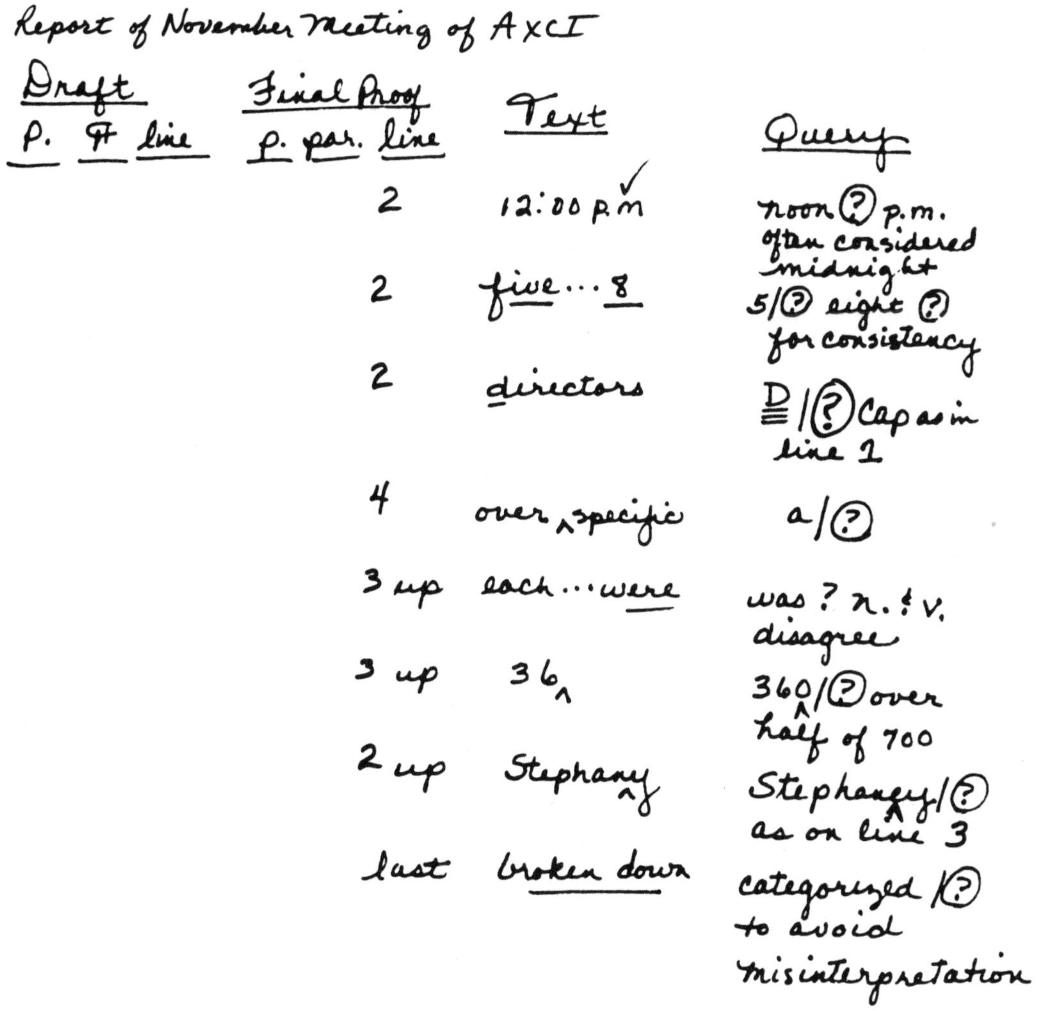

Report of November Meeting of AxCI

Draft	Final Proof	Text	Query
P. ¶ line	p. par. line		
	2	12:00 p.m ✓	noon ⟨?⟩ p.m. often considered midnight
	2	five...8	5/⟨?⟩ eight ⟨?⟩ for consistency
	2	directors	D≡ /⟨?⟩ Cap as in line 1
	4	over ∧specific	a/⟨?⟩
	3 up	each...were	was? n. & v. disagree
	3 up	36∧	360/⟨?⟩ over half of 700
	2 up	Stephany∧	Stephany/⟨?⟩ as on line 3
	last	broken down	categorized /⟨?⟩ to avoid misinterpretation

Figure 27. Handwritten query list

Some queries, of course, don't lend themselves to a yes-or-no form; for example:

> (where goes closing quote?)

Some queries lend themselves to a yes-or-no answer only when you add "OK," for example:

> (closing quote here OK?)

If you question a statement of fact, an unusual spelling, or a quotation's accuracy, underscore (or note) it and ask the author (Au) to verify it; for example:

> In the United States, 1.045 boys are (Au: verify) born for every 1,000 girls.

Any query can be addressed specifically to the author or to the editor (Ed); for example:

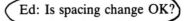

Ed: Is spacing change OK?

A query must be clear and specific, and it must answer these three questions:

1. *Where's the problem?* Pinpoint the place. For queries written directly in the margin, make checkmarks, underscores, or carets in the text. On query slips, place a ringed question mark in the margin or cite page, paragraph, and line number. On query lists, cite page, paragraph, and line numbers, and quote a bit of the text.

2. *What's the problem?* The query itself should explain.

3. *Why is it a problem?* Such phrases as "for consistency," "as previously," "per style sheet," and even "punc error" or "noun and verb disagree" are invaluable aids to the person who must decide what to do about queries. Unless you're certain the reason for a query is obvious (for example, when you've dealt with the same editor for a long time or when you've made the same query in the same job several times before), explain every query.

Recurring errors

When you see the same problem many times throughout the copy, mark each instance with a checkmark in the margin and write a separate query list, as shown in Figure 28.

```
programing--
Is one m only per old GPO style OK/?
 See pp 3
          9
         14
         22
         35
         96
```

Figure 28. List of recurring errors

Special abbreviations

Some editors are used to seeing (G?) for questions of grammar, (F?) for questions of fact, and (M?) to ask "meaning?" But use these abbreviations only where you're sure they'll be understood:

 "Darien peaks" <u>are</u> the name given the experiences of revelation or discovery seeming to be as great as that of <u>Cortez</u>, when, as Keats described him, "with eagle eyes he star'd at the Pacific . . . upon a peak in Darien."

Balboa (F?)
Keats got it wrong

We must follow Gertrude Stein's advice when she says,
"nobody visits as much as they who visit them." (M?)

Speed in querying

Querying slows down proofreading significantly. Querying must be done efficiently or the time loss is unacceptable.

Team proofreaders must decide quickly whether to query a point; the senior member may rule. When in doubt, query.

If you can't immediately figure out how to word a query, mark the live copy (perhaps with "problem here") so you can find the spot later and try again in a separate step.

Cautions in querying

Restrain your editing instincts. Don't rewrite anything. (*Rewriting* is defined as crossing out a whole sentence and writing a whole new one.) If a sentence is clear enough for you to know how to rewrite it, leave it alone. For example, although the following sentence is badly written, the query suggesting a rewritten sentence is unacceptable from a proofreader:

Text	Unacceptable query
Of the approximately 30,000 foundations that exist in this country, most of the major ones number between three and five hundred.	*(Change to—) There are 300–500 major foundations among the 30,000 or so in this country/(?)*

This query would be valid:

Text	Valid query
Of the approximately 30,000 foundations that exist in this country, most of the major ones number between three͜and five hundred.	*hundred/(?) (or "300 and 500" (?))*

(The error of omitting the first "hundred" or "thousand" or "million" in expressing range is common; watch for it.)

In querying, there's no point in being a purist. Never gratuitously query which (that/ (?)), will (shall/ (?)), or wish (want/ (?)).

Be cautious about querying a comma unless its presence or absence affects the meaning.

She showed me her new, pretty͜expensive shoes. */(?) (to clarify)*

Be cautious about querying style unless you can back up the query with a rule from the specified style guide:

memoránda *memorandums/(?) (per Chicago style)*

Query lightly, if at all (excluding unmistakable errors), when copy has been prepared by a professional copy editor; when copy is technical, scientific, or mathematical; when copy is a legal or financial document such as a contract, mortgage, or transcript of testimony; or when copy is quoted matter.

Query sexism when it could offend readers and embarrass the publisher. Suggest a graceful alternative when you can do so quickly; for example:

Every district manager must turn in his monthly report promptly.

A schoolteacher's relationship to her students is critical.

Changing the meaning is the greatest sin in editorial work; be wary. Never suggest a change that will change the meaning unless you're sure you're on solid ground. An illogical statement such as the following (from a safety manual) rates a query:

It is in the best interest of the corporation for its employees to incapacitate themselves on the job. *worst /(?) (for sense)*

Use the dictionary to avoid querying perfectly good words used correctly. For example, these queries are invalid because the words are used correctly:

Kissinger's apparat *C us /(?)*

A concern with death informs this very original work. *permeates /(?)*

Don't try to change a published quotation.
Know your grammar:
- It would be shameful to change good grammar to bad, as shown here:

Space as a focus of foreign policy is one of those subjects that are a direct result of technological advance.

The true antecedent of "that" is "those subjects," not "one." Turn the sentence around in your mind to make this clear: Of those subjects that are a direct result of technological advance, space is one.
- It would be humiliating to be caught querying needlessly, as shown here:

When bureaucratic politics works badly, the president's choice is narrowed. *work /(G?)*

"Politics" is a collective noun, and either a singular or plural verb is correct. Figure 29 shows examples of a few valid queries.

> For practice in querying,
> turn to Exercise 35.

The advent of the automobile heightened the rise of the State police force. Earlier State police efforts had occurred in Texas, which organized Rangers and Massachusetts, which appointed State constables.

∧/(?)
∧/(?)
∧/(?)

HELP YOUR DRYCLEANER SUPPORT MUSCULAR DYSTROPHY

Support the muscular dystrophy foundation/(?)

Sunbelt women from Georgia to California here share with you their traditional beauty secrets. And to help you concoct your own off-the-kitchen shelf cosmetics, see the chart of natural ingredients that follow.

=/(?)

Chart ... follows/(?)

SEAPINE CHESTS

These beautifully crafted chests, in dark weathered finish, bound with antique brass bindings and handles will look as good in a land setting as it does on a luxury yacht.

chests (plural)

they do/(?)

There are many possible ways to organize the United States government for the conduct of foreign policy. The choice between them will be influenced by the personalities of the President and his principal collaborators, but it should also reflect the nation's basic foreign policy priorities.

between among/(?)

As he marched around the FTC building during the protest, Raymond R. Nuckles, a 23-year-old American Safety Razor employee, declared: "That's my livelihood. If the plant closes down, I don't know what I will do. I've got to support my family (of four). Jobs are hard to find. You just don't go and find a job at age 45."

∫ 23-year/
∫ old
employee/(?)
∧ (?)

ABC*heating*

 # so it does not look like "cheating"/(?)

Deterring crime: By failing to execute a convicted murderer do we risk prevention of other murders?

By I s/(?)

jeopardizing/(?)
do we risk

prevention of murders would be a desirable risk

Figure 29. Valid queries (assuming the live copy matches the dead copy)

Alterations and corrections

A commercial typographer is responsible for making *corrections** at no charge to any unauthorized deviation from the dead copy or from specifications. (Some small shops don't accept this responsibility.) The traditional name for these deviations is *printer's errors* (PEs).

A commercial typesetter is not responsible for correcting an error that's found in dead copy, not even an obvious misspelling.

When an error in the dead copy is repeated in the live copy, and that error is then marked for correction, the change is called an *alteration* (traditionally, an *AA* or *alt,* short for *author's alteration***). The same term applies to any change from the dead copy made after the live copy is printed out in near-final form, such as page proofs.

If you work for a publisher who gives you the authority to mark for correction, or if you work with copy on which queries have been answered and changes approved, you may need to distinguish PE's, which the typographer pays for, from AA's, which the customer pays for.

To distinguish one from the other, you may use different implements (pen and pencil) or different colors; you may label each mark AA or PE; or you may mark AA's in one margin and PE's in the other.

If you work for a typographer, you may be required to mark up revises to show where alterations were made according to a customer's wishes and where space and type have been moved to accommodate the alterations; these revises go back to the customer along with the bill for them.

What if a publisher's proofreader misses an error at an early stage of the production process and catches it later? When does a correction become eligible to be charged as a change? The answer depends on where the typographer draws the line.

Some publishers insist that, until the job is photographed, a typographer's error be corrected at no extra charge—through page proofs—and some typographers will oblige customers that far. However, because corrections become more costly at every successive stage, some typographers start charging at an earlier stage. Once a job is marked "OK," "OK with corrections," or "OK with alterations," further changes are always charged for.

As a proofreader, you must know the policy for each job, because you must know what constitutes an AA. After the first round of reading, you may have to return to the original dead copy to discover when the error was first made.

> For practice in distinguishing between corrections and changes, turn to Exercise 36.

---

* *Corrections* are defined as "changes in composition and other work performed by the typographer due to errors by the typographer."

**Alterations are defined as "any addition, change or modification of work in progress made by the customer in copy, style, or specifications originally submitted to the typographer."—*Trade Customs of the Typographic Industry,* issued jointly by the Typographers International Association (TIA) and the Advertising Typographers Association of America (ATA).

Summary of errors and problems to mark or query (or ignore)

The following list summarizes many of the problems proofreaders look for. If you can catch everything on the list and decide correctly whether to mark, query, or ignore a problem, you'll be well on the way to doing work of professional quality.

Mark the following for correction:

- Unauthorized deviations from the dead copy
- Unauthorized deviations from specifications
- Typos, including omissions of letters, transpositions of letters and words, doublets, repeaters, and outs

Decide whether to *mark, query,* or *ignore* the following. Where levels *a, b,* and *c* (or just *a* and *b*) are listed, decide at which level to mark or query:

- *Mechanical faults* (misaligned characters, broken or dirty characters, rivers or lakes, smudges, dots, uneven ink color, and so on)
    a. Glaring (conspicuous to an untrained eye)
    b. Moderate (instantly conspicuous to a trained eye)
    c. All (conspicuous to a trained, searching eye)
- *Spacing errors:* bad appearance or inconsistencies in analogous items where there are no specs for indention, justification, line spacing, type page and column width and depth, word spacing, letter spacing, balance of facing pages, or equal space around displayed matter on facing pages
    a. Glaring (conspicuous to an untrained eye)
    b. Moderate (instantly conspicuous to a trained eye)
    c. All (conspicuous to a trained, searching eye)
- *Positioning faults:* knotholes, failure to clear for 10, faults in horizontal and vertical alignment, in position of folios, in running heads, and in any displayed matter
- *Word division errors,* including ladders (up to three consecutive end-of-line hyphens are usually acceptable)
- *Widows and orphans at page or column top and bottom*
    a. A heading at page bottom has fewer than the specified lines of text (2–6) following it
    b. The last line of a paragraph starts a page or column
       —A widow line of less than two-thirds measure
       —Any widow line, no matter how long
    c. The first line of a paragraph ends a page or column
- *Widows at paragraph bottom*
    a. The last line of a paragraph is the end of a divided word or a broken compound expression (*page 3, L.B. Johnson*)
    b. The last line of a paragraph is less than the specified limit, which may be, for example, one-third the line width or 2–6 characters
    c. The last line of paragraph is any single word
- *Other bad breaks:* head is not broken for sense, text line starts with a dash or ellipsis, a short page hasn't the required number of lines (usually five), and so on
- *Type style errors:* bad appearance or inconsistencies in analogous items where there are no specs for typeface, type size, caps, Clc, italics or underscores—in text, heads, running heads, folios, and so on
- *Poor graphics*

- *Nonstandard grammar or usage*
  a. Glaring only
  b. Moderate faults (use discretion)
  c. All (nitpick)
- *Punctuation errors and inconsistencies*
  a. Glaring only
  b. Moderate faults (use discretion)
  c. All (nitpick)
- *Editorial style discrepancies*: inconsistencies in analogous items where there are no specs for compound words, capitalization, number style, cross references, abbreviations, symbols, units of measure, treatment of proper names, use of italics or underscores, and so on
  a. Glaring (different styles for the same item within several lines of each other)
  b. Conspicuous (different styles for the same item on the same page)
  c. All
- *Poor exposition*
  a. Material that makes no sense, obvious omissions and discrepancies, apparently incorrect or incomplete sentences
  b. Somewhat confusing sections
  c. Turgid, awkward, or needlessly repetitious sections; peculiarities of language
- *Errors in alphabetical or numerical sequence* (folios, footnotes, illustrations, tables, lists, bibliographies, and so on)
- *Faulty reference:* referenced matter that doesn't follow its first reference, doesn't correspond to its description (footnotes, illustrations, tables, and so on), or doesn't match a reference list or bibliography (as in dates and spelling of names)
- *Missing material:* pages, illustrations, graphics, and so on
- *Faulty headings:* inappropriate or incorrect headings, running heads, titles, captions, and so on
- *Incorrect arithmetic* (such as addition in tables)
- *Errors in equations and formulas:* incorrect breaks, wrong symbols, and so on
- *Problems in tables, charts, graphs, exhibits:* inconsistencies in analogous items where there are no specs for style or format (spacing, punctuation, abbreviations, capitalization, notation for unavailable data, and so on). Also, lack of clarity (bad split, need for straddle rules) and typographical faults (broken or crooked rules, misalignments, transpositions, and so on)
- *Errors in front-matter listings:* table of contents doesn't match chapter or section headings or page numbers; list of illustrations doesn't match illustration titles or page numbers
- *Blanks in text* (items to be inserted, such as page number references)

For practice in general proofreading,
turn to Exercise 37.

8 Tips, Traps, and Reminders
(in alphabetical order)

Alignment

In a list, an outline form, or a format where indents hang, arabic or roman numerals may be cleared for 10, like this:

9.	xxxxxxxxxxx	I.	XXXXXXXX
	xxxxxxxxxxx	II.	XXXXXXXXXX
10.	xxxxxxxxxxx	III.	XXXXXXXX
	xxxxxxxxxxx		

In tabular material, the usual vertical alignment of columns containing figures looks like the following examples, with (a) parentheses, (b) fractions, (c) superscripts, (d) decimal points, (e) en dashes, (f) slashes, (g) colons (or ratio signs), or (h) minus signs.

(a)	(b)	(c)	(d)	(e)	(f)	(g)	(h)
3	$4\frac{1}{2}$	10^2	3.1216	1–27	6/80	6:56	–1.0
(20)	17	450	45	22–6	10/65	49:4	10.5
89	5	98	17.06	34–76	8/79		–.3

The characters in the column at the extreme left of some tables are aligned flush left, as in column (a) below. Items in totally different categories can either be aligned at the left, as in column (b), or centered, as in column (c):

(a)	(b)	(c)
Jan 1	3.1416	3.1416
Feb 10	6–4	6–4
Mar 25	42,000	42,000
Apr 5	1 ton (metric)	1 ton (metric)

Communicator's signals

Use the international communicator's alphabet and numbers whenever you spell words or give numbers orally. These signals, designed for optimum clarity and used in such applications as aviation radio and voice-input computer systems, are especially helpful on the telephone.

alpha	Juliette	Sierra	zero
bravo	kilo	tango	wun
Charlie	Lima (Leema)	uniform	too
delta	mike	Victor	tree
echo	November	whiskey	foe-er
foxtrot	Oscar	X-ray	fife
golf	Papa	yankee	six
hotel	Quebec	zulu	seven
India	Romeo		ate
			niner

Composition codes

Every change of type and every character a typewriter or word processor doesn't provide must be coded. But in most cases, the coding does not appear on printouts. Once in a while, you may see a code that appears in error. Here's one that was supposed to tell the computer to print an en dash:

Elizabeth I (1533<en>1603)

Confusion, sources of

Among the things novice proofreaders misunderstand are the differences in the following:

—Full caps and small caps
—Hyphens, en dashes, em dashes, minus signs
—Underscores, italics, baseline rules
—Proofmarks and editing marks
—Uses of the dele and the closed-up dele
—Closing up (tying) all space and reducing space
—Typed and typeset copy
—Style choices (such as "the chairman" or "the Chairman") and conventions that seldom allow a choice (such as beginning every sentence with a capital letter).

Diacritical marks

Many styles specify that diacritical marks aren't used for words that are completely anglicized, such as *cafe, vis a vis,* and *smorgasbord.* Some styles don't even put accents on foreign words (e.g., manana, Espanol, touche). Some styles use diacritical marks in text but omit them from all-cap heads.

Electronic copy problems

Some problems in electronic transmission relate to the keyboarder's (usually the writer's or editor's) inability to adjust to a word processor's capabilities. You may see—

- A lowercase *l* where a figure *1* belongs (see Figure 30). This error occurs when a keyboarder is used to a typewriter that doesn't provide a separate character for figure *1.*

**Can you think of a way the trust could
legally make this disbursement during
calendar 1985 but defer the receipt of
same by the beneficiary until 1986?**

The characters are nearly identical, but the spacing is different.

Can you think of a way the trust could
legally make this disbursement during
calendar 1985 but defer the receipt of
same by the beneficiary until 1986?

The characters are similar but not identical.

Figure 30. An "el" for a "one"

- A short line where a line of full measure belongs. This error occurs when the keyboarder hits the return key at the end of a line (which inputs a "hard" line break) instead of allowing the computer's "word wrap" feature to decide where a line should end.
- A short page where a full page belongs. This error occurs when the keyboarder inputs a hard page break instead of allowing the computer to decide where a page should break.

Certain typos may recur because of the typical computer's differences from a typewriter in the use of the shift key. On word-processed copy you may see—

```
< instead of ,
> instead of .
; instead of :
```

Some problems relate to a change in a line's width when edited or translated. You may see—

- A hyphen where it doesn't belong, because the word was once divided at the end of a line
- No hyphen where one belongs in a compound word, because the hyphen was lost when it left the end of a line.

In some equipment, these problems relate to the input of hard (permanent) or soft (temporary) hyphens.

Some problems relate to the translation or coding of material to be typeset. The following table shows some of the typewriter characters that represent DTP or typeset characters. Some are exact equivalents, but many characters aren't available on a typewriter or on certain word-processing fonts; if the change isn't accounted for in translation tables or codes, the typed equivalent will be set instead of the correct characters.

Typed	Typeset
hyphen	hyphen
	en dash
	minus sign
two hyphens	em dash
multiple hyphens	2-em or longer dashes
underscore	baseline rule
	italic
hyphen-and-slash	*shilling fraction* (e.g., ¾, as in 1¾)
fraction (e.g., 1-3/4)	*em fraction* (stand-up or stack fraction, like this: $\frac{3}{4}$)
	en fraction (*piece fraction,* made up of separate parts, e.g., 3/ and 4 = 3/4)
full caps	full caps
	small caps
double quotes,	open double quotes
same open as close	close double quotes
	(e.g., " and " or ″ and ")
apostrophe,	apostrophe and
open single quote,	close single quote
and close single quote	both the same (')
all the same	open single quote
	(' or ')
prime, minute, or inch	prime, minute, or inch symbol
symbol same as single	(′)
quote	
double prime, second,	double prime, second, or foot symbol
or foot symbol same	(″)
as double quote	
bullet: lc *o*	center dot (·)
or degree sign	large bullet (●)
or period	small bullet (•)
	etc.
no equivalent	ligatures
	kerning
	ornamental initials
	many special characters

Ethics

Ethical proofreaders always keep the information they read confidential.

Fact checking

Some proofreaders act also as fact checkers. It's their job to check any quotation against its source and to verify bibliographic references, spelling of proper names, statistics, and the like. It may be part of their job to query or verify any statement that raises a question (for example, "Crime decreased 4% this year"— Decreased from when? What kind of crime?).

A fact checker must have access to a good reference library, including an encyclopedia, an almanac, and an atlas. Library information services answer a few questions by telephone so long as the service isn't abused. (One fact checker in Washington, D.C., phones every library in the area in turn, asking each the allotted three questions.) Most helpful of all are cooperative authors who provide details on their sources, including page numbers and sometimes even photocopies.

Figures

To correct one figure in a group, some editors and proofreaders insist that the entire group must be marked for correction—to avoid any possibility of misunderstanding. Another school of thought believes in marking only the offending figure—to help avoid the possibility of additional error by the marker or by the person at the keyboard. Take your choice:

$$12 \times 12 = \cancel{145} \quad 144$$

(or)

$$12 \times 12 = 14\cancel{5} \quad 4$$

Read all figures and all spelled-out numbers at least twice.

"$1,250,000" is the same as "$1.25 million," and "2,554,000,000 shares" is the same as "2.554 billion shares."

If a dollar figure is both written out and given in figures, be sure the two correspond.

Watch prices for inconsistency (as when $30 is given for a former listing of $20) and for sense (as when a sale price is greater than the manufacturer's list price).

Handwriting

Some authors and editors have undecipherable handwriting. You may have to query, but try the following suggestions first:

- Consider the context.
- Read on. Mark the place and see if the same word or expression is used later.
- Use a magnifying glass.
- Count the humps or peaks. There will be more, for example, in "portioning" than in "parting":

partioning parting

Make sure your own handwriting is legible. If anyone has trouble reading what you write, it may help if you switch from cursive writing to print-script.

In basic print-script, upright letters are formed of straight lines, circles, and parts of circles.

This is an example of *print-script:*

The quick brown fox jumped over the lazy dog.

This is an example of *cursive* writing:

The quick brown fox jumped over the lazy dog.

Clearly written figures are essential:

1 2 3 4 5 6 7 8 9 0

Illustrations

Be sure the title and the caption correspond with an illustration; for example, be sure the number of names in a caption matches the number of faces in a photograph.

Insurance

Here are some of the accidents that could happen and ways to avoid them or at least recover from them:

- Damaged proofs from spilled coffee: never put anything spillable on the same surface as proofs.
- Lost proofs: make photocopies before shipping or transporting proofs.
- Illegible proofreading marks on photocopies: mark proofs in a photocopyable color, such as deep red or black.
- Mixed-up pages from a spill: number unnumbered pages as soon as you get them.
- Lost query slips: make photocopies that include query slips, or make a list that duplicates the slips.
- Damaged *slicks* (typeset copy on shiny photographic paper, also called *glossies* or *repro proofs*) or other camera-ready copy from heavy pressure with a nonphoto-blue pen or pencil: use a light touch; if need be, find an implement that requires only a light touch (such as a felt-tip pen).

Proverbs for proofreaders

1. *Love is nearsighted.* When you are the writer, editor, or keyboard operator proofreading your own work, you will almost certainly suffer from myopia. You are too close to see all the errors. Get help.

2. *Familiarity breeds content.* When you see the same copy over and over again through the different stages of production and revision, you may well miss new errors. Fresh eyes are needed.

3. *If it's as plain as the nose on your face, everybody can see it but you.* Where is the reader most likely to notice errors? In a headline, in a title, in the first line, first paragraph, or first page of copy; and in the top lines of a new page. These are precisely the places where editors and proofreaders are most likely to miss errors. Take extra care at every beginning.

4. *When you change horses in midstream, you can get wet.* It's easy to overlook an error set in type that is different from the text face you are reading. Watch out when type changes to all caps, italics, boldface, small sizes, and large sizes. Watch out when underscores appear in typewritten copy.

5. *Don't fall off the horse in the home stretch.* Errors often slip by at the ends of tables, chapters, sections, and unusually long lines.

6. *Mistakery loves company.* Errors often cluster. When you find one, look hard for others nearby.

7. *The more, the messier.* Be careful when errors are frequent; the greater the number of errors, the greater the number of opportunities to miss them.

8. *Glass houses invite stones.* Beware copy that discusses errors. When the subject is typographical quality, the copy must be typographically perfect. When the topic is errors in grammar or spelling, the copy must be error-free. Keep alert for words like *typographical* or *proofreading.*

9. *The foot bone conneckit to the kneebone?* Numerical and alphabetical sequences often go awry. Check for omissions and duplications in page numbers, footnote numbers, or notations in outlines and lists. Check any numeration, anything in alphabetical order, and everything sequential (such as the path of arrows in a flowchart).

10. *It takes two to boogie.* An opening parenthesis needs a closing parenthesis. Brackets, quotation marks, and sometimes dashes belong in pairs. Catch the bachelors.

11. *Every yoohoo deserves a yoohoo back.* A footnote reference calls out for its footnote; a first reference to a table or illustration calls out for the table or the illustration. Be sure a footnote begins on the same page or column as its callout. Be sure a table or illustration follows its callout as closely as possible.

12. *Figures can speak louder than words.* Misprints in figures (numerals) can be catastrophic. Take extraordinary care with dollar figures and dates and with figures in statistics, tables, or technical text. Read all numerals character by character; for example, read "1993" as "one nine nine three." Be sure any figures in your handwriting are unmistakable.

13. *Two plus two is twenty-two.* The simplest math can go wrong. Do not trust percentages or fractions nor the "total" lines in tables. Watch for misplaced decimal points. Use your calculator.

14. *Don't use buckshot when one bullet will do.* Recurring errors may need only one instruction instead of a mark at each instance.

15. *Sweat the small stuff.* Watch strings of little words (if it is as bad as he says ...), and watch the inside letters of words. A simple transposition turns *marital strife* into *martial strife, board room* into *broad room.* One missing character turns *he'll* into *hell, public* into *pubic.*

16. *Above all, never assume that all is well.* As the saying goes, "ass-u-me makes an ass out of u and me."

Publishing conventions

Callouts

A common typographic style puts superscripts and other callouts for footnotes or endnotes following all punctuation except a dash and, if the callout applies to matter inside parentheses, a closing parenthesis.

Footnote callouts follow most punctuation.[1]

Other styles, however, place superscripts and callouts outside periods and commas and inside dashes, colons, and semicolons. If one method is consistently used, follow that style.

Manuscript formatting

A professional manuscript may have formatting like this:

- No end-of-line word division
- Only one space after a period
- Footnotes, tables, tabular material, illustrations—any material that must be fitted to pages in the final document—on separate pages or in a separate file
- Added pages or insertions marked A B C (for example, "page 8A," or "insert A, page 8"
- Headings marked at A B C or 1 2 3 levels of subordination according to a *hedsked* (heading schedule)

Pagination

This is a typical pagination scheme:

Right-hand pages (*recto*) have odd numbers; left-hand pages (*verso*) have even numbers. Usually, but not always, each new chapter or major section begins on a right-hand page, so the preceding page may be blank. Blank pages are counted, but the page number isn't shown (*blind folios,* they're called); these pages also do not carry running heads or rules.

The first page of the main text is usually a right-hand page. The main text and *back matter* (material following the main text, such as an appendix, end notes, a bibliography, and the index) are numbered in Arabic numerals.

The *front matter* or *preliminaries* (material preceding the main text, such as a dedication page, an acknowledgments page, a table of contents, and a preface) are numbered in lowercase Roman numerals; the half title page (if any) and the title page are blind; the first page number shown may be *iii,* for example.

The table of contents lists only the sections following it, not those preceding it.

Punctuation inside closing quotes

Although a few people resist the rule and some seem not to have heard of it, a long-standing American convention puts periods and commas inside closing quotation marks and other punctuation marks outside unless they are part of the quotation.

> "Commas," I'm told, "and periods go inside closing quotes."

Exceptions occur only in certain specialized contexts, such as instructions for computer programs where a comma or a period may be part of a file name or a command; for example: Please check all files starting with "SYS.", all files ending ".TXT", and all files on disk "027".

Punctuation in italic and boldface

Some typists have learned to underline stopping short of punctuation marks. In copy prepared for DTP or typesetting, however, an underline is a type mark calling for italic and should include periods, commas, colons, and semicolons.

The convention is that these punctuation marks appear in the type style of the character preceding them—roman, italic, or boldface.

> Thank you, *danke,* and *merci.*

Some typographic styles include exclamation points and question marks in the convention; other styles put them in italic or boldface according to the context of a sentence.

Set quotes in italic according to the overall context:

> *"Why, why, why?"* he asked.

> New Production of *'King Lear'* Proceeds
> (headline)

In body type, follow italic with roman in plurals and possessives like these:

> Dot your *i*'s and cross your *t*'s.

> three *Hamlet*s, one in each theater.

> the *Washington Post*'s front page.

Some styles call for roman parentheses with italic:

> Among the Latin expressions still in use are these: e.g. (*exempli gratia*), which means "for example," and i.e. (*id est*), which means "that is."

Quality of type

The proofs you see may not reflect the type quality of the final product. They may be imperfect copies from a copying machine; they may be on low-quality paper, like newsprint. Some typesetting systems provide a "proof mode" of lower typographic quality than the final mode will be.

Don't be misled by the appearance of *mechanicals,* that is, boards (of cardboard) on which the various components of a page, including artwork, headings, and text, are pasted up separately, like patchwork, and on which you may see many blue marks. If the paste-up artist is knowledgeable, the boards will photograph well; the printer's camera neither sees "nonphoto-blue" nor detects the patchwork.

Don't expect reproductions of photographs to be good quality in early proofs. And don't expect galleys or page proofs to have the specified margins; wide margins may be there for your proofreading marks.

Quotations

Quotations may be treated according to their length. One style guide, for example, calls for 50 words or more to be treated as an *extract*—displayed without quotation marks and indented right and left—and for 49 words or fewer to be treated as part of the text—enclosed in quotation marks but not otherwise set off. Extracts, of course, don't need quotation marks.

Recurring errors

Be suspicious when you see the same error recurring repeatedly. Maybe it's not an error, maybe you didn't get a thorough style sheet, or maybe you didn't absorb all the instructions. Maybe it's a problem that doesn't need marking at every instance because it can be corrected with one adjustment; for example, one switch on a certain model word processor changes an apostrophe to a degree sign; if a proofreader sees degree signs instead of apostrophes, one instruction tells the corrector to set the switch correctly for the next printout.

Scanner copy

On copy that has gone through a text scanner, or optical character reader (OCR), you might see wrong characters if the characters in the copy the scanner read weren't sharply defined. For example, a scanner might mistake a slightly defective *h* for an *n,* a *y* for a *v,* a *g* or a *p* for an *o,* or an *I* for an *1,* like this:

1s anv orinciole involved nere?

Spacing

In a well-designed document, line spacing is visually at least a little greater than word spacing; word spacing, of course, is greater than letter spacing; and letter spacing is neither too loose nor too tight.

Legibility suffers when letters fit too tightly, when a letter pair can be confused with another letter—*rn* for *m,* for example. Readability suffers when letters fit so tightly or so loosely that a word loses its distinctive pattern:

lost pattern

l o s t   p a t t e r n

Good letter spacing produces even color throughout the text; tight letter spacing produces dark clumps here and there. Loose word spacing produces lakes and rivers of white.

Spelling

Watch especially for errors a computer spellcheck will not catch—misspellings resulting from simple spacing errors (*a cross* for *across, day today* for *day to day*) or wrongly used homophones (words that sound alike but differ in meaning—*Here, here!* for *Hear, hear!* or *Their, their!* for *There, there!*).

Be aware that many words have more than one accepted spelling in use today, and the choice among them is a matter of style. To set standards, you need a dictionary, preferably one that your employer specifies.

Because dictionaries from different publishers differ, as do different editions from the same publisher, it's good to use only one edition and to be thoroughly familiar with it. For example, you should know how its front matter explains *equal variants* (such as "theater *or* theatre," "judgment *or* judgement," "toward *or* towards," "traveler *or* traveller") and *secondary variants* (such as "lovable *also* loveable," "zeros *also* zeroes," "story *also* storey").

You need to know whether the first listed definition is the one most often used or the historically oldest. And you may need the dictionary to identify British usage and spelling (labeled, for example, *chiefly Brit*) if you need to change words like *whilst* to *while,* or *favour* to *favor.*

You may have to choose one of several variants in foreign language transliterations such as these: Beijing/Peking/Peiping, Tchaikovsky/Tchaikowsky, Viet Nam/Vietnam, Chanukah/Hanukkah.

You may have to exercise judgment: some misspellings, such as *alright* or *dependance,* have occurred so often that they're listed in many dictionaries, but most people still consider them misspellings.

Where style is specified, it may call for the use of the first listing or the main entry among equal variants; where style is unspecified, sensible proofreaders (and broad-minded copy editors) will usually ignore their own preferences and let an author's equal or secondary variants remain—if the author's choices are consistent.

Consistency is the trick. If you have a choice, stick to one of the variants.

Style, editorial

Editorial style rules aim to eliminate inconsistencies that may distract the reader and lower a publication's quality. English allows many style choices, but few can be decided by a proofreader; the authority is the author or the editor or the publisher's specified style guide.

Knowledge of style, however, is a major advantage to a proofreader. If you know what the many equally correct choices are, you know more than most writers, most English teachers, and many editors.

You can learn about editorial style by becoming familiar with at least two style guides, perhaps choosing among *The Chicago Manual of Style, The Associated Press Stylebook,* the *U.S. Government Printing Office Style Manual, Words Into Type,* and *Webster's Standard American Style Manual.* Webster's is derived from G. & C. Merriam's large data base and describes the way questions of style are usually handled in this country. The others in large part prescribe a preferred style.

One of the reasons you need to be familiar with the details of editorial style is so you can tell if an author's individual, uncodified style is consistent. If the publisher doesn't insist on a prescribed style, or if no style is specified, all you need to look for is inconsistency. Here's an obvious example:

> The galleys seem to be O.K.: the type looks OK, the breaks look o.k., and I think everything is okay.

But consistency is tricky. Here are examples of consistent style:

> The specs call for a one-pica sink.
> The specs call for a sink of one pica.

> Today President Clinton appointed a new ambassador.
> The president appointed Ambassador McCall today.

> Fifty miles away is the state capital.
> The capital is 50 miles away.

Among the points of editorial style that should be consistent are these:

Abbreviations and acronyms, signs and symbols. Current trends favor fewer periods and capitals in abbreviations along with fewer abbreviations in general writing but more in technical writing. Most style guides give detailed rules. The short form may be used in headings even though the long is preferred in text. Some choices:

> %   percent   per cent
>
> square meters   sq. m.   sq m m^2
>
> United Nations   U.N.   UN
>
> the eighties   the '80s   the 80's   the 80s

Alphabetization. Which method—word by word or letter by letter? (See Chapter 6.)

Capitalization. Proper nouns are capped; common nouns are lowercased. But different styles define proper nouns differently, and the rules for capitalization may be fairly complex. Here are examples of the extremes:

Up style	Down style
Executive Secretary Matthews	Executive Secretary Matthews
the Executive Secretary	the executive secretary
Tim Matthews, Executive Secretary	Tim Matthews, executive secretary
Editor-in-Chief Jones	editor-in-chief Jones
Bidder To Be Tax-Exempt	Bidder to Be Tax-exempt

Compounding. A compound word may be solid (one word), hyphened, or open (two words). The same word may be compounded differently as a noun and as a verb (e.g., the cutout, to cut out) or as an adjectival compound before the noun (called a *unit modifier*) and as a predicate adjective (e.g., higher-priced goods, goods that are higher priced).

Dictionaries list permanent compounds. For temporary compounds, such as many unit modifiers, some style guides give detailed rules.

Documentation. Style for references, notes, bibliographies, and so on, which determines the sequence of data and the use of caps, punctuation, quotation marks, or italics, is complex (*The Chicago Manual of Style* devotes more than 100 pages to documentation style).

Italics and underscores. Style choices include treatment of foreign words and titles of publications. In some styles, certain kinds of titles are quoted instead of italicized.

Numbers. Number style decrees whether numbers are to appear in sentences as words or as figures. Some styles generally spell out numbers from one to nine and use figures starting with 10; some spell out numbers under 100. Many exceptions to the general rule are detailed in style manuals. One rule you can count on: in running text, always spell out the first word in a sentence.

Punctuation

Commas. Newspaper styles don't use the serial comma (red, white and blue); technical and academic styles do (red, white, and blue), although not always within an extremely short series.

Unless you can't make sense out of what you're reading, it's a poor idea to query or correct commas apart from their serial style; their use is highly individual.

Ellipses. Ellipsis points that indicate omitted material may be set with periods or with a symbol of three dots. (The symbol has the advantage of being unbreakable at the end of a line.) Usage and spacing vary from style to style, and some of the rules, especially those for punctuation, are complex. It may help to know that in a common style, three periods are equally spaced; and, if a sentence ends before an omission, the three periods follow a fourth period—the one that ends the sentence.

Tricks of the trade for proofreaders

(This list of tricks is adapted from an article by Barbara Hart and Peggy Smith published in *The Editorial Eye* in late March 1983.)

1. *Follow proven procedures.*

   - When you can, use either standard proofreading or editing marks; which kind depends on the amount of space between lines and on the stage of production.
   - Be sure to use marks or instructions the corrector understands.
   - As you did in the second grade, read one word at a time—the opposite of speed reading. Read unfamiliar words letter by letter.
   - Maintain a good, steady pace, not too slow but not so fast that you miss errors.
   - When you work solo, read aloud to yourself, especially when the material is difficult.
   - Do different tasks separately; for example, after you've gone over the whole text, look for end-of-line errors; then check for widows and orphans; next check alphabetical or numerical sequences—first, check folios; next, lists; next, footnotes and their callouts; and last, tables and their callouts. Combine tasks only when you're sure of your skill. (Partners in team proofreading can do separate tasks so that both keep busy.)
   - Adjust your effort to the job. A memo to the office down the hall needs only a cursory check; a legal document or a budget may need team proofreading and several readings.
   - Take a five-minute break every hour and spend some of the time looking into the distance. Never read for more than three hours straight without at least a 15-minute break.

2. *Take extra precautions.*

   - Take nothing for granted. Read everything except boilerplate.[1] Even with boilerplate, scan for garbled material. Read addresses, salutations, and signature lines in correspondence; read any recurring material that's become so familiar you're tempted to accept it unread. Don't just mark "wf" on passages set in the wrong font, but read the passages to spot typos that would otherwise remain when the font is changed.
   - Watch for errors in prominent places—where pages, paragraphs, and sections begin; where lines and pages break; and where type size or typeface changes (as in footnotes and heads). Pin up heads and title pages on the wall and stand back to read them.
   - Watch for errors where other errors occur; typos often come in groups.
   - Watch for errors where they would be particularly embarrassing, such as in copy about quality or advice on how to avoid errors.
   - Watch for new errors in corrected copy; correction frequently breeds new errors.
   - Look at live copy upside down and sideways to find spacing errors and misalignments.

---

[1] Boilerplate is text standardized for repeated use.

- When proofreading columnar material—an index, a table, or a table of contents—read first across to find format problems or dropped punctuation and then read down for content.
- When you work alone on tables or revises, slug them (or put revises and their previous galleys on a *light table*[2]) to find respaced lines so you can check for misplaced or dropped copy and new word divisions.
- Double-check each handwritten insertion in the dead copy against the live copy to be sure none was missed.
- When the dead copy is a collection of scraps of paper, count the number of paragraphs in both dead and live copy to be sure none was missed.
- If you become fascinated with the content, read the manuscript once for pleasure, then proofread.
- Never, never put anything that could spill (coffee, tea, food) on the surface with the copy you are proofreading. Replacing damaged copy can be costly.

3. *Use several tools, not just a pencil.*

- Keep your place and focus your attention with a guide such as a straight-edge or one of the tools mentioned in Chapter 5.
- When you're interrupted, use a pencil mark, a self-stick note, or a colored sheet to mark the place where you stopped.
- Use a magnifying glass to decipher bad handwriting (see "Handwriting" in this chapter) or to identify the typeface.
- Check alignment or centering with a *pica grid.*[3]
- Check centering with a *centering rule.*[4] Or fold the paper in half and hold it to the light to see if the type's left and right edges align. Or measure the width of each margin with the tip of a pencil and your thumbnail against the pencil's body.
- Use a light table to check the *register*[5] of folios, running heads, and running feet and to check that boilerplate matches its model.
- Use a calculator to verify the totals in tables and other simple arithmetic.
- Flag places you want to go back to (for example, when you plan to write all queries in one step) with a small checkmark in the margin and a paper clip or self-stick note on the page, or write down the page, paragraph, and line numbers.

4. *Keep notes.*

- If no style is specified, keep notes, especially on capitalization, compounds, and number style.
- If you have no spec sheet for head levels, type size, spacing, and so on, make your own from what you see.
- Keep a list of words often misspelled or found as misprints. Look at them twice when you find them in text. Here's a start: cavalry, calvary; conservation, conversation; from, form; it is, is it; is, in, it, if; or, on, of; simulation, stimulation.

---

[2] A light table is a made of a piece of glass with a light underneath and is used to see a bottom sheet through a top sheet.
[3] A pica grid is a transparent sheet printed with vertical and horizontal lines one pica apart.
[4] A centering rule is marked with measurements from its center to its edges.
[5] Register is exact alignment from page to page.

Among the hardest typos to find are real words that are wrong in context. Unless you are somewhat aware of the sense of what you're reading, you'll miss these errors.

5. *Keep improving.*

- Learn from your mistakes. Keep a record of what you've missed. Analyze the record to learn your weaknesses and correct them.
- Improve your eye for letterforms: collect and classify examples of typefaces (start a file or scrapbook).
- Read. Study. Learn all you can about language and typography. Keep up with the world. Odd facts, unusual spelling, general information—nearly everything you know comes in handy sooner or later.

Word division

Word division in this country is based on pronunciation (e.g., ba-rom-e-ter), not on a word's derivation, although sometimes pronunciation and derivation coincide (e.g., cen-ti-me-ter). In the most helpful word breaks, the part of the word left behind suggests the whole word (dura-ble is preferred to dur-able) and neither of the two parts of the word is easily misread (e.g., service-man, not serviceman).

Marks

You can mark wrong word division in differing ways, ranging from the specific to the general.

1. *Give specific instructions, character by character.* Mark like this if you are an experienced proofreader marking for a corrector (a typist or typesetter) who is familiar with standard proofmarks.

Deletion and insertion: Insertion and deletion:

............the typog-   ....the typ-
raphic eye   graphic eye

2. *Write out the correct syllabication.* Consider using these marks when both you and the corrector are inexperienced with the work or the equipment, or when the corrector is more experienced than the proofreader.

............the typog-
raphic eye   ty-po-graph-ic

3. *Identify the problem, and mark breaks, runovers, or runbacks.* Use these marks only when they are the office style, and when the corrector can be depended upon to place the hyphen correctly.

Style differences

Different organizations, different style guides, and different publications have different rules for word division. Only two rules are invariable:

1. *Divide only between syllables.*
   Breaks in one-syllable words are unacceptable:

Breaks within syllables are unacceptable:

2. *Leave behind or carry over at least two characters:*

Rule 1 seems simple, but authorities don't agree on what makes a syllable. You need a single authority to prevent the same word from appearing with different divisions (e.g., wo-men, wom-en); when this happens on the same page, it's especially distressing to a proofreader.

You also need to know whether certain divisions are unacceptable even though they fall between syllables—contractions (does-n't), acronyms (AL-COA), or proper names (Bos-ton, Linc-oln).

Rule 2 can be extended in different ways—to specify that only words of five or more characters may be divided, or that three characters must be left behind or carried over, or that two can be left behind but three must be carried over, or that two can be carried over except for *-ed,* even when it is a syllable (as in depended).

Many variations depend on line width. In narrow measure, as in a newspaper or a news magazine, for example, it may be acceptable to divide proper names and to carry forward two letters.

You need to be familiar with many other rules. For example, the 33 rules in the U.S. Government Printing Office booklet, *Word Division,* represent commonly accepted standards, including those for breaking figures and equations. (The booklet's list of word divisions, however, is unique to GPO style and agrees with no dictionary.)

Many proofreaders find it convenient to check word division or spelling with a speller-divider like GPO's *Word Division* or one of those put out by dictionary publishers.

Frequent errors

Word division as we practice it in this country is, to a computer, less than 100 percent logical. But some *H&J* (hyphenation and justification) programs depend entirely on logic; others add an "exception dictionary" to their logic; but only very large programs can account for all the exceptions.

Errors often found include these:

— Breaks after the first syllable where there's room for another: in-troduction, per-sonnel
— Wrong breaks in past participles. Watch any word that ends in *-ed;* the division may break a syllable: pul-led, pull-ed, wat-ched, consider-ed, recal-led, embos-sed
— Wrong breaks in present participles: pul-ling, fin-ding, or in other words ending in *-ing:* scaffol-ding, no-thing
— Wrong breaks in one-syllable endings. Watch that the following aren't broken: -ceous, -cial, -cient, -cion, -cious, -geous, -gion, -gious, -scious, -sial, -sion, -tial, -tion, -tious
— Wrong breaks after a letter group that would be a prefix in other words: trans-cribe, anti-cipation, pro-blem, pro-fit, re-commend
— Wrong breaks between consonants: bet-ween, ins-tance
— Wrong breaks after a vowel: opi-nion, so-meone
— Wrong breaks in homographs. These are correct: pro-gress (verb), prog-ress (noun); di-vers (several), div-ers (people who dive); even-ing (making even), eve-ning (end of day)
— Typos (doubles or outs) in words of three or more syllables: consti-tu-tionality, consti-tionality.

A good way to catch many errors is to read every word break aloud, as if it were two words.

Take extra care with the following:

— Proper names (wrong—Kiss-inger; right—Kis-singer)
— Foreign languages. Division is very different from English, for example:
  (French) abs-trac-ti-on, bi-blio-thé-que
  (Spanish) cons-ti-tu-cio-nal, in-te-rro-ga-ción
  (German) eu-ro-pa-i-sche, Ka-me-ra-den
— Medical and pharmacological terms
— Scientific, mathematical, and technical terms.

Appendixes

A Proofmarks: A Cheat Sheet

This cheat sheet is intended for you only if you have good reasons to use it instead of the list of standard marks; for example, if you must begin proofreading before you can study the complete list or if you proofread your own work and make your own corrections. To be fully informed about marks, see Chapters 2, 3, and 4; to begin to be fully professional in the use of marks, read this whole book.

Summary

Rules

1. Mark every error twice—first in the text, then in the margin.
2. Separate outside marks in the margin with slashes.
3. Mark in both margins, using the margin nearer the error.
4. Mark from left to right.
5. Ring instructions and explanations.

In-text marks

/	slash: delete or replace
—	crossbar: delete or replace
∧	caret: insert
⌒	close up mark (tie): close up extra space
⌒/	tied slash: delete and close up
⌒=	tied crossbar: delete and close up
∿	double loop: transpose

Marginal marks

#	space
ℐ	delete
⌒	close-up mark, close up extra space
ℐ⌒	delete and close-up mark
ⓣⓡ	transpose
◯	(ring around instruction): follow instruction; don't type or set ringed characters

Examples of marks

_a_	Repla̸ce character or ring word	(tr) (words) Transpose	
#	Add⋏space	Align	
⌒	Close up sp⌢ace entirely	(align) at the margin.	
ℐ	Delete a̸y character		
ℐ	Delete ch characters	(cap) Change to a capital letter	
ℐ⌒	Close up deleted char̸acter		
⋏a	Insert c⋏racters	(period) Insert a period⋏	
ch⌒C	Insert and close up ⋏aracters	(lessen) Lessen space	
(tr)	Tra⋏nspose characters	(ital) Set in (italic)	

129

Explanation

Five general rules

1. Mark every error twice. First, mark in the text to show *where* the error is. Second, mark in the margin to show *what* correction is needed.

   ɾ   Mak every error twice.

2. Separate marks in the margin with slashes.

   ɛ/ℓ   Ue sashes to separate.

3. Mark in both margins, using the margin nearer the error.

   ɾ   Mak in both margns.   *ι*

4. Mark from left to right.

   ɾ/o   Mak frm left to right.

5. Ring instructions and explanations so they won't be mistaken for letter-for-letter corrections.

   R ing instructio ns and exp la na tio ns.   *(check spacing)*

The ring allows you to start proofreading when you have learned only a few marks—those described below and listed above. You just mark inside the text to show where the problem is; then, outside in the margin, write out the explanation of what you want and put a ring around your explanation.

Basic Marks

Replacement

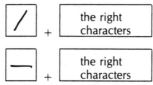

Slash a single wrong character and write the right one in the margin:

a   Repl/ce a wrong character.

Cross through a whole word with more than one wrong character or with more than one error and write the entire correct word outside:

wrong   Replace ~~ring~~ words.

Cross through a longer group of wrong characters and write the correct group outside:

wrong phrase   Replace a ~~etpmh ljtsdr~~ or line.

Use replacement freely. It fits many kinds of errors and problems and is often the clearest way to mark.

Adding space

Mark an upward caret in the text and a space sign in the margin to add space between characters:

> ⌗   Add space‸between characters.

Use replacement where it seems a clearer way to mark:

> space between   ~~spacebetween~~ characters

Mark a sideways caret inside the text and a space sign outside in the margin to add space between lines:

> ⌗   ⟩ Add space
> between lines.

Closing up space entirely

Put close-up marks (also called ties) in the text and in the margin to mean "close up entirely; take out all extra space":

> Tie characters that be⌒long together.   ⌣

Use replacement where it seems a clearer way to mark:

> characters that ~~be long~~ together   *belong*

Simple deletion

In the text, slash or cross through the character(s) to be deleted. In the margin, mark a dele (rhymes with steely):

> Slash to delete⁄ one character.   ꝃ

> Cross through to delete more than ~~than~~ one character.   ꝃ

> Cross through to delete~~lete~~ more than one character.   ꝃ

Use replacement for a short deletion if it seems clearer:

> *delete*   ~~deleter~~ one character.

Deletion with close-up mark

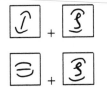

Put a close-up mark on both the in-text and the marginal marks for characters deleted from the middle of words or groups of characters:

ℨ   Close up char/acters deleted from between others.

Use replacement if you can't quickly figure out how to mark for deletion:

characters   ~~charractacters~~ deleted from between others

Simple insertion

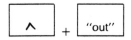

An omission is called an "out." Outs are corrected by insertion. In the text, mark a caret; in the margin, write the characters to be inserted:

k   A caret mars the spot for insertion.

Use replacement for a short insertion where it seems clearer:

marks   ~~mars~~ the spot

Insertion with close-up mark

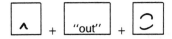

Attach a close-up mark (a tie) to a marginal mark where an insertion belongs at the beginning or end of a word. Put a left-hand close-up mark on an insertion to be attached at the end of a word—that is, to the insertion's left. Put a right-hand close-up mark on an insertion to be attached to the beginning of a word:

left-han tie   ⊃d

    ⌐⊃   ight-hand tie

Use replacement if you can't quickly figure out how to mark for insertion:

left-hand   ~~left han~~ tied insertion

right-hand   ~~ight hand~~ tied insertion

Long insertion

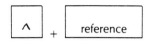

Don't write an insertion longer than seven words in the margin. First, mark a caret where the insertion goes. Then what you do depends on what kind of work you're doing and what will happen next.

If you're reading by comparison and you know that the corrector will see the original copy, refer in the margin to the copy, like this:

(out, see copy, p. X)

But if you're proofreading without an earlier copy to compare with, or if you're not sure the corrector will have the earlier copy to refer to, carefully type the long insertion or make a photocopy of it, attach it to the page or galley, and write this reference in the margin:

(out, see attached)

Transposition

Mark a double loop around adjacent characters or words to be transposed (exchanged), and write "tr"—the abbreviation for "transpose"— in the margin. Put a ring around the "tr" to be sure the letters won't be set by mistake:

(tr)   Transpose characters.

(tr)   (words. Transpose)

Use replacement where transpositions aren't adjacent, where more than one transposition occurs in a word or a group of words, and wherever you think replacement makes the correction clearer:

Use replacement freely.   m/n

Use replacement forely.   freely

Any other correction

In the text, mark a caret, a bracket, a ring—any mark that clearly shows exactly where the problem is. (Reserve the slash and the crossbar for deletion and replacement.) Then, in the margin, write a ringed instruction that says exactly what you want. Here are some examples:

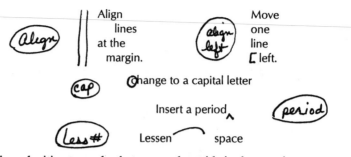

Some legitimate marks that are used outside in the margin are easy to learn because they are nothing but abbreviations. You already know that "tr" stands for *transpose* and "cap" for *capital letter.* Here are some other common abbreviations used in the margin:

bf = boldface type
ital = italic type
lc = lowercase
wf = wrong font of type

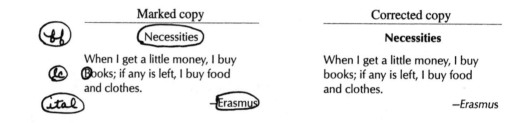

Marked copy	Corrected copy

Necessities

When I get a little money, I buy
books; if any is left, I buy food
and clothes.

—Erasmus

The kitestring system

For most copy, you should prefer the *book system* of marks, which calls for separate in-text and marginal marks, as described so far in this cheat sheet. For most copy, kitestrings (guidelines) connecting inside and outside marks are at best untidy and at worst confusing. But use them where it's sensible to do so; for example, in wide tables, spreadsheets with many columns, or illustrations with many labels. Kitestrings look like this:

Kitestrings

B Proofreader's Job Description

(for solo comparison)

Compares newest version of copy to previous version and, at each stage, marks the newer version for correction or queries the author or editor, as follows:

- In the first proof—
  - —Marks deviations from the original manuscript's contents
  - —Marks deviations from specifications and instructions
  - —Marks deviations from the typographic quality standards applicable to the job and to the first proof
  - —Where authority is given, marks or queries blatant errors overlooked by the author or editor, such as misspelling
- In later proofs—
  - —Marks again corrections not made or improperly made
  - —Marks new errors (for example, in word division in respaced lines)
  - —Marks deviations from specifications and quality standards applicable to the stage of proof (for example, specs and standards for page proofs are more detailed than those for galleys)
- At every step—
  - —Maintains speed, accuracy, and production flow
  - —Meets deadlines
  - —Follows job specifications exactly, marking and querying selectively and ignoring problems irrelevant to the particular job
  - —Uses specified proofreader's marks neatly with specified writing implement
  - —Follows office procedures
  - —Keeps supervisor informed of progress and problems

C Standards for Proofreaders

Accuracy

Errors made by typists and typesetters

More than a hundred years ago, a printer's reader named Watts studied 60 two-column pages of small type, and classified errors by type and frequency. The errors fell into the groups shown in the following table.

Watts' Count of the Frequency of Error

	Instances	Words Affected
Omissions	98	256
Substitutions	101	101
Doubles	14	30
Insertions	8	8
Transpositions	2	4
	223	399

Note that omissions account for more than 60 percent of the words affected by error. Current studies indicate that omissions are still the most frequent problem.

The 223 errors that Watts found affected 397 different words, or about one in 1,750 characters. But of course, the training and the technology were very different. Watts was proofreading the work of craftsmen who had taken six years to become journeyman printers, and who set type manually, reaching into a type case, picking up metal characters and spacing materials one by one, and placing them in a composing stick to form words and lines.

Even so, that rate of error is only a little smaller than the average found among today's keyboard operators—one or two errors per 2,000 characters.

Some publishers' standards are high: the specifications for the input of the new edition of the *Oxford English Dictionary,* which required many tags and codes, allowed a maximum of seven errors per 10,000 keystrokes. That rate equates to one error per 1,429 keystrokes, but the 50 British proofreaders who read the copy input by American workers found a lower error rate.

Errors missed by proofreaders

Studies show that comparison proofreaders miss one or two errors every 7,000 keystrokes, which amounts to missing about one error in 10.

The standards for comparison proofreading differ from shop to shop. Here are four shops' maximum allowable number of proofreading misses:

1 per typeset page
1 for every 10 keyboarding errors
2 in 10,000 ems of type
1 every hour

The first in this list is a low standard; the second agrees with the average; the third and fourth are high standards.

Speed

Proofreading usually takes two-thirds to three-quarters of the time it takes to key the material.

Proofreading speed, however, can't always be determined by keyboarding speed. For example, jobs with many typographic commands usually take proofreaders proportionately less time than keyboarders. But jobs with hard-to-read type (for example, 6-point type, long lines, or unusual typefaces) will take longer to proofread than to set.

And proofreading speed is directly related to keyboarding accuracy: the more keyboarding errors, the slower the proofreading.

Conditions that slow both keyboarding and proofreading include the following:

- Hard-to-read dead copy, such as manuscript that's all caps or italics, that's printed in coarse dot-matrix type, or that's handwritten or heavily edited
- Hard-to-handle dead copy, such as index cards, fanfold paper, or wide paper
- Content including foreign language, technical terminology, or many *pi* characters (characters not found on a standard keyboard or in an ordinary font, such as the symbols used in higher mathematics)
- Any need for an unusual amount of coding, including caps and small caps, ornamental initials, tables, rule forms, or outlines.

For straightforward copy, with no relation to keyboarding speed, one company requires a solo worker to proofread 4,000 words an hour and a team, 5,000 words an hour. This is extremely fast. Many companies would accept half that rate.

Equivalents

Each manuscript page of $8\frac{1}{2} \times 11$ inches typed double spaced with 1-inch margins is roughly equivalent to 2,000 characters, or 250 words, depending on type size and style. (By another method of measurement, each such page is about equivalent to 750 ems.)

Summary

An average keyboarder will make an error once or twice every manuscript page; an average solo proofreader will read 6 to 10 manuscript pages an hour against the accompanying live copy and will miss an error or two in the live-copy equivalent of every $3\frac{1}{2}$ pages of dead copy.

> To determine your proofreading speed relative to keyboarding, turn to Exercise 38.

D Tools for Measuring Type

Graphic arts supply shops sell several kinds of gauges and rulers. Haberule and C-Thru are two of the brand names.

To serve temporarily, use the rulers pictured here.

LEADING AND LINE GAUGES
Use the leading gauges to measure size of type plus leading from baseline to baseline.

PICA AND AGATE RULERS

Note that ½ pica equals 6 points, 1 pica equals 12 points.

PICAS (12-point scale)	AGATES (5½-point scale)
0	0
1	
2	5
3	
4	10
5	
6	15
7	
8	20
9	
10	25
11	
12	30
13	
14	35
15	
16	40
17	
18	45
19	
20	50
21	
22	55
23	
24	60
25	
26	65
27	
28	70
29	
30	75
31	
32	80
33	
34	85
35	
36	90
37	
38	95
39	
40	100
41	
42	105
43	
44	110
45	
46	
47	

E Editing Marks and Proofmarks Compared

Because editing marks go right in the text, they are practical only where there is room for them; for example, between the lines of double-spaced copy.

Because proofmarks take little space between lines, they are practical in single-spaced or typeset copy. In the text they mark only the exact spot *where* a correction or change is needed; it is in the margin that they identify *what* correction or change is needed.

When you mark a manuscript (ms.) that will be rekeyed, keep in mind that some errors will not be reproduced and therefore need not be marked; for example, wrong font, defective characters, and some spacing errors such as unequal wordspace.

The following chart shows both kinds of marks side by side.

See Chapter 4 for examples of standard and modified editing marks and proofmarks.

Instructions	Editing Marks (in text only)	Proofmarks (in text and margin)	
Operations			
Delete	to err is ꬶhuman	to err is ꬶhuman	ℊ
	to err is ~~not~~ human	to err is ~~not~~ human	ℊ
Delete & close up	to err is humṃan	to err is humṃan	ℨ
Insert	to err ˌhuman	to err ˌhuman	*is*
	(for a long out)		(out, see copy, p.x)
Insert & close up	to eˌr is ˌuman	to eˌr is ˌuman	cᴧ/hᵔ
Replace	to err iₓ human	to err iₓ human	s
	to ~~hum~~ is human	to ~~hum~~ is human	err
Transpose	to err ⟨human is⟩	to err ⟨human is⟩	⟨tr⟩
	to err is ⟨uh⟩man	to err is ⟨uh⟩man	⟨tr⟩
	(or)	(or)	
	to err is ⧸u⧸h⧸man	to err is ⧸u⧸h⧸man	h/u

Instructions	Editing Marks (in text only)	Proofmarks (in text and margin)	
Special Marks			
Message ring: Don't set ringed explanation in type	(Same as proofmark)	Ring around message for example: $5	
Let it stand (ignore marked correction)	To err is human	To err is human	
Query to author	(Same as proofmark)	To roar is human	
		(or)	
		To roar is human	
Counting slashes	(Not applicable)	Example: Mke sme correction consecutively as many times as slashes	a//
Spell out	2nd Ave.	2nd Ave	
Abbreviate or use symbol	Second Avenue	Second Avenue	2nd Ave.
End of document	*end* (or) *30* (or) *#*	(Same as editing mark)	
Retain hyphen at end of line	...twenty- six letters	(Same as editing mark)	
Delete line-end hyphen & close up word	...mis/ takes do happen	...mis/ takes do happen	
Space and Position			
Close up space	to err is hu man	to err is hu man	
Insert space	to erris human	to erris human	
	(or)		
	to erris human		
Lessen space	to err is human	to err is human	
Equalize word spaces	(Same as proofmark)	to err is human	
Insert line space	(Same as proofmark)	Xxxxxxxx xx xxxx xx Xxxx xxx xxxx	#
Take out line space	(Same as proofmark)	Xxxxxxxxx xx xxx xxxxx xxxxx xxx	

Instructions	Editing Marks (in text only)	Proofmarks (in text and margin)	
Move right	Ab‌cd efgh ijkl	Ab‌cd efgh ijkl	⏋
Move down	Abcd⌊efgh⌋ijkl	Abcd⌊efgh⌋ijkl	⊔
Move left	⌐Abcd efgh ijkl	⌐Abcd efgh ijkl	⊏
Move up	Abcd⌐efgh⌐ijkl	Abcd⌐efgh⌐ijkl	⊓
Center	⏋Xxxx Xxxx⊏	⏋Xxxx Xxxx⊏	*ctr*
Straighten	Ab‾cde‾f‾gh	Ab‾cde‾f‾gh	*straighten*
Align	‖ Xxxx xxx xx ‖xxxxx xxx xxx ‖ xxx xxxx xxx	‖ Xxxx xxx xx ‖xxxxx xxx xxx ‖ xxx xxxx xxx	*align*

Line Breaks

Instructions	Editing Marks	Proofmarks	
Run on	(Same as proofmark)	Xxxxx xxxx ⌐ xxx xx xxxxx xxx xxx	*run on*
Break	Xxxx⌐xxxxxxxxx	Xxxx⌐xxxxxxxxx	*break*
Run over	(Same as proofmark)	Xxxxx xxxx x xx⌐xxx xxxxx xxx xxx	*run over*
Run back	(Same as proofmark)	Xxxxx xxxx *run back* xxxxx⌐xxxxx xxx xxx	
New paragraph	xxxx xxxxxx. ¶Xxxx (or) xxxx xxxxxx. ⌐Xxxx	xxxx xxxxxx. Xxxx	¶
No new paragraph	xxxx xxxxxx xxx.⌐ *run on* ⌐Xxx xxx xxxxxxxx	xxxx xxxxxx xxx. ˄Xxx xxx xxxxxx	no ¶
Insert 1-em space	(Same as proofmark)	▯ Xxxx xxx xxx xxx	
Insert 2-em space	(Same as proofmark)	▢ Xxxx xxx xxx xxx	
Insert 3-em space	(Same as proofmark)	③ Xxxx xxx xxx xxx	
Correct word division	Perfection is inh-˄uman Perfection is inhum-˄an	Perfection is inh-uman Perfection is inhum-an (or) Perfection is ~~inh-uman~~	*in-hu-man*

Instructions	Editing Marks (in text only)	Proofmarks (in text and margin)
Type Style		
Italic	Abcdef	Abcdef *ital*
Small caps	abcdef	abcdef *sc*
Full caps	abcdef	abcdef *caps*
Boldface	Abcdef	Abcdef *bf*
Caps & small caps	Abcdef	Abcdef *c+sc*
Lowercase letter	Abcdef	Abcdef *lc*
Lowercase word	ABCDEF	ABCDEF *lc*
Capital letter	ABCdEF	ABCdEF *D*
Caps and lowercase	abcdef	abcdef *clc*
Caps and lowercase	ABCDEF	ABCDEF *clc*
Wrong font	(Same as proofmark)	abcdefghijkl *wf*
Subscript	H₂0	H₂0
Superscript	3²=27	3²=27
Ligature	(Same as proofmark)	fly off *lig*
Kern	(Same as proofmark)	Valued work *kern*
Punctuation		
Apostrophe	abcs	abcs
Colon	Hamlet To be or not to be...	Hamlet To be or not to be... :
Comma	To err, I say is human.	To err, I say is human.
Dashes, typeset		
en (short) dash	pages 10 20	pages 10 20 $\frac{1}{N}$
em (long) dash	To err well, it's only human.	To err well, it's only human. $\frac{1}{M}$
3-em (extra-long) dash	Shakespeare, *Comedies* $\frac{3}{M}$ *Tragedies*	Shakespeare, *Comedies* *Tragedies* $\frac{3}{M}$
Dashes, typewritten		
short dash (same as hyphen)	pages 10 20	pages 10 20 =/
long dash (2 hyphens)	To err well, it's only human.	To err well, it's only human. --/

Instructions	Editing Marks (in text only)	Proofmarks (in text and margin)	
Dashes, typewritten *(continued)*			
extra-long dash	Shakespeare, *Comedies* Tragedies	Shakespeare, *Comedies* Tragedies	= 6x
Exclamation point	Wow. !	Wow	set !
Hyphen	Nobody is error free.	Nobody is error free.	= /
Parenthesis, opening	To err is lamentably) human.	To err is lamentably) human.	⊀
Parenthesis, closing	To err is (lamentably human.	To err is (lamentably human.	⅂
Period	Proofreaders live by error⊙	Proofreaders live by error	⊙
Question mark	Why ?	Why	set ?
Quote marks, single*			
opening	'BATMAN' SIGHTED	'BATMAN' SIGHTED	⸜
closing	'BATMAN SIGHTED	'BATMAN SIGHTED	⸝
Quote marks, double			
opening	"To err is human" ?	Who said, To err is human" ?	"
closing	Who said, "To err is human ?	Who said, "To err is human ?	"
Semicolon	Chicago, Ill. St. Louis, Mo.	Chicago, Ill. St. Louis, Mo.	;
Virgule (slash, shill)	$20/bushel (slash)	$20bushel	/ (slash)

---

* As in a headline.

Proofreading Exercises

Proofreading aptitude test

SPELLING

Write <u>G</u> next to any spelling you guess at and would look up in a dictionary if you were proofreading.

A. <u>Recognition</u>: Cross through every misspelled word and write out the entire word with correct spelling in the righthand column.

The occurrence of a misspelled word in print is totaly _____

impermissible. The affect is disastrous, an embarrass- _____

ment to the printer, a distraction to the reader, and a _____

slurr on the writer's competence. Misspelling is a sign _____

that the role of the proofreader has been slighted or _____

misunderstood. Although the proofreader is principly _____

committed to see that the proof follows the copy _____

accurately, there is a further committment to prevent _____

the author, editor, or printer from looking rediculous. _____

A proofreader is never presumtuous in correcting (or-- _____

better--querying) an incorrect spelling. Let no _____

conscientious proofreader wholey acquiesce to the rule _____

of "follow copy" in regard to spelling.

B. <u>Choosing between letters</u>: Fill in the missing letter, choosing one of the two in parentheses.

1.	comput__r	(e;o)	6.	inadvert__nt	(a;e)
2.	deduct__ble	(a;i)	7.	indispens__ble	(a;i)
3.	defend__nt	(a;e)	8.	resist__nt	(a;e)
4.	depend__nt	(a;e)	9.	sep__rate	(a;e)
5.	super__ede	(c;s)	10.	tox__n	(e;i)

C. <u>Choosing among words</u>: Underline the correct spelling.

    1,2. I look foreword/foreward/forword/forward to writing
           the foreword/foreward/forword/forward to your book.

- (continued)

3,4,5,6. As principal/principle of this school, my first
principal/principle is to balance the budget.
My principal/principle concern is to avoid reducing
our endowment's principal/principle.
7. accommodate; acommodate; accomodate
8. changeable; changable
9. chrystal; crystal
10. conscensus; concensus; consensus
11. conscience; consience; concience
12. cooly; coolly
13. drunkeness; drunkenness
14. engineering; enginneering
15. harass; harras; harrass
16. hypocracy; hypocrisy
17. irresistable; irresistible
18. liason; liaison; laiason; laison
19. limousine; limosine
20. managable; manageable
21. necesary; necessary; neccessary; neccesary
22. parallel; parralel; paralell
23. preceed; precede
24. prefering; preferring
25. privilege; priviledge
26. proceed; procede
27. publicly; publically
28. questionaire; questionnaire
29. receive; recieve
30. recomendation; recommendation; reccomendation; reccommendation
31. seize; sieze
32. siege; seige
33. vaccum; vacuum; vacumn
34. weird; wierd

D. Assessment of results

Although as a proofreader you are allowed to refer to a dictionary
occasionally, you should not need to look up many of the words in this
test. Compare your answers with the correct answers given in the
key. (In some cases, the "correct" answers are the preferred
spelling; another alternative is possible but will be unacceptable to
traditionalists.)

Proofreading Exercises

Exercise 1. Simple deletion

In-text marks: slash for one or two characters, crossbar for two or more characters

Marginal mark: dele

Examples:

Some think too little and write̸ too much.　　ℐ

Some ⫽think too little and write too much.　　ℐ//

Some ~~who~~ think too little and write too much.　　ℐ

Some think too ~~lit~~little and write too much.　　ℐ

Instructions: Mark the following live copy to match the dead copy. Keep marginal marks in the right-hand margin.

Dead copy

```
Some think too little and
write too much.
Some think too little and
write too much.
Some think too little and
write too much.
Some think too little and
write too much.

The proof-reader's position is
not an enviable one.  When he
does his best and makes his
book correct he does no more
than his duty.  He may correct
ninety-nine errors out of a
hundred, but if he misses the
hundredth he may be sharply
reproved for that negligence.
                --Theodore De Vinne
```

Live copy (to be marked)

```
Some think too little and
writer too much.
Some ththink too little and
write too much.
Some who think too little and
write too much.
Some think too litlittle and
write too much.

The proof-reader's position is
not at all an enviable one.
When he does his very best and
makes his book correct he does
no more than his duty.  He may
correct ninety-nine errors out
off a hundred, but if he misses
the hundred, but if he misses
the hundredth he may be sharply
reproved for that negligence..
                --Theodore De Vinne
```

Exercise 2. Deletion with the close-up mark (in the middle of words or groups of characters)

In-text mark: closed-up slash or closed-up crossbar

Marginal mark: closed-up dele

Example:

Proofƒreading is essentential for perfection.   ℨ //

Instructions: Mark the following live copy to match the dead copy. Keep marginal marks in the right-hand margin.

Dead copy

Proofreading is essential for
perfection.

The proof-reader's position is
not an enviable one. When he
does his best and makes his
book correct he does no more
than his duty. He may correct
ninety-nine errors out of a
hundred, but if he misses the
hundredth he may be sharply
reproved for that negligence.
            --Theodore De Vinne

Live copy (to be marked)

Proofereading is essentential
for perfection.

The proof-reader's possition
is not an enviable one. When
he does his beast and makes
his book correct he does no
more than his duty. He may
correct ninety-nine errors out
of a hundered, but if he
misses the hundredth he may be
sharply reproved for that
negegligence.
            --Theodore De Vinne

Exercise 3. Simple deletion and deletion with the close-up mark

Instructions: Mark the following live copy to match the dead copy. Keep marginal marks in the right-hand margin.

Dead copy

```
The proof-reader's position is
not an enviable one.  When he
does his best and makes his
book correct he does no more
than his duty.  He may correct
ninety-nine errors out of a
hundred, but if he misses the
hundredth he may be sharply
reproved for that negligence.
              --Theodore De Vinne
```

Live copy (to be marked)

```
The proof-reader's position is
not an unenviable one.  When he
he does his best and makes his
books corrrect, he does no more
than his duty.  He may correct
no more than his duty.  He may
correct ninety-nine errors out
of a hundred, but if he misses
the hundredth he may be sharply
reaproved for that negligence.
              --Theodore De Vinne
```

Exercise 4. Simple insertion

```
 ^
```

In-text mark: caret

Marginal mark: the insertion

Example:

p̭oofreading   *r̫*

Instructions: Mark the following live copy to match the dead copy. Keep marginal marks in the right-hand margin.

Dead copy

Patty Piper proofread a perfect
page. If Patty Piper proofread
a perfect page, where is the
perfect page that Patty Piper
proofread?

Live copy (to be marked)

Patty Piper poofread a perfect
page. If Patty Piper proofread
a perfect page, where is the
page that Patty Piper proofread?

Exercise 5. Insertion with the close-up mark (at the beginning or end of a word or group of characters)

In-text mark: caret

Marginal mark: the insertion, with left-hand or right-hand close-up mark

Examples:

proofreadin︿   ⌐ℊ
︿roofreading   𝒫⌐

Instructions: Mark the following live copy to match the dead copy. Keep marginal marks in the right-hand margin.

Dead copy

Patty Piper proofread a perfect
page. If Patty Piper proofread
a perfect page, where is the
perfect page that Patty Piper
proofread?

Live copy (to be marked)

Patty Piper roofrea a perfect
page. If Patty Piper proofread
a perfect page, here is the
perfect page that Patty Pipe
proofread?

Exercise 6. Long and short outs

Here's how to treat insertions longer than about seven words:

In-text mark: caret

Marginal mark:

If you're sure the corrector will have the dead copy, write this, with a ring around it, in the margin: "Out, see copy p. x." Then mark brackets around the insertion in the dead copy and write "set" (in a ring) near the opening bracket.

If the corrector won't be able to get the copy, or if you're not sure, write "Out, see attached" inside a ring in the margin. Then provide the attachment: either type the insertion carefully and label it "Insert for p. x" or get a photocopy of the dead copy and mark the insertion with brackets and the ringed word "set."

Instructions, Exercise 6A: Proofread the following, assuming that the person who will be making the corrections will have access to the dead copy. Keep marginal marks in the right-hand margin.

Dead copy

```
Elegance in prose composition
is mainly this:  a just admis-
sion of topics and of words;
neither too many nor too few of
either; enough of sweetness in
the sound to induce us to enter
and sit still; enough of illus-
tration and reflection to change
the posture of our minds when
they would tire; and enough of
sound matter in the complex to
repay us for our attendance.
          --Walter Savage Landor
```

Live copy (to be marked)

```
Elegance in prose composition
is mainly this:  a just admis-
sion of. topics and words; nei-
ther too many nor too few of
either; enough of sweetness in
the sound to induce us to sit
still; and enough of sound
matter in the complex to repay
us for our attendance.
          --Walter Savage Landor
```

Instructions, Exercise 6B: Proofread the following, assuming that the person who will be making the corrections will *not* have access to the dead copy. Keep marginal marks in the right-hand margin.

Dead copy

Elegance in prose composition
is mainly this: a just admis-
sion of topics and of words;
neither too many nor too few of
either; enough of sweetness in
the sound to induce us to enter
and sit still; enough of illustration and reflection to change
the posture of our minds when
they would tire; and enough of
sound matter in the complex to
repay us for our attendance.
          --Walter Savage Landor

Live copy (to be marked)

Elegance in prose composition
is mainly this: a just amis-
sion of topics and words; neither too many nor too few of
either; enough of sweetness in
the sound matter in the complex to repay us for our
attendance.
          --Walter Savage Landor

Exercise 7. Inserting and deleting space

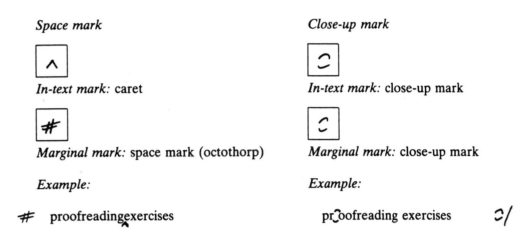

Space mark

$\wedge$

In-text mark: caret

#

Marginal mark: space mark (octothorp)

Example:

proofreadingexercises

Close-up mark

⌒

In-text mark: close-up mark

c

Marginal mark: close-up mark

Example:

pr⌒oofreading exercises   ⌒/

Instructions: Mark the following live copy to match the dead copy. Use the space mark (#) and the close-up mark (⌒) to solve the spacing problems. Keep marginal marks in the right-hand margin.

Dead copy

```
Our transition from barbarism
to civilization can be attrib-
uted to the alphabet.--Otto Ege
```

Live copy (to be marked)

```
O urtransition from barbarism
to civilization can beat trib-
uted tothe alphabet.--Otto Ege
```

Exercise 8. Deletion and insertion

Instructions: Mark the following live copy to match the dead copy. Keep marginal marks in the right-hand margin.

Dead copy

Bacon cautions writers not "to hunt more after words than matter, and more after the choiceness of the phrase, and the round and clean composition of the sentence, and the sweet falling of the clauses, and the varying and illustration of their works with tropes and figures, than after the weight of matter, soundness of argument, life of invention or depth of judgment."

Live copy (to be marked)

Bacon cautions writers "to hunt more after words than matter, and more after words than matter, and more after the choice-choiceness of the phase, and the round and clean composition of the sentence, and the sweet falling of the clauses, and the varying and illusteration of their work with tropesand figures, than after the weight of matter, sound ness of argument, life of invention, or depth of judgment."

Exercise 9. Replacement

In-text mark: slash or crossbar

Marginal mark: the replacement

Examples:

proof~~l~~eaf~~t~~ing
~~preafdooring~~   r/d
                    proofreading

Instructions: Mark the following live copy to match the dead copy. Keep marginal marks in the right-hand margin.

Dead copy

My Lord, I do here, in the
name of all the learned and
polite persons of the nation,
complain to Your Lordship as
First Minister, that our language is extremely imperfect;
that its daily improvements
are by no means in proportion
to its daily corruptions; that
the pretenders to polish and
refine it have chiefly multi-
plied abuses and absurdities;
and that in many instances it
offends against every part of
grammar.   --Swift

Live copy (to be marked)

My Lord, I do hear, in the
name of all the learned and
polite people of the nation,
complain to Your Lordship as
First Minister, that our language is extremely inperfect;
that its daily improvements
are by no means in preportion
to its daily corruptions; that
the pretenders to polish and
refine it have chiefly multi-
plied abuses and absurdities;
and that in many cases it
offends against every part on
grammer.   --Swift

Exercise 10. Transposition

In-text mark: double loop

Marginal mark: "tr"—in a ring

Example:

 Pofreading essential is for perfection. (tr)

Instructions: Mark the following live copy to match the dead copy. Keep marginal marks in the right-hand margin. Use transposition for adjacent characters or words, use replacement for those that are not adjacent.

Dead copy	**Live copy** (to be marked)

ITALIC

Dead copy:

The italic letter claims an origin quite independent of the roman to which it is an accessory. It is said to be an imitation of the handwriting of Petrarch. Aldus Manutius, seeking a letter that took less space than roman, introduced italic for the printing of the entire text of a series of classics which otherwise would have required bulky volumes.

The original font is lowercase only; it was used with roman capitals in the six sizes that Aldus produced.

Italic was later used to distinguish front and back matter-- such as introductions, prefaces, indexes, and notes--from the roman text itself.

Still later it was used in the text for quotations; and finally it served the double purpose of emphasizing words and, in some works, chiefly translations of the Bible, of marking words not properly belonging to the text.

Live copy:

ITALIC

The italic letter claims an origin quite indepednent of the roman which it is an accessory to. It is said to be an imitation of the handwriting of Petrarch. Aldus Manutius, seeking a letter that took less space than roman, intorduced italic for the printing of the entire text of a series of classics which otherwise would have required bukly volumes.

The orinigal font is lowercase only; it was used with roman capitals in the six sizes that Aldus produced.

Italic was used later to distinguish front and back matter-- such as prefaces, introductions, indexes, and notes--from the roman text itself.

Still later it was used in the text for quotations; and finally it served the dobule purpose of emphasizing words and, in some works, chiefly tralanstions of the Bible, of marking words not belonging properly to the text.

Exercise 11. Replacement, including special replacement marks

Defective characters

In-text mark: ring

Marginal mark: "X"—in a ring

Spelled-out short forms

In-text mark: ring

Marginal mark: "sp"—in a ring

Instructions: Mark the following live copy to match the dead copy. Keep marginal marks in the right-hand margin.

Dead copy

```
    At the mill, a ream--500
sheets--of 17 x 22-inch paper
of the heaviest general office
bond weighs 24 pounds.  When
this paper is cut into 8-1/2
x 11-inch sheets, it's called
24-pound bond--but, of course,
it takes four reams to weigh
24 pounds.  The following chart
shows the common weights and
uses of business papers:
```

Weight	Use
9 lb	carbon copies
13 lb	legal documents, court briefs
16 lb	general office reports, second sheets, file copies
20 lb	letterhead
24 lb	heavy letterhead

Live copy (to be marked)

```
    At the mill, a ream--500
sheets--of 17 x 22-inch paper
of the heaviest general office
bond weighs 24 lbs.  When this
paper is cut into 8-1/2 x 11-
inch sheets, it's called 24-
pound bond--but, of course, it
takes 4 reams to weigh 24
pounds.  The following chart
shows the common weights and
uses of business papers:
```

Wt.	Use
9 lb	carbon copies
13 lb	legal documents, court briefs
16 lb	genl office reports, 2nd sheets, file copies
20 lb	letterhead
24 lb	heavy letterhead

Exercise 12. Review

Instructions: Use proofreader's marks for the indicated changes. If transposition is required, use loops in this exercise. Keep all marks in the right-hand margin.

A. Words

This exercise is designed to help you see word patterns, including words within words. As you work the sections on deletion and replacement, save as many characters as you can.

Change "an" to "manual."   ∧^an^∧   *mc/cual*

Deletion

1. Change "now" to "no."   now

2. Change "there" to "here."   there

3. Change "pencil" to "pen."   pencil

4. Change "grandchild" to "child."   grandchild

5. Change "friend" to "fiend."   friend

6. Change "exist" to "exit."   exist

7. Change "adulterate" to "adulate."   adulterate

8. Change "proofreading" to "read."   proofreading

9. Change "English" to "is."   English

10. Change "language" to "an."   language

11. Change "complete" to "let."   complete

12. Change "renewal" to "new."   renewal

Insertion

13. Change "no" to "now."   no

14. Change "here" to "there."   here

15. Change "pen" to "pencil."   pen

16. Change "child" to "grandchild."   child

17. Change "fiend" to "friend."   fiend

18. Change "exit" to "exist."   exit

19. Change "adulate" to "adulterate."   adulate

20. Change "read" to "proofreading."   read

21. Change "is" to "English."   is

22. Change "an" to "language."   an

23. Change "let" to "complete."   let

24. Change "new" to "renewal."   new

Replacement

25. Change "sensible" to "sensibly."   sensible

26. Change "unto" to "into."   unto

27. Change "type" to "typical."   type

28. Change "borrow" to "tomorrow."   borrow

29. Change "use" to "usage."   use

30. Change "survey" to "surveillance."   survey

31. Change "father" to "mother."   father

32. Change "near" to "far."   near

33. Change "exercise" to "exorcise."   exercise

34. Change "flour" to "flower."   flour

35. Change "example" to "exemplary."   example

Transposition

36. Change "casual" to "causal."   casual

37. Change "marital" to "martial."   marital

38. Change "trial" to "trail."   trial

39. Change "united" to "untied."   united

Correct the spelling of items 40-45 by transposition:

40.   preceed

41.   procede

42.   beleive

43.   sieze

44.   Feburary

45.   perscription

46.   Change "sky blue" to "blue sky."   sky blue

47.   Change "human being" to "being human."   human being

B.   Sentences

Mark the following sentences so each will be corrected to read as follows:

Proofreading is quality control.

48.   Proofreading and editing are forms of
      quality control in publishing.

49.   Proofing is qualified control.

50.   Proofreaders form the core of our business,
      a business that is known for its quality.

C. Paragraph

51. Mark the following live copy to match the dead copy. Keep marginal marks in the right-hand margin.

Dead copy

Over the office door of Aldus
Manutius (1450-1515), founder
of the Aldine Press in Venice,
appeared this legend: Whoever
you are, you are earnestly requested by Aldus to state your
business briefly and to take
your departure promptly. In
this way you may be of service
even as was Hercules to the
weary Atlas, for this is a
place of work for everyone who
enters.

Live copy

Over the office door or Aldus
Manutius (1450-1515), founder
of the Aldine Press in Vienna,
appeared this motto: Whosoever
you are, you are eanestly requested by Aldus to state your
business briefly and take your
departure promptily. In this
this way you may be of service
even as Hercules was, for this
is a place of Atlas for this
is a place of worship for you
and everyone who enters here.

Exercise 13. Punctuation: Humpty Dumpty

In-text marks: same as for deletion (Exercises 1-3), insertion (Exercises 4 and 5), replacement (Exercise 9), and transposition (Exercise 10).

Marginal marks:

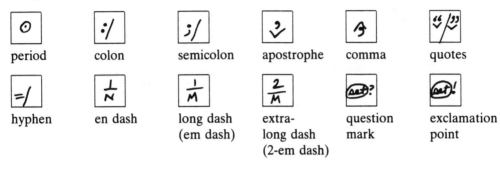

period	colon	semicolon	apostrophe	comma	quotes

hyphen	en dash	long dash (em dash)	extra-long dash (2-em dash)	question mark	exclamation point

Instructions: Proofread by comparing the dead copy on this page with the live copy on the next page. Mark only on the live copy with proofreading marks for insertion, replacement, deletion, and transposition, as needed. Use both left and right margins.

Dead copy

"When *I* use a word," Humpty Dumpty said, in rather a scornful tone, "it means just what I choose it to mean—neither more nor less."

"The question is," said Alice, "whether you *can* make words mean so many different things."

"The question is," said Humpty Dumpty, "which is to be master—that's all."

Alice was too much puzzled to say anything; so after a minute Humpty Dumpty began again. "They've a temper, some of them—particularly verbs: they're the proudest—adjectives you can do anything with, but not verbs—however, *I* can manage the whole lot of them! Impenetrability! That's what *I* say!"

"Would you tell me please," said Alice, "what that means?"

"Now you talk like a reasonable child," said Humpty Dumpty, looking very much pleased. "I meant by 'impenetrability' that we've had enough of that subject, and it would be just as well if you'd mention what you mean to do next, as I suppose you don't mean to stop here all the rest of your life."

"That's a great deal to make one word mean," Alice said in a thoughtful tone.

"When I make a word do a lot of work like that," said Humpty Dumpty, "I always pay it extra."

Live copy (to be marked)

"When *I* use a word," Humpty Dumpty said in rather a scornful tone, "it means just what I choose it to mean-neither more nor less."

"The question is, said Alice, "whether you *can* make words mean so many different things!"

"The question is," said Humpty Dumpty, "which is to be master-that's all.".

Alice was too much puzzled to say anything, so after a minute Humpty Dumpty began again. "They've a temper, some of them—particularly verbs; they're the proudest—adjectives you can do anything with but not verbs—however, *I* can manage the whole lot of them! Impenetrability! That's what *I* say."

"Would you tell me please," said Alice, "what that means."

"Now you talk like a reasonable child," said Humpty Dumpty, looking very much pleased. I meant by impenetrability that we've had enough of that subject, and it would be just as well if youd mention what you mean to do next, as I suppose you don't mean to stop here all the rest of your life".

"That's a great deal to make one word mean," Alice said, in a thoughtful tone.

"When I make a word do a lot of work like that," said Humpty Dumpty, "I always pay it extra.."

Exercise 14. Punctuation, capitals, and lowercase: Inaugural Address

Capitals

In-text mark

Marginal mark

Lowercase

In-text mark

Marginal mark

Instructions: Proofread the following by comparison. Mark the live copy in both left and right margins.

Dead copy

John Stuart Mill's inaugural address (as rector of the University of St. Andrew) on February 1, 1867, included the following words:

"To question all things;--never to turn away from any difficulty; to accept no doctrine either from ourselves or from other people without a rigid scrutiny by negative criticism; letting no fallacy, or incoherence, or confusion of thought, step by unperceived; above all, to insist upon having the meaning of a word clearly understood before using it, and the meaning of a proposition before assenting to it;--these are the lessons we learn from ancient dialecticians."

Live copy (to be marked)

John stuart Mills inaugural address (as Rector of the University of SAINT Andrew) on february 1, 1867, included the following words:

To question all things;—never to turn away from any difficulty; to accept no doctrine either from ourselves or from other people without a rigid scrutiny by negative criticism; letting no Fallacy, or incoherence, or confusion of thought, step by unperceived. Above all, to insist upon having the meaning of a word clearly understood before using it, and the meaning of a proposition before assenting to it—these are the lessons we learn from Ancient Dialecticians.

Exercise 15. Proofreading practice:
Eugene Field on Printers' Blunders

Instructions: Proofread the following by comparison. Mark the live copy in both left and right margins.

Dead copy

EUGENE FIELD ON PRINTERS' BLUNDERS*

The most distressing blunder I ever read in print was made at the time of the burial of the famous antiquary and littérateur, John Payne Collier. In the London newspapers of Sept. 21, 1883, it was reported that "the remains of the late Mr. John Payne Collier were interred yesterday in Bray church-yard, near Maidenhead, in the presence of a large number of spectators." Thereupon the Eastern daily press published the following remarkable perversion: "The Bray Colliery Disaster. The remains of the late John Payne, collier, were interred yesterday afternoon in the Bray churchyard in the presence of a large number of friends and spectators."

Far be it from the book-lover and the book-collector to rail at blunders, for not unfrequently these very blunders make books valuable....The genuine first edition of Hawthorne's "Scarlet Letter" is to be determined by the presence of a certain typographical slip in the introduction. The first edition of the English Scriptures printed in Ireland (1716) is much desired by collectors, and simply because of an error. Isaiah bids us "sin no more," but the Belfast printer, by some means or another, transposed the letters in such wise as to make the injunction read "sin on more."

The so-called Wicked Bible is a book that is seldom met with, and, therefore, in great demand. It was printed in the time of Charles I, and it is notorious because it omits the adverb "not" in its version of the seventh commandment; the printers were fined a large sum for this gross error....

Once upon a time the Foulis printing establishment at Glasgow determined to print a perfect Horace; accordingly the proof sheets were hung up at the gates of the university, and a sum of money was paid for every error detected.

Notwithstanding these precautions the edition had six uncorrected errors in it when it was finally published. Disraeli says that the so-called Pearl Bible had six thousand errata! The works of Picus of Mirandula, Strasburg, 1507, gave a list

---

*From Eugene Field, <u>The Love Affairs of a Bibliomaniac</u>, Charles Scribner's Sons, New York, 1896.

of errata covering fifteen folio pages, and a worse case is
that of "Missae ac Missalis Anatomia" (1561), a volume of one
hundred and seventy-two pages, fifteen of which are devoted to
the errata. The author of the Missae felt so deeply aggrieved
by this array of blunders that he made a public explanation to
the effect that the devil himself stole the manuscript, tampered with it, and then actually compelled the printer to misread it....

We can fancy Richard Porson's rage (for Porson was of
violent temper) when, having written the statement that "the
crowd rent the air with their shouts," his printer made the
line read "the crowd rent the air with their snouts." However,
this error was a natural one, since it occurs in the "Catechism
of the Swinish Multitude."

Live copy (to be marked)

EUGENE FIELD ON PRINTER'S BLUNDERS

The most distressing blunder I ever read in print was made at the time of the burial of the famous antiguary and litteateur, John Payne Collier. In the London newspapers of Sept. 21, 1883, it was reported that "the remains of the late Mr. John Payne Collier were yesterday interred in Bray church-yard, near Maidenhead, in the presence of a large number of spectators." There upon the Eastern daily press published the following remarkable perversion: "The Bray Colliery Disasters. The remains of the late John Payne, collier, were interred yesterday afternoon in the Bray churchyard in the presence of a large number of friends and spectators."

Far be it from the book-lover and the book-collector to rail at blunders, for not unfrequently these very blunders make books valuable. . . . The genuine first edition of Hawthorne's "Scarlet Letter" is to be determined by the presence of a certain typograhical slip in the introduction. The first edition of the English Scriptures printed in Ireland (1716) is much desired by collectors, and simply because of an error. Isaiah bids us "sin no more," but the Belfast printer, by some means or another, transposed the letters in such a way as to make the injunction read "sin on more."

The so-called Wicked Bible is a book that is seldom met with, and, therefore, in great demand. It was printed in the the time of Charles I., and it is notorious because it omits the adverb "not" in its version of the seventh commandment; the printers were fined a large sum for this gross error. . . .

Once upon a time the Foulis printing establishment at Glasgow determined to print a perfect Horace; accordingly the proof sheets were hung up at the gates of the university, and a sum of money was paid for every error detected.

Notwithstanding these precautions the edition had six uncorrected errors in it when it was finally published. Disraeli says that the so-called Pearl Bible had six thousand errata The works of Picus of Mirandula, Strasburg, 1507, gave a list

---

*From Eugene Field, *The Love Affairs of a Bibliomaniac*, Charles Scribner's Sons, New York, 1896

of errata covering fifteen folio pages, and a worse case is that of "Missae ac Missalic Anatomia" (1561), a volume of one hundred and seventy-two pages, fifteen of which are devoted to the errata. The author of the Missea felt so deeply aggrieved by this array of blunders that he made a public explanation to the effect that the devil himself stole the manuscript, tampered with it, and then actually compelled the printer to misread it. . . .

We can fancy Richard Porson's rage (for Porson was of a violent temper) when, having written the statement that "the crowd rent the air with their shouts," his printer made the line read "the crowd rent the air with their snouts." However, this error was a natural one, since it occurrs in the "Catechism of the Swinish Multitude."

Exercise 16A. Changes in space: Letter spacing

Instructions: Test your eye: Mark a ring around the letter spaced lines.

These apparently conflicting words from a famous archi- tect and an American president can apply to the nitpicking quality of proof- reading. Interpret them as you like:

All the difficulties of this world are in t h e details.—Pres- ident Clinton

God is in the de- tails.—Ludwig Mies van der Rohe

Exercise 16B. Changes in space: Unequal word space

Instructions: Mark for unequal word spacing in this justified copy.

Not just large errors need to be watched for; small ones, too, cause trouble. Fowler's thoughts on the results of the use of wrong words (*insuccess* for *failure, deplacement* for *misplacement, unquiet* for *unrest*) can apply to any of the small mistakes to which writing is subject.

These are "mere slips, very likely," he wrote, and "indeed quite unimportant in a writer who   allows himself only one such slip in fifty or a hundred pages; but one who is unfortunate enough to make a second before the first has faded from memory becomes at once a suspect. We are uneasily on the watch for his next lapse, wonder whether he is a foreigner or an Englishman not at home in the literary language, and fall into that critical temper which is the last he would choose to be reading."

—H. W. Fowler, *The King's English*

Exercise 16C. Changes in space: Ligatures

Instructions: The following take-off on ligatures was found on a bulletin board. The author is unknown.

    To train your eye to see character spacings, ring every pair of ligatured letters, and write the number of rings you've marked at the right of every line. The first two lines have been done as examples. Note that "the" comprises two ligatures.

A ligature is a character that contains two or more   9
letters. Ligatures were employed by the medieval   6
scribes since they could be easily constructed with
a pen and enabled them to write at a more rapid
rate. Gutenberg's movable type included an extensive
assortment of ligatures because he wanted to create
a printed page that was undistinguishable from the
hand drawn manuscript. The number of ligatures
decreased as time went on for economic rather than
esthetic reasons.

Computer-aided photocomposition systems have
made possible a different approach to the design of
letterforms. We are no longer restricted to the 26-
character alphabet since an unlimited number of
letters can be stored in the memory of the computer.
The use of ligatures in the design of letterforms is the
next evolutionary step in the development of modern
reading systems.

Exercise 17. Word division

Instructions: Proofread, marking the live copy to conform exactly to the dead. Mark on both left and right sides of the live copy, as shown in the first lines.

Dead copy

                    The proof

              of the print-

        ing is in the read-

                      ing.

                    "To ques-

        tion all things;--nev-

        er to turn away

        from any dif-

        ficulty; to ac-

        cept no doc-

        trine either from our-

        selves or from other peo-

        ple without a rigid scru-

        tiny by negative criti-

        cism; letting no fal-

        lacy or inco-

        herence or con-

        fusion of thought,

        step by unper-

        ceived; above

        all, to in-

Live copy (to be marked)

                    The proof

              of of the prin-

        ting is in the readi-

                      ng.

                    "To que-

        stion all things;—ne-

        ver to turn a-

        way from any diff-

        iculty; to acc-

        ept no doctr-

        ine either from ourselv-

        es or from other pe-

        ople without a rigid scrut-

        iny by negative critic-

        ism; letting no fall-

        acy or incoh-

        erence or co-

        nfusion of thought,

        step by unperc-

        eived; ab-

        ove all, to ins-

211

sist upon hav-

ing the mean-

ing of a word clear-

ly understood before

using it, and the

meaning of a prop-

osition before as-

senting to it;--these

are the les-

sons we learn from

an-

cient dia-

lecticians."

ist upon ha-

ving the mea-

ning of a word clea-

rly understood bef-

ore using it, and t-

he meaning of a pro-

position before asse-

nting to it;—the-

se are the less-

ons we learn fr-

om anci-

ent dial-

ecticians."

Exercise 18. Spacing and positioning

Practice A

Marginal marks   *In-text marks*

c⁀/   clo⁀se up space; make one word

insert⌄space; make two words

(less #)   less ⌄ space between words

Instructions: Use the marks shown above to correct spacing problems. (There is no dead copy.)

> At oneside is the author's and editor's work; at
> the otheris the typesetter's work. My work goes
> be tween the two. I'm the cheese betweentwo
> slices of bread to make a sand wich.

Practice B

Marginal marks   *In-text marks*

⊐   [move] right

⊔   move ⌊down⌋

⊏   ⌈ move left

⊓   move ⌈up⌉

⊐⊏   ⊐center⊏

Instructions: Use the marks shown above to correct spacing problems. (There is no dead copy.)

> TO THE SCRIBES AT
> SAINT MARTIN'S
> MONASTERY,
> TOURS, FRANCE
> (circa 782 A.D.)
> Here let the scribes beware of making
>   mistakes through haste. Let them dis-
> tinguish the proper sense by colons
> and commas, and let them set down
> the points, each one in its due place,
> and let not him who reads the words
> to them either read falsely or pause
> suddenly.

Practice C

Marginal marks

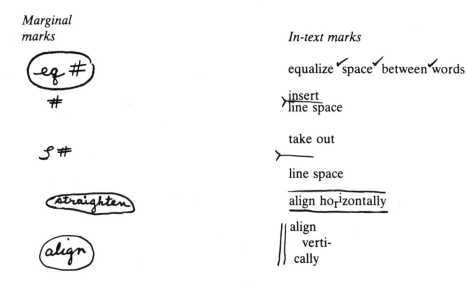

In-text marks

equalize ✓space✓ between✓words

insert
line space

take out

line space

align ho_rizontally

align
verti-
cally

Instructions: Mark to correct spacing problems. (There is no dead copy.)

Proofreading is my vocation and my obsession. I search for
errors on cereal boxes and in travel folders, mail order catalogues, and greeting cards. I write proofreader's corrections
on letters from friends and query the instruction sheets that
come with new appliances. Some dark night I will take a
can of red paint and a brush to the nearby street sign
that reads "Greenfied Rd." and paint a caret between the
e and the *d* and an *l* at the side.   —Proofreader

Practice D

Marginal marks

run on

break

run over

run back

¶

no ¶

In-text marks

No
new line

break. Begin new line

carry over to
next line

carry
back to previous line

start new paragraph. Here

no new paragraph.
Here

Instructions: Mark the following live copy to match the dead copy. Keep marginal marks in the right-hand margin.

Dead copy

MARKING FAULTS
CITED IN
GPO STYLE MANUAL

"The manner in which correction marks are made on a proof is of considerable importance," says the U.S. Government Printing Office Style Manual.
It goes on to list some faults in marking, as follows:
● straggling, unsymmetrical characters
● disconnected marks placed in the margin above or below the lines to which they relate
● irregular lines leading from an incorrect letter or word to a correction
● large marks
● marks made with a blunt pencil
● indistinct marks
● frequent use of the eraser to obliterate marks hastily or incorrectly made.
Some proofreading supervisors would add, "not-thorough-enough use of the eraser." Obliterated marks must be infrequent--and invisible.

Live copy (to be marked)

MARKING
FAULTS CITED IN GPO
STYLE MANUAL

"The manner in which correction marks are made on a proof is of considerable importance," says the U.S. Government Printing Office *Style Manual*. It goes on to list some faults in marking, as follows:
● straggling, unsymmetrical characters
● disconnected marks placed in the margin above
or below the lines to which they relate
● irregular lines leading from an incorrect letter or word to a correction ● large marks
● marks made with a blunt pencil
● indistinct marks
● frequent use of the eraser to obliterate
marks hastily or incorrectly made.
Some proofreading supervisors would add, "not-thorough-enough use of the eraser."
Obliterated marks must be infrequent—and invisible.

Exercise 19. Moving type and space:
Ben Franklin's Complying Temper

Instructions: Mark the following copy for spacing and positioning errors. Be sure to mark word division errors as in Exercise 17. (Note that there is no dead copy.)

**Benjamin Franklin's Complying
Temper**

In "An Apology to Printers," Benjamin Franklin asked all
who were angry with him "on the account of printing things they don't
like" to consider a list of twelve particulars. Number seven of the
particulars was this:

It is unreasonable to imagine printers approve of
everything they print, and to censure them on any
particular thing accordingly; since in the way of
their business they print such a great variety of

things opposite and contradictory. It is likewise
as unreasonable what some assert, "That printers
oughtnot to print anything but what they approve";
since if all of that business should make such a
resolution and a bide by it, an end would thereby
be put to free writing, and the world would afterwards have nothing to read but what happened to
be the opinions of printers.

Franklin went on to tell this story:

A certain well-meaning man and his son were
travelling towards a market town with an ass which
they had to sell. The road was bad, and the old man
therefore rode, but the son went afoot. The first
passer by they met asked the father if he was not
ashamed to ride by himself, and suffer the poor lad
to wade along through the mire; this induced him to
take up his son behind him. He had not travelled
far, whenhe met others, who said, they are two un-
merciful lubbers to get both on the back of that
poor ass in such a deep road. Upon this the old
man got off, and let his son ride alone. The next
they met called the lad   a graceless, rascally
young jackanapes, to ride in that manner through
the dirt, while his aged father trudged along on
foot; and they said the old man was a fool for su-
ffering it. He then bid his son come down, and
walk with him, and they travelled on leading the

ass by the halter, till they met with another company, who called them a couple of senseless block-
heads, forgoing both on foot in such a dirty way,

221

when they had an empty ass with them, which they
might ride upon. The old man could bear it no
that we cannot please all these people. Le tme
longer. 'My son,' said he, 'it grieves me much
throw the ass over the next bridge, and be no further troubled with him.' Franklin concluded:
Though I have a temper almost as complying as [the
old man's] . . . I intend not to imitate him. . . .
I consider the variety of humors among men, and
despair of pleasing everybody; yet I shall not therefore leave off printing. I shall continue my business.
I shall not burn my press and melt my letters.

Exercise 20. Review of marks

A. In-text and marginal marks

Instructions: Fill in the blanks with the correct numbers, matching the marks shown in the right-hand column with the descriptions in the left-hand column. Note: A number may be used more than once, and more than one number may fit a blank.

Marks used only in the text

_____ delete or replace a word of two or more characters per marginal mark

_____ insert character or word per marginal mark

_____ fix spacing problem between lines per marginal mark

_____ move to center

Marks used in both the text and the margin

_____ close up

_____ move right

_____ move down

_____ move left

_____ move up

_____ *in text*: delete or replace one character per marginal mark
in margin: separates marginal marks; indicates how many times to make a correction; concludes an inconspicuous mark

Mark used in the margin for deletion

_____ delete

(1) sideways caret ——◁

(2) crossbar ——

(3) upright caret ∧

(4) slash /

(5) ⌐¬

(6)]

(7) ⌇

(8)]⌐

(9) ⌣

(10) ⌐

(11) ⌢

Marks used in the margin

_____	insert omission longer than one line	(1)	(16)
_____	insert word space	(2)	(17) / (shill)
_____	insert line space		
_____	set superscript 2	(3)	(18)
_____	set subscript 2		
_____	apostrophe	(4)	(19) no
_____	colon		
_____	comma	(5)	(20) (set) ?
_____	opening bracket		
_____	hyphen	(6)	(21) (set) !
_____	short dash on typewriter		
_____	en dash	(7)	(22) -- /
_____	long dash on typewriter		
_____	em dash	(8)	(23) [(bracket)
_____	exclamation point		
_____	opening parenthesis	(9)	(24)
_____	closing parenthesis		
_____	period	(10) - - - -|	(25)
_____	question mark		
_____	opening double quotes	(11)	(26) (out see copy, p. x)
_____	closing double quotes		
_____	opening single quote	(12)	
_____	closing single quote		
_____	semicolon	(13)	
_____	slash, shill, virgule		
_____	paragraph	(14)	
_____	no paragraph		
_____	2-em dash	(15) =|	
_____	typewritten equivalent of 2-em dash		

B. Corresponding marks that differ in the text from in the margin

Instructions: Mark the live-copy column in the text and in the margin to make each item match its counterpart in the dead-copy column.

Meaning of mark	Dead copy	Live copy
spell out	four feet	4 ft.
wrong font	proofreading	proofreading
defective character	proofreading	proofreading
delete and close up	proofreading	prooofreading
transpose characters	proofreading	proofraeding
transpose words	proofreading manual	manual proofreading
align horizontally	proofreading	p r o o f r e a d i n g
align vertically	proof- reading manual	proof- reading manual
run on	proofreading manual	proofreading manual
carry back to previous line	Editorial Experts Proofreading Manual	Editorial Experts Proofreading Manual
carry down to next line	Editorial Experts Proofreading Manual	Editorial Experts Proofreading Manual
insert space between lines in typing	Proofreading Manual	Proofreading Manual
insert space between lines in typeset copy	Proofreading Manual	Proofreading Manual
equalize space	proofreading	proofreading
set in roman	proofreading	*proofreading*
set in italic	*proofreading*	proofreading
set in lightface	proofreading	**proofreading**
set in boldface	**proofreading**	proofreading
set in caps	PROOFREADING	proofreading
set in lowercase	proofreading	PROOFREADING
set in caps and lowercase	Proofreading Manual	PROOFREADING MANUAL
set small caps	PROOFREADING	**PROOFREADING**
set caps & small caps	PROOFREADING MANUAL	Proofreading Manual
use ligature	**fly off**	**fly off**

C. Abbreviations

Instructions: Write out what the following abbreviations stand for.

1. sp   _____

2. wf   _____

3. rom   _____

4. lf   _____

5. tr   _____

6. ital   _____

7. sc   _____

8. bf   _____

9. lc   _____

10. Clc   _____

11. C+sc   _____

12. eq #   _____

13. stet   _____

14. ctr   _____

15. shill   _____

16. cap   _____

17. ltr #   _____

18. lig   _____

Exercise 21. Practicing proofreading: Benjamin Drew

Instructions: Mark the following live copy to match the dead copy. Mark *only* the live copy. Use both margins as necessary. Do not edit the material; it is a quotation from a published book and cannot be changed.

Note that the marks for replacement in this exercise should follow the principles shown in the following examples.

● Add no close-up mark to a mark for a replacement at the end (or beginning) of a word if no change in marginal word spacing is involved. Here, the replacement should be attached to the word just as the characters being replaced were:

Proofreade~r~ without tears?   *ing*

Follow the same principle when you replace punctuation marks with other characters:

Copy with error	Copy with proofmarks
Yes, no, or may, so	Yes, no, or may/ so. *be*

● Add a close-up mark to a marginal mark for replacement only when the replacement should be attached to a word but the characters being replaced aren't attached. You need the close-up mark to avoid spacing errors. Here, the replacement must be closed up although the characters being replaced are separated from the word with space:

Proofreading with ~no~ tears?   *Cout*

You needn't follow the same principle when you mark to replace other characters with punctuation marks because the spacing before and after punctuation marks is standard:

Yes ~or~ no, or maybe so.   ⌃

"No fears, no tears, my dears. ~ears~   "

Dead copy

Excerpts from Benjamin Drew

In the 1880's, Benjamin Drew, classical scholar, printer, educator and, latterly, proofreader for the U.S. Government Printing Office, in a book entitled Pens and Types, wrote down "the results of a proof-reader's experience, and such suggestions derived therefrom as may...be useful to all who prepare reading-matter for the press (and) to all who assist in printing and publishing it...."

Some of the material in the second edition of 1889 is still instructive, including the following excerpts:

On Querying

Many errors in spelling, made by men who probably know better, but write hastily, are silently corrected in the printing-office. Contradictions, errors of fact, anachronisms, imperfect sentences, solecisms, barbarisms, are modestly pointed out to the author by the proof-reader's "quaere," or by a carefully worded suggestion; and, most usually, the proof is returned without comment,--and none is needed,--corrected according to the proof-reader's intimations. Dickens, and a few other writers of eminence, have acknowledged their indebtedness in such cases; but we know one proof-reader--whose experience embraces an infinite variety of subjects from bill-heads to Bibles--who can remember but three cases in which his assistance, whether valuable or otherwise, was alluded to in a kindly manner. On the other hand, the correction in the proof is sometimes accompanied by some testy remark: as, "Does this suit you?" or, "Will it do now?" The proof-reader is, however, or should be, perfectly callous to all captious criticisms and foolish comments; he need care nothing for "harshness" or other nonsense, provided his work is well and thoroughly done. Let no nervous or touchy man meddle with proof-reading.

On Style

The proof-reader knows, that...every printing-office has a style of its own; that, if left to itself, its style would be practically uniform and always respectable,--and he soon learns that some writers for the press have very firm opinions about matters of little or no consequence, and are very tenacious, if not pugnacious, in preferring tweedledee to tweedledum; not because it is written with more e's, but because it is more correct--in their opinion....

We have known two works to be in hand at the same time, one with directions to "Capitalize freely," the other, to "Use capitals sparingly." The "Directions" are sometimes quite minute, almost microscopic; still, it is the duty of the proof-reader to follow them into the very extremities of their littleness. One writer says, "Put up 'eastern,' 'western,' etc., in such cases as this: 'The purple finch sometimes passes the cold season in Eastern Massachusetts, and even in Northern New Hampshire'"; another directs, "Put compass-points down, as 'In northern Nevada.'" If the office style is "Hudson and Connecticut Rivers," a direction will be sent in thus: "In all my works, print 'Weber and Sevier rivers,' 'Phalan's and Johanna lakes'--not Lakes." One author wants "VIII-inch gun and 64-pounder"; another looks upon this as numerically and typographically erroneous, and insists on an "8-inch gun and a LXIV-pounder"; still another prefers arabic figures throughout, and prints an "8-inch gun and 64-pounder"; yet another likes best the first of the above styles but wishes a period placed after the roman numerals, so it shall read, an "VIII.-inch gun"; one more dislikes "double pointing," and would retain the period, but strike out the hyphen. "In my novel, spell 'Marquise De Gabriac' with a big D, and 'Madame de Sparre' with a little 'd,'"....

Suppose half-a-dozen works going through the press at the same time, embracing three styles of orthography, and four or five styles in capitalization; one style which requires turned commas at the beginning only, of a quotation, and one which requires them at the beginning of every line of an extract,--you see at once that a proof-reader, so beset, must needs have his wits about him....

The publishers of the "Life of John" desire to have it in uniform style with their "watch-pocket series," in which names of ships were put between quotation-marks; the author of the "Life of James" insists, that, in his work, names of ships shall not be quoted, and shall be set in roman; the "Life of William," being in office style, requires names of ships to be in italics....

The "Life of John" has "backwards," "forwards," "towards," all with the final <u>s</u>; and the proof-reader has just received from the outside reader of the "Life of James," a sharp note, stating that he has stricken the <u>s</u> from "towards," as many as ten times, and coolly assuring the said proof-reader that there is no such word as "towards" in the English language....

Among these literary foolishnesses and idle discriminations, are inter-readings of pamphlets on the leather trade; the Swamptown Directory, the copy being the pages of an old edition, pasted on broadsides of paper, half the names stricken out, and new ones inserted haphazard on the wide margin, their places in the text indicated by lines crossing and recrossing each other, and occasionally lost in a <u>plexus</u> or ganglion; reports of the Panjandrum

Grand Slump Mining Company, the Glenmutchkin Railway Company, and the
new and improved Brown Paper Roofing Company; Proceedings of the
National Wool-Pulling Association, and of the Society for Promoting
the Introduction of Water-Gas for Culinary and Illuminating Purposes;
likewise auction-bills, calendars, ball-cards, dunning-letters (some
of these to be returned through the post-office, the proof-reader's
own feathers winging the shaft), glowing descriptions of Dyes,
Blackings, Polishes, and Varnishes; in short, proofs of the endless
variety of matters which constitute the daily pabulum of a book and
job office,--and, in all these, style has its requirements.... We
have known more than forty special directions to be sent to a
printing-office with the manuscript copy of one book. An author may
fancy that numerous minute rulings will ensure uniformity and beauty
to his book; but the chances of discrepancy and mistake are increased
in direct ratio to the number of such of his rulings as run counter to
the office style. His "more requires less," but produces "more."

Live copy (to be marked)

EXCERPTS FROM BENJAMIN DREW

In the 1880s, Benjamin Drew, classical scholar, printer, educator and, latterly, proofreader for the US Government Printing Office, in a book entitled "Pens and Types," wrote down "The results of a proof-reader's experience, and such suggestions derived therefrom as may... be useful to all who prepare reading-matter for the press (and) to all who assist in printing and publishing it..."

Some of the material in the second edition of 1899 is still instructive, including the following concepts:

On Quering

Many errors in spelling, made by men who probably know better, but write hasily, are silently corrected in the printing office. Contradictions, errors of fact, anachronisms, imperfect sentences, solecisms, barbarisms, are modestly pointed out to the author by the proof-reader's "quaere," or by a carefully-worded suggestion; and, most usually, the proof is returned with no comment,—and none is needed,—corrected according to the proof-reader's intimations.

Dickens, and a few other writers of eminence, have acknowledged their indebtedness in such cases, but we know one proofreader—whose experience embraces an infinite variety of subjects from bill-heads to Bibles—who can remember but 3 cases in which his assistance, whether valuable or otherwise, was alluded to in kindly manner.

On the other hand, the correction in the proof is sometimes accompanied by some testy remark, as, "Does this suit you?" or, "Willit do *now*?" The proof-reader is, however, or should be, perfectly callus to all captious criticism and foolish comment; he need care nothing for "harshness" or other nonsense, provided his work is well done. Let no nervous or touchy man meddle with proof-reading.

On Style

The proof-reader knows, that... every printing office has its own style and that, if left to itself, its style would be practical, uniform, and always respectable,—and he soon learns that some writers for the press have very firm opinions about matters of little or no consequence, and are very tenacious, if not pugnacious, in preferring *tweedledee* to *tweedledum*; not because it is written with more *e's*, but because it is more correct—in their opinions...

We have known two works to be in hand at the same time, one with directions to "capitalize freely," the other, to "use capitals sparingly." The "Directions" are sometimes quite minute, almost microscopic; still, it is the duty of the proof-reader to follow them into the very extremities of their small-ness. One writer says, "Put up 'eastern,' 'western,' etc. in such cases as this: 'The purple finch sometimes passes the cold season in Eastern Massachusetts, and even in Northern Nevada'"; another directs, 'Put compass points down, as 'In northern New Hampshire." If the office style is "Hudson and Conneticut Rivers," a direction will be sent in thus: "In all my works, print 'Weber and Severn rivers,' 'Phalan's and Johannah lakes'—not Lakes." One author wants "VII-inch gun and 64-pounder"; another looks upon this as numer-ically and typographically erroneous and insists on "8-inch gun and LXIV-pounder"; still another prefers Arabic figures throughout, and prints an "8-inch gun and 64-pounder"; yet another likes best the first of the above styles but wishes a period placed after the Roman numerals, so it shall read, an "VIII.-in. gun"; one more dislikes double pointing," and would retain the period, but strike out the hyphen. "In my novel, spell 'Marquis De Gabriac' with a big D, and 'Madame de Sparre' with a small 'd,'" . . .

Suppose half a dozen works going through the press at the same time, embracing three styles of orthography, and four or five styles in capitalization; one style which requires turned commas at the beginning only of a quotation, and one which requires them at the beginning of every line of an extract,— you see at once that a proof-reader, so beset, must have his wits about him . . .

The publishers of the "Life of John" desire to have it in uniform style with their "watch-pocket series," in which names of ships were put between quotation-marks; the author of the "Life of James" insists, that, in his work, names of ships shall not be quoted, and shall be set in roman; the "Life of William," being in office style, requires names of ships to be in italics . . .

Among these literary foolishnesses and idle discrimi-nations, are inter-readings of pamphlets on the leather trade; the Swamtown Directory, the copy being the pages of an old edition, pasted on broadsides of paper, half the names stricken out, and new ones inserted haphazardly on the wide margin, their places in the text indicated by lines crossing and recrossing each other, and occasionally lost in a plexus organglion; reports of the Panjandrum Grand Slum Mining Co., the Glenmuchkin Railroad Company, and the new and improved Brown Paper Roofing Company; Pre-ceedings of the National Wool-Pulling Association, and of the Society for Promoting the Introduction of Water-Gas for Culinary and illuminatory Purposes; likewise auction-bills, calendars, ball-cards, dunning-letters (some of these to be returned through the post-office, the proof-reader's own

feathers winging the shaft), glowing descriptions of Dyes, Blackings, Polishes, and Varnishes; in short, proofs of the endless variety of matters which constitute the daily pabulum of a book and job office,—and, in all these style has its requirements ...We have known more than 40 special directions to be sent to a printing-office with the manuscript copy of one book. An author may fancy that numerous minute rulings will insure uniformity and beauty to his book; but the chances of discrepancy and mistakes are increased in direct proportion to the number of such rulings as run counter to the office style. His "more requires less," but produces "more."

Exercise 22A. Specifications: Type specimens

Instructions: Check the live copy against the dead copy's typemarks specifying typeface, line width, and leading. Use the type specimen sheet below and the appropriate measuring tools from Appendix D. Mark only the live copy; use both margins.

Type specimen sheet
TYPE STYLES, all shown in 14 point

Century Schoolbook
ABCDEFGHIJKLMNOPQRSTUVWXYZ
abcdefghijklmnopqrstuvwxyz
1234567890 ⅛ ¼ ⅜ ½ ⅝ ¾ ⅞
?/:;,."""''–-–c L o @ # $ % ¢ & * ()+-=

Helvetica
ABCDEFGHIJKLMNOPQRSTUVWXYZ
abcdefghijklmnopqrstuvwxyz
1234567890 ⅛ ¼ ⅜ ½ ⅝ ¾ ⅞
?/:;,."""''–-–c L o @ # $ % ¢ & * ()+-=

Oracle
ABCDEFGHIJKLMNOPQRSTUVWXYZ
abcdefghijklmnopqrstuvwxyz
1234567890 ⅛ ¼ ⅜ ½ ⅝ ¾ ⅞
?/:;,.'''''–-–c L o @ # $ % ¢ & * ()+-=

ENGLISH TIMES
ABCDEFGHI JKLMNOPQRSTUVWXYZ
abcdefghi jklmnopqrstuvwxyz
1234567890 ½ ⅓ ⅔ ¼ ¾
?.;:'',.&[ ]- - —! □ % /ᶜ___

Garamond
ABCDEFGHIJKLMNOPQRSTUVWXYZ
abcdefghijklmnopqrstuvwxyz
1234567890 ⅛ ¼ ⅜ ½ ⅝ ¾ ⅞
?/:;,."""''–-–c L o @ # $ % ¢ & * ()+-=

Dead copy

Not only alphabets (including figures, punctuation, and other special characters) are used as type specimens; many specimens are text, and many of these texts can be informative or amusing.

The following specimen of Century Schoolbook type provides information on how typefaces may be compared. This text is repeated in 48 different typefaces with each one's name introducing the information (in Type and Typefaces by J. Ben Lieberman, The Myriade Press, New Rochelle, NY, 2nd edition, 1978).

Century
10
12 X 20

set line breaks exactly as shown

CENTURY SCHOOLBOOK MAY BE COMPARED   *(sc)*
with other typefaces in many ways. First is readability: some faces help the eye more than others.
Second is color: letters in mass can appear light or
dark, dull or sparkling. Third is tone: faces suggest
authority, richness, modernity, simplicity, etc.
Fourth is efficiency for a given job--fitness for the
size of type and sheet required, the kind of paper,
the printing process to be used. Since no one typeface
is likely to be best in every respect, these matters have *(ital)*

The following specimen of Helvetica carries a message extolling photocomposition. The same message also appears in specimens of 26 other typefaces in a book on typeface recognition (Primer of Typeface Identification, by A.S. Lawson and Archie Provan, National Composition Association, 1976).

HELVETICA

Helvetica
9 X 14
12

same line breaks

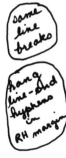

hang end-line hyphens in RH margin

Photocomposition offers the advantages of razor sharp crispness, proportional spacing, a wider selection of type
styles in a greater variety of sizes, better
type alignment and an unequalled uniformity of density.
Typesetting itself offers a number of
advantages: typeset copy is more legible; thus it increases comprehension;
reading speed and retention of the message are improved; typeset copy lends
authority and professionalism to the
written word; typestyles contribute to
the spirit of the message--from serious
to humorous; typeset copy is more compact, reducing printing and distribution
costs; and, finally, typeset copy is more
inviting, encouraging wider readership.

Some specimens keep the word spacing even by continuing from line to line without regard to hyphens or the rules of word division. (The following example is from The TypEncyclopedia by Frank J. Romano, R.R. Bowker Company, New York and London, 1984.)

Oracle
8/9 X 13
same line breaks

ORACLE
The history of writing is, in a way, the hist
ory of the human race, since in it are bou
nd, severally and together, the developm
ent of thought, of expression, of art, of int
ercommunication, and of mechanical inv
ention. Indeed, it has been said that the in
vention of writing is more important than

The previous example also shows how many specimens break off in
the middle of a word or sentence. Different typefaces set at the same
measure will break at different words or sentences, even though the
type is the same size. For example, here's almost the same text as
that above in a different face:

ENGLISH TIMES

Times
8/9 X 13
same line breaks

The history of writing is, in a way, the history
of the human race, since in it are bound, sev
erally and together, the development of tho
ught, of expression, of art, of intercommun
ication, and of mechanical invention. It has
been said that the invention of writing is of
more importance than all the victories ever

In 18th-century issues of <u>The Inland Printer</u> are type specimens
conveying some flights of fancy and some expressions of the continuous
enmity between typesetters and editors (the typefaces used aren't the
same as those in the original):

Century
10/12 X 19

A hat is the canopy of thought, the roof of imagination.
A high hat is a proper loft for lofty ideas and things to skip
around in. A soft hat often covers hard thoughts.

Garamond
6/7

DOES THE EDITOR SIT IN HIS SANCTUM GRIM
NOT MUCH, MY SON, NOT ANY FOR HIM. AMID SYLVAN GROVES AND
PASTURES GREEN, WHERE HILLS RISE UP THE VISTAS BETWEEN

8/9

THE EDITOR SITS BENEATH THE SKIES,
DOTH FISH AND WISH DEATH UNTO THE FLIES: TO-MORROW HIS PAPER
WILL SWARM WITH--NOT LIES, BUT FISH STORIES

10/12

A WASP CAME BUZZING TO HIS WORK
AND VARIOUS THINGS DID TACKLE: HE STUNG A BOY AND
THEN A DOG, THEN MADE A ROOSTER CACKLE

12/14

AT LAST UPON AN EDITOR'S CHEEK HE
SETTLED DOWN TO DRILL: HE PRODDED THERE FOR
HALF-AN-HOUR AND THEN HE BROKE HIS BILL

Garamond
9/10 x 12

Waiting for Purchasers: One male and eight female unicorns; seven sea serpents; three griffins, fully developed; four mermaids, extremely beautiful; seven dragons, descendants of the one slain by St. George; one hippogriff, just weaned; four salamanders, basking in the glow of an anthracite furnace; eleven sphynxes, very docile and amiable; three centaurs, lately domesticated; with many other interesting curiosities.
Open for inspection on Monday, April 6, 1894

INJUNCTION THAT SHOULD BE GENERALLY HEEDED

Century
8/10 x 11

The Chicago Society of Proofreaders recommends the abrogation of the diphthongs in words which have been incorporated in our language, including legal and medical terms, and the substitution of e for them; hence, spell archeological, diarrhea, subpena, eolian, etc.; also in proper names, thus: Cesar, Etna, Esculapius, Linnean, etc.

Live copy (to be marked)

Not only alphabets (including figures, punctuation, and other special characters) are used as type specimens; many specimens are text, and many of these texts can be informative or amusing.

The following specimen of Century Schoolbook type provides information on how typefaces may be compared. This text is repeated in 48 different typefaces with each one's name introducing the information (in *Type and Typefaces* by J. Ben Lieberman, The Myriade Press, New Rochelle, NY, 2nd edition, 1978).

CENTURY SCHOOLBOOK MAY BE COMPARED with other typefaces in many ways. First is readability: some faces help the eye more than others. Second is color: letters in mass can appear light or dark, dull or sparkling. Third is tone: faces suggest authority, richness, modernity, simplicity, etc. Fourth is efficiency for a given job—fitness for the size of type and sheet required, the kind of paper, *the printing process to be used. Since no one typeface is likely to be best in every respect, these matters have*

The following specimen of Helvetica carries a message extolling photocomposition. The same message also appears in specimens of 26 other typefaces in a book on typeface recognition (*Primer of Typeface Identification,* by A.S. Lawson and Archie Provan, National Composition Association, 1976).

Photocomposition offers the advantges of razor sharp crispness, proportional spacing, a wider selection of type styles in a greater variety of sizes, better type alignment and an unequalled uniformity of density.

Typesetting itself offers a number of advantages: typeset copy is more legible, thus it increases comprehension; reading speed and retention of the message are improved; typeset copy lends authority and professionalism to the written word, typestyles contribute to the spirit of the message—from serious to humorous; typeset copy is more compact, reducing printing and distribution costs; and, finally, typeset copy is more inviting, encouraging wider readership.

Some specimens keep the word spacing even by continuing from line to line without regard to hyphens or the rules of word division. (The following example is from *The TypEncyclopedia* by Frank J. Romano, R.R. Bowker Company, New York and London, 1984.)

ORACLE
The history of writing is, in a way, the hist
ory of the human race, since in it are bou
nd, severally and together, the developm
ent of thought, of expression, of art, of int
ercommunication, and of mechanical inv
ention. Indeed, it has been said that the in
vention of writing is more important than

The previous example also shows how many specimens break off in the middle of a word or sentence. Different typefaces set at the same measure will break at different words or sentences, even though the type is the same size. For example, here's almost the same text as that above in a different face:

ENGLISH TIMES
The history of writing is in a way the history of the human race, since in it are bound, sev erally and together, the development of tho ught, of expression, of art, of intercommun ication, and of mechanical invention. It has been said that the invention of writing is of more importance than all the victories ever

In 18th-century issues of *The Inland Printer* are type specimens conveying some flights of fancy and some expressions of the continuous enmity between typesetters and editors (the typefaces used aren't the same as those in the original):

A hat is the canopy of thought, the roof of imagination. A high hat is a proper loft for lofty ideas
and things to skip around in. A soft hat often covers
hard thoughts.

DOES THE EDITOR SIT IN HIS SANCTUM GRIM
NOT MUCH, MY SON, NOT ANY FOR HIM. AMID SYLVAN GROVES AND
PASTURES GREEN, WHERE HILLS RISE UP THE VISTAS BETWEEN

THE EDITOR SITS BENEATH THE SKIES,
DOTH FISH AND WISH DEATH UNTO THE FLIES; TO-MORROW HIS PAPER
WILL SWARM WITH—NOT LIES, BUT FISH STORIES

A WASP CAME BUZZING TO HIS WORK
AND VARIOUS THINGS DID TACKLE: HE STUNG A BOY AND
THEN A DOG, THEN MADE A ROOSTER CACKLE

AT LAST UPON AN EDITOR'S CHEEK HE
SETTLED DOWN TO DRILL: HE PRODDED THERE FOR
HALF-AN-HOUR AND THEN HE BROKE HIS BILL

INJUNCTION THAT SHOULD
BE GENERALLY HEEDED

The Chicago Society of Proofreaders recommends the abrogation of the diphthongs in words which have been incorporated in our language, including legal and medical terms, and the substitution of *e* for them; hence, spell archeological, diarrhea, subpena, eolian, etc.; also in proper names, thus: Cesar, Etna, Esculapius, Linnean, etc.

Waiting for Purchasers: One male and eight female unicorns; seven area serpents; three griffins, fully developed; four mermaids, extremely beautiful; seven dragons, descendants of the one clain by St. George; one hippogriff, just weaned; four salamanders, basking in the glow of an anthracite furnace; eleven sphynxes, very docile and amiable; three centaurs, lately domesticated; with many other interesting curiosities.

Open for inspection on Monday, April 6, 1894

Exercise 22B. Specifications: Marks for type style

Marginal mark	In-text mark	Corrected copy
(ital)	Set in italic	*Set in italic*
(sc)	Set in small caps	SET IN SMALL CAPS
(caps)	Set in capitals	SET IN CAPITALS
(bf)	Set in boldface	**Set in boldface**
(bf ital)	Set in boldface italic	***Set in boldface italic***
(bf caps)	Set in boldface caps	**SET IN BOLDFACE CAPS**
(C + sc)	Set in caps and small caps	SET IN CAPS AND SMALL CAPS
(Clc)	Set in caps and lowercase	Set in Caps and Lowercase
(Clc)	SET IN CAPS AND LOWERCASE	Set in Caps and Lowercase

Instructions: Use proof marks to correct any errors in type style you may find in "A Writer's Goals" and to put it into the following format:

> Main Head—Full caps, BF
> Subheads—Clc, BF
> Titles of Books—Clc, ital
> In citations, author's names—C+SC

A Writer's Goals

Maugham on Fiction
It seems to me that I must aim at lucidity, simplicity, euphony.
I have put these three qualities in the order of the importance I
assigned to them.——SOMERSET MAUGHAM, *THE SUMMING UP*

SHIPLEY ON NONFICTION
hAd he been speaking of nonfiction, Maugham might have replaced
euphony with verity.——Joseph T. Shipley, ORigins of English Words

Exercise 22C. Specifications: Wrong font

This is the alphabet in Times, roman and italic:

ABCDEFGHIJKLMNOPQRSTUVWXYZ   abcdefghijklmnopqrstuvwxyz

ABCDEFGHIJKLMNOPQRSTUVWXYZ   *abcdefghijklmnopqrstuvwxyz*

Instructions: Find and mark the wrong fonts in the quotation below. Note that there is no dead copy.

Live Copy

If I do not clearly express what I mean, it is either for the reason that,
having no conversational powers, I cannot express what I mean, or
that having no meaning, I do not mean what I fail to express.

      —Mr. Grewgious, in Dickens' *The Mystery of Edwin Drood*

Exercise 23. Edited copy: Continuing Need for Proofreading

Instructions: Mark the following live copy to match the dead copy. Mark *only* the live copy. Use both margins as necessary. Assume that your level of authority doesn't permit any editing of the material.

Dead copy

THE CONTINUING NEED FOR PROOFREADING

You see words in type, printed materials, are everywhere, not just in books, pamphlets, magazines, catalogues, and newspapers, but also in many other forms--in the products of job printing--handbills, calendars, greeting cards, tickets, checkbooks, office forms, and business stationery; on display at the side of the road--posters, billboards, road signs; on your pantry shelves--boxes, tin cans, and bottles; in decorative and novelty printing on paper, cloth, and plastic--napkins, towels, playing cards, baseball cards, game boards, yarn goods, shower curtains, shopping bags, tee shirts; and in music, maps, and stamps.

Type and printing are everywhere, from our birth certificates to our death notices. And every word is subject to the gaucheries results of writers and typists and typesetters ignorance and carelessness, that is, to the horror of misspelling, typographic error, and careless sloppy printing.

Even the best writers suffer from a loss of word sense now and then; even the best most up-to-date technology help fails to offers "prove" the quality of authors and typesetters. a work's in all typographic and linguistic respects.

no ¶

As a scholar-proofreader wrote ~~more than a century ago~~ *in 1889*, "So long as authors the most accomplished are liable to err, so long as compositors the most careful make occasional mistakes, so long as dictionaries authorize various spellings, just so long must there be individuals trained and training to detect errors . . . proofreaders."

Good proofreading can preserve quality and can even turn a bad job into an acceptable one and a good job into an excellent one. ~~But~~ failure to catch problems can ruin a well written, well edited, well designed job. *But*

Proofreading is true quality control. Don't slight it.

<u>**Live copy**</u> (to be marked)

The Continuing Need for Proofreading

Words in type, printed materials, are every where, not only in books, pamphlets, magazines, catalogues, and newspapers, but inthe products of job printing—handbills, calendars, greeting cards, checkbooks, office forms, and business stationary; on display at the roadside—posters, billboards, road signs; on our pantry shelves—boxes, tin cans, and bottles; in decorative and novelty printing on paper, cloth, and plastic—napkins, towels, playing cards, basball cards, game boards, yard goods, shower curtains, shopping bags, tee shirts; and in music, maps, and stamps. Type and printing are everywhere, from our birth certficates to our death notices. And very word is subject to the gaucheries of misspelling, typographic errors, and care less printing.

Even the best writers suffer a loss of word sense now and then; even the best help technology offers fails to "prove" a work's quality in all typograhic and linguistic respects. As a scholar-proofreader wrote in 1889, "So long as authors the most accomplished are liable to err, so long as compostiors the most careful make occasional mistakes, so pong must there be individuals trained and training too detect errors,..proofreaders."

Failure to catch problems can ruim a well written, well edited, well desinged job.But goood proofreading can preserve quality and can even turn a bad job into an accepable one and a good job into an excellent one. Proofreading is true guality control.

Exercise 24. Modified marking techniques

General instructions: Your marks in any of the parts of this exercise may be somewhat different from the answer keys. The reason for the differences is that no single absolutely correct way exists for marking in a nonstandard technique.

Remember that your goals are, first, to find all the errors and, second, to mark errors in such a way that the corrector knows at a glance exactly what needs fixing. The answer keys for this exercise, unfortunately, can tell you only how well you've met the first goal.

All parts of this exercise use the following dead copy:

Dead copy

```
    He, whose business it is to offer this unusual
apology, very well remembers to have been sitting with
Dr. Johnson, when an agent from a neighboring press
brought in a proof sheet of a republication, requesting
to know whether a particular word in it was not
corrupted.
    "So far from it, sir," (replied the Doctor with
some harshness), "that the word you suspect, and would
displace, is conspicuously beautiful where it stands,
and is the only one that could do the duty expected of
it by Mr. Pope."
                    --From an apology for errors in a book
                    published in 1793
```

Exercise 24A. Writing out instructions

Instructions for the exercise: Compare the live copy with the dead copy on the previous page. Use standard in-text marks except for type style: carets, slashes, crossthroughs, and rings require no special knowledge to interpret. In the margin, write explicit instructions to the corrector.

Example:

*take out and
change o to p*

The art of art, the glory expression and ~~and~~ the sunshine of the light of letters is simplicity.

—Whitman

add of

cap w

Live copy

He, whose busness it is to offer this unusual apology, very well rembers to have been sitting with Dr. Johnson, when an agent from a neigh-boring press brought in a proof sheet of a re-publication, requesting to know whether a par-particular word in it was not corrupted.

"So far from it, sir," (replied the doctor with some harshness), "that the word you suspect, and would displace, is conspicuously beautiful where it stands, and is the only one that would do the duty expected of it by Mr. Pope"

—From an apology for errors
in a book published in 1793

Exercise 24B. Marking in the margins only

Instructions: Compare the live copy with the dead copy on page 271. Mark in the margin only.

To insert or replace one or two characters, write the entire word in the margin and use a caret to point to the change:

Marginal mark	Error in text
insert	inset
replace	replece

To insert or replace an entire word, write the previous word in the margin (sometimes the following word, too) and point a caret to the change:

Marginal mark	Error in text
an entire word	insert an word
an entire word	replace an whole word

To delete something, write the error in the margin and use a looped slash or crossthrough as a kind of combination in-text and marginal mark or, if necessary, a closed-up dele:

Marginal mark	Error in text
del	del delete
deleted	deletee
delete	deleete

Example:

and the
simplicity

The art of art, the glory expression and and the sunshine of the light of letters is simolicity.

—whitman

glory of

Whitman

Live copy

He, whose busness it is to offer this unusual apology, very well rembers to have been sitting with Dr. Johnson, when an agent from a neigh-boring press brought in a proof sheet of a re-publication, requesting to know whether a par-particular word in it was not corrupted.

"So far from it, sir," (replied the doctor with some harshness), "that the word you suspect, and would displace, is conspicuously beautiful where it stands, and is the only one that would do the duty expected of it by Mr. Pope"

—From an apology for errors in a book published in 1793

Exercise 24C. Making a handwritten correction list

Instructions: Handwritten lists lend themselves to the use of standard proofmarks. If you follow the format shown in the example, the last two columns almost amount to in-text and marginal marks.

Compare the live copy with the dead copy on page 271. On a sheet of 8-1/2 x 11-inch paper, write a correction list according to the format in the example.

Example:

Live copy from which sample list was made

The art of art, the glory expression and
and the sunshine of the light of letters
is simolicity.
                                    —whitman

Handwritten list

Live copy

He, whose busness it is to offer this unusual apology, very well rembers to have been sitting with Dr. Johnson, when an agent from a neighboring press brought in a proof sheet of a re-publication, requesting to know whether a par-particular word in it was not corrupted.

"So far from it, sir," (replied the doctor with some harshness), "that the word you suspect, and would displace, is conspicuously beautiful where it stands, and is the only one that would do the duty expected of it by Mr. Pope"

—From an apology for errors
in a book published in 1793

Exercise 24D. Making a typed correction list

Instructions: In the format shown in the example, the last two columns of a typed correction list amount to spelling out the instructions to the corrector.

Compare the live copy with the dead copy on page 271, and type a correction list on a sheet of 8-1/2 x 11-inch paper according to the format in the example.

Example:

Live copy from which sample typed list was made

The art of art, the glory expression and
and the sunshine of the light of letters
is simolicity.
                                    —whitman

Correction list for Whitman quotation

Dead copy p para line	Live copy p para line	Corrected error	Correction to make
	1	glory of	add "of"
	2	and the	delete extra "and"
	3	simplicity	change o to p
	4	Whitman	cap W

Live copy

He, whose busness it is to offer this unusual apology, very well rembers to have been sitting with Dr. Johnson, when an agent from a neighboring press brought in a proof sheet of a re-publication, requesting to know whether a par-particular word in it was not corrupted.

"So far from it, sir," (replied the doctor with some harshness), "that the word you suspect, and would displace, is conspicuously beautiful where it stands, and is the only one that would do the duty expected of it by Mr. Pope"

—From an apology for errors
in a book published in 1793

Exercise 24E. Making corrections yourself

Instructions: Compare the live copy with the dead copy on page 271. Make the corrections right on the copy. Avoid proofmarks that an uninitiated person wouldn't understand. If there's room, write missing characters right on the line; there's always room for punctuation marks. If a missing character or word belongs at the end of the line, write it in place. Write other short outs above a caret. If the space between lines would become very crowded, use guidelines. Type long outs and cut and paste them in place.

Example:

The art of art, the glory ᵒᶠ expression and

~~and~~ the sunshine of the light of letters

is simplicity.

—Whitman

Live copy

He, whose busness it is to offer this unusual

apology, very well rembers to have been sitting

with Dr. Johnson, when an agent from a neigh-

boring press brought in a proof sheet of a re-

publication, requesting to know whether a par-

particular word in it was not corrupted.

"So far from it, sir," (replied the doctor with

some harshness), "that the word you suspect,

and would displace, is conspicuously beautiful

where it stands, and is the only one that would

do the duty expected of it by Mr. Pope"

—From an apology for errors

in a book published in 1793

Exercise 24F. Using editing marks with checkmarks in the margin

Instructions: Compare the live copy with the dead copy on page 271. Use editing marks inside the text. (Consult the list of editing marks in Chapter 4.) For *every* editing mark in the text, write a checkmark in the nearest margin; you may need more than one checkmark in any one line.

Example:

The art of art, the glory expression and ✓

✓ and the sunshine of the light of letters

✓ is simplicity.

—whitman ✓

Live copy

He, whose busness it is to offer this unusual
apology, very well rembers to have been sitting
with Dr. Johnson, when an agent from a neigh-
boring press brought in a proof sheet of a re-
publication, requesting to know whether a par-
particular word in it was not corrupted.

"So far from it, sir," (replied the doctor with
some harshness), "that the word you suspect,
and would displace, is conspicuously beautiful
where it stands, and is the only one that would
do the duty expected of it by Mr. Pope"

—From an apology for errors
in a book published in 1793

Exercise 25A. Dry reading: The simplest answer

Instructions: Instead of just marking "Break up," suggest a solution to break up the knothole:

```
This step involves transferring or integrating the new system into
an operational status.  New system operating instructions are
prepared, and the completed system documentation is turned over to
appropriate personnel.  The system is then considered operational,
and control passes from the system-development function to the
Department.
```

Exercise 25B. Dry reading: The Mississippi

Instructions: Proofread at level 2. Mark to correct the problems; query inconsistencies.

The Route Of the Mississippi River

From Minnesota, the Mississippi river flows southward along the borders of Wisconsin, Illlinois, and seven other states, past Dubuque, St. Louis and Memphis, past the State that bears the river's name towards its source at New Orleans, La.

Exercise 25C. Dry reading: Renaissance printing

Instructions: Dry read the live copy at level 2, but do not query. Correct typos, misspellings, and blatant copy errors; when style is inconsistent, choose the form used most often. Although you may find this to be dense, cumbersome prose in need of editing, do *not* attempt to copy edit or rewrite. Use editing marks.

Printing in the Renaissance

Stimulated to reaction against ecclesiastical and feudal tyranny and responding to influences possibly brought to life by the influx of scholars from Byzantium, Italy had already done much to ward rehabilititating the classical products of antiquity when the balance of Europe began to throw off the shackles of intellectual despotism and to succumb to those mighty spiritual energies that ended in the emancipation of reason, the freedom of thought, and the recognition of natural rites.

The coarse of the Renaissance, determined by the revival of learning, vitalized the Italian scholarship of the fifteenth century, afforded tremendous impetus to the rise of Greek and the accumulation of its classical documents, and encouraged the new art of typography that gave to Italy an Aldus Manutius and to France the Estiennes.

The awakening that came to mankind first entered the Italian mind first as the arts of Italy reflected the humanistic spirit of her letters and as science and philosophy bridged the chasm between the ancient and the 15th-century worlds. The Turkish threat against Constantinople more and more influenced the emigration of learned Greeks into Italy, and with them came the literature of Greece—the writings of Pindar, Plato, and Aristotle. As scholars sought to evolve a new critical apparatus to express the renascent culture, a classical education became a necessity, and the knowledge of antiquity was indefatigably explored.

From Italy the tidal wave swept across the Alps into Germany, where where modifications akin to the nature of the sturdy Teutonic inhabitants effected a liberty of religious conviction and a license in expressing it that were powerfully enlarge by the agency of the printing press.

The achievements and aims of Froben, at Basle, reflect the position of printing in Germany at the time. As the power of the Press spread through out Europe, the Pulpit began to lose its claim to be the supreme center from which all knowledge emanated. France however was effected differently.

In fifteen-century France, the terror of classical learning, of the Oriental, Hebrew and Greek studies that encourage Biblical criticism, held sway the longest. Only to art was liberty accorded: in architecture, the fine arts, and, to a limited extent,
literature, through the patronage of Francis I, shone forth a genius that was wanting in the domain of biblical study. But the press, that is, the printing industry, was governed by the ecclesiastical body of the time, the college of the Sorbonne.

On the one hand, the patron age of the sovereign developed the material beauty and splendor of books: Grolier was encouraged to bind; Robert Stephens was encouraged to print; a magnificent Greek type was cast at they expense of the royal treasury; and, when a sumptuary law prohibited gilding houses and furniture, book binding was, by a special clause, exempted. The enrichment of the physical aspects of books—the expanse of margin, the thick-wove paper, and the brilliant type—all that came from the idea that Rosso and Cellini formed of their royal master's patronage of letters. The king's taste had a materialistic direction, expressed in his oft-quoted saying to Cellini, *"Je l'etoufferai dans l'or"* (I'll smother it in gold). So it is that the magnificence of the revival left it's mark in the Greek additions from the press of Robert Stevens, printer to the king.

On the other hand, the spirit of curiosity that had arisen among the public made other demands on the press. The pubic wanted to learn. The people desired books, not to place in a cabinet but to read in order to know—first and foremost, to know the truth in the matter of religion; next to know the causes and remedies of the evils, moral and material, by which they felt themselves crushed; and finally, to know how to struggle with nature, how to rest from her more comforts and more enjoyment.

But the press as a media of knowledge—as an arena for debating spiritual and social problems—was not the press that Francis I would encourage. This is the explanation of the apparent inconsistency in the public acts of that monarch, the acts that have caused him to be represented in such different lights.

While Francis I is invoked by some historians as the Father of Letters, others brand him as a bigot and persecutor whose zealous despotism would not tolerate the least dissent or the gentlest criticism. The truth is that Francis the First was both at once.

Exercise 25D. Dry reading: Reading ease and comfort

Instructions: Dry read at level 3 and correct errors with editing marks.

How to Foster Ease and Comfort in Reading

Douglas McMurtrie, a well known typographer and book designer, tells us (in *The Book,* Dorset Press, 1943) that "the average reader demands a book easy and comfortable to read, easy and comfortable to handle, and easy and comfortable to purchase."

The following list, based on his proscriptions for ease and comfort in reading, apply to many kinds of publication.besides books

Design Elements

- A typeface "free of affectation or labored drawing."
- Type size "large enough to read with ease under average lighting, or worse, by readers of average acuity of eyesight, or worse."
- Line spacing enough "to direct the eye back from the end of one
  line to the beginning of the next without
  possibility of confusion."
- Spacing that is "reasonably snug" between words & sentences.
- Lowercase rather than capitals so far as possible in chapter heads, subheads, and so on.
- Margins with traditional proportions, especially when specified by "designers of modest ability." Tradition calls for the gutter margarine to be the narrowest, and the margins at the top, outer edge, and bottom of the page to increase progressively.

Editorial Elements

- Frequent paragraph brakes to give the eye of the reader a pause that refreshes."
- Books for study or reference "as liberally provided with sign posts in the way of subheads, and so forth, as the well-marked highway."

Production Elements

- Pages printed "sharply and clearly in good black ink, and uniform color and strength of impression maintained."
- Pages that line up accurately.
- pages that back up accurate.

Instructions: Dry read and mark at level 3 to correct the problems you find in this advertisement, which is designed to appear on a paper bag that will be distributed door to door. Use proofmarks.

Bag It at Householder's Hardware—

Shop with this discount bag

and get 10 % off everything in it!

- ■ All merchandise must fit inside the bag, all at one time.

- ■ Indivudual items up to twice the height of the bag allowed.

- ■ Multiple items must fit inside the bag. No stacking allowed beyond the height of the bag.

- ■ All merchandise must remain in it's original packaging.

- ■ All currently sale priced merchandise is not eligible for the discount.

- ■ Offer applies to in stock products only.

- ■ Offer limited to one bag per cutomer per visit.

- ■ Bag only may be used one time.

- ■ Discount bags are not available at store.

- ■ No rain checks, no special orders honored for this event

Exercise 25F. Dry reading: Editorial problems to catch

Instructions: The following list gives names and examples of only a few editorial problems out of the many a dry reader may encounter.

For this exercise, proofread at level 4 and add the editing marks (or write the queries) that make the point. Item 1, below, is an example.

A dozen kinds of editorial problems to catch

1. Typos:
    *   typose

2. Misspellings:
    *   mispellings

3. Wrong word use.
    *   Every day I lay down and take a nap.
    *   Bee especially careful of homophones.

4. Faulty thinking:
    *   The price of coffee dropped 100 percent.

5. Factual inaccuracy:
    *   In 1493, Columbus sailed the ocean blue.
    *   "Beauty is truth, truth beauty"
        —Ode to a Grecian Urn, John Keats

6. Mismatch of references to what they refer to—
    *   Descriptions should fit what they describe (for example, in headings, captions, and tables)
    *   Lables should match what they label in words, editorial style, and alphabetical or numerical sequence (for example, footnotes should match their callouts; tables of contents and lists of illustrations should match the heads and captions they list)
    *   Cross-references should be accurate (for example, see the related items, 4 and 5, below, on illogic and factual inaccuracy).

6. Errors in alphabetical order or numerical sequence.

8. Punctuation faults, including the following:
    *   misleading punctuation, including "needless" quotation marks
    *   excessive punctuation!!!
    *   too little punctuation for example missing commas
    *   marks' of punctuation used incorrectly

8. Substandard grammar and usage:
    *   Not every proofreader writes good.

9. Disagreement between a singular subject and a plural verb:
    *   Knowledge about grammar and spelling are a big part of successful editing.

10. Disagreement between a plural verb and a singular subject:
    *   With the job of an editor comes a need for sensitivity and an absolute requirement for courtesy to the writer.

11. Pronoun problems, including problems of case, agreement, and indefinite antecedents:
    *   To who do I give the correct answer?
    *   Who do I give the correct answer to?
    *   Every editor should be able to cite an appropriate authority for every error they correct.

- Margaret told the editor that one of her sentences was brilliant.

12. Modifier problems:
    - Using an adjective when an adverb is the proper form looks badly.
    - The comparative, not the superlative, degree is the correct choice when two things are being compared, as in "He is the tallest of her two sons."
    - Modifiers that could have two possible meanings are called "squinting." Modifiers that squint often confuse the reader.

13. Parallel construction.

14. Inconsistent Editorial Style

Exercise 25G. Dry reading: Pronouns

Instructions: Proofread the following table at level 5. Correct the problems; do not query.

PERSONNEL PRONOUNS
(arranged by case, number, person, and case)

	Singular			Plural		
	1st	*2nd*	*3rd*	*1st*	*2nd*	*3rd*
Nominative	I	you thou	he she it	we	you ye	they
objective	me	you thee ye[2]	him her it	us	you you-all[1] ye[2]	them
Posssessive[3]	my mine	your thy yours thy thine	his her his hers it's	our ours thy thine	your thy yours	them theirs

[1] (or "y'all"). Acceptable colloguialism in the southern United States
[2] Nominative ye is used sometimes in literature also as objective, as in Shakespeare and others.
[3] Some grammarians classify these possessives as adjetives, not pronouns; some only classify the first two rows (my-their, thy-the) as adjectives and consider the rest to be pronouns.

Exercise 26. Excerpts from the *U.S. Government Printing Office Style Manual*

Instructions: Proofread Parts A, B, and C by comparison. Mark the live copy in both left and right margins.

A. Early Correctors of the Press

Note that a computer program for spelling or "proofreading" would catch none of these errors.

Dead copy

It does not appear that the earliest printers had any method of correcting errors before the form was on the press. The learned correctors of the first two centuries of printing were not proof-readers in our sense; they were rather what we should term office editors. Their labors were not chiefly to see that the proof corresponded to the copy, but that the printed page was correct in its Latinity--that the words were there, and that the sense was right. They cared little about orthography, bad letters, or purely printer's errors, and when the text seemed to them wrong they consulted fresh authorities or altered it on their own responsibility. Good proofs, in the modern sense, were impossible until professional readers were employed--men who first had a printer's education and then spent many years in the correction of proof.

B. Standardized Spelling

"Railroading" would probably miss these errors.

Dead copy

The orthography of English, which for the past century has undergone little change, was very fluctuating until after the publication of Johnson's Dictionary, and capitals, which have been used with some regularity for the past 80 years, were previously used on the hit or miss plan. The approach to regularity, so far as we have it, may be attributed to the growth of a class of professional proofreaders, and it is to them that we owe the correctness of modern printing.

C. The Printer's Wife

A computer program for spelling and proofreading would catch all these errors. Probably it would also list *Narr* and *Herr*; they wouldn't be in its dictionary. And some programs would stop at the two *Ands* because they have capitals but don't begin a sentence.

Dead copy

```
     The story is related that a certain woman in Germany, the wife of
a printer, who had become disgusted with the continual assertion of
the superiority of man over woman which she had heard, hurried into
the composing room while her husband was at supper and altered a sen-
tence in the Bible, which he was printing, so that it read "Narr" in-
stead of "Herr," thus making the verse read "And he shall be thy fool"
instead of "And he shall be thy lord."
```

A. Early Correctors of the Press

Live copy

It does not a pear that the earliest printers had any method of correcting errors be fore the form was on the press. The learned correctors of errors before the form was on the press. The learned correctors of the first twenty-two cen- turies of printing were not proof readers in our cents; they were rather what we would term off ice editors. There labors were chiefly to sea that the proof corresponded to the copy, but that the printed page was correct in it's Latinity—that the words were there, and that they sense was right? They care little about orthography, bad letters, or purely printer's errors, and where the text seem to them wrong, they consulted fresh authority or altar it on their one responsibility. Good proofs, in the modern sense, were possible until professional readers where employed—men who first had a printers education and than spent many months in the correction of proof. —U.S. Government Printing Office Style Manual

B. Standardized Spelling

Live copy

The orthography of English, which for the past century has undergone little change, was very fluctuating until after the publication of Webster's Dictionary, and capitals, which have been used with some regularity for the past 90 years, were previously used on the hit or miss plan. The approach to regularity, so far as we have it, may be attributed to the growth of modern printing.

C. The Printer's Wife

Live copy

The story is related that a certian woman in Germany, the wife of a printer. who had become disgusted with the continual assertion of the superiority of man over woman which she had heard,, hurried into the composing room while her husband was at supper and altered a sence in the Bible, which he was printing, so that it read "Narr" instead of of "Herr", thus making the vers read "And he shall be thy fool" instead of "And he shall be thy lord".

Exercise 27. Standard marks

Instructions: Proofread the live copy of *Errors in Early Printed Work* by comparing it with the dead copy. Mark only the live copy; do not edit the material. (In this exercise, the live copy has been typewritten from a typeset document. Typeset italic should be typed as underscored roman.)

Use standard proofreading marks in the text and in both margins. Don't query. Treat transpositions within a word as replacements; use loops only for adjacent words.

Dead copy

] ERRORS IN EARLY, [
(PRINTED WORK [

Fℓ # (set brackets)
[an erroneous]

~~Another~~ belief has been fostered in the mind of the reader: that printing in its early days was done much better than it is now; that books were printed more accurately when the methods and machinery of the art were simpler, when printers and publishers were men of high scholarship and had more intimate intercourse with the literati of their time. This belief has no good basis. The demigods of typography are like the demigods of so-called history: the greatest are those who are at the greatest distance. Not much research is needed to show that demigods of all kinds do not belong to history but to fiction, and that errors of the press were, to say the least, quite as common in the early days of typography as they are now.

With a few exceptions, the early printers were foolishly boastful. They bragged of the superior beauty of their types and the greater accuracy of their texts. Gutenberg, first and best of all, seems to have been the only one who refused to magnify himself. Printing had been practised less than twenty years when Peter Schoeffer, the surviving member of the triumvirate who developed the art, in his edition of the *Institutes of Justinian* of 1468, reminded his readers that he paid great sums to the wise men who corrected his texts, but he adds that there were even then rival printers who did not take proper precautions against errors of the press. It may be assumed that Gabriel Petrus of Venice was one of the growing number of negligent printers, for he published a book in 1478 with two pages of errata. Before the fifteenth century

closed, lists of errata were frequent. Sometimes errors were so numerous that the faulty book had to be reprinted. Robert Gaguin of Paris was so disgusted with the mistakes made by a printer of that city in an edition of French legends (1497) that he ordered a second edition from a printer of Lyons, but the change of printer was not happy: the reprinted book was as faulty as the first.

Cardinal Bellarmine of Rome had a provoking experience in 1581. He cancelled the first edition of his book printed at Rome, and sent an amended copy to a printer of Venice, hoping to get absolutely perfect work, but the new edition was also full of errors.

A book of Picus Mirandola, printed at Strasburg in 1507, in the real cradle of typography, contains fifteen pages of errata.

The fullest list of errata known is that of a book called *The Anatomy of the Mass*, printed in 1561. This book of one hundred and seventy-two pages is followed by errata covering fifteen pages. In apology, the writer says the errors were caused by the malice of the devil, who had allowed the manuscript to be drenched with water and made almost illegible before it was placed in the hands of the printers. Not content with this, the devil instigated the printers to commit a surprising number of inexcusable blunders.

Books of authority and reference made in the sixteenth century were quite as full of errors as more unpretentious work. Joseph Scaliger said that he would frequently make a bet that he could find an error on any chance-selected page of the *Greek Lexicon* of Robert Constantine, and that he always won the bet. Chevillier adds that Constantine was responsible for as many errors as the printer.

In his *Memoirs*, Baron de Grimm tells of a French author who died in a spasm of anger after he had detected more than three hundred typographical errors in a newly printed copy of his work.

The Bible, as a bulky and frequently reprinted book, presents exceptional opportunity for error. An edition of the Vulgate printed in 1590, and said to have been made under the supervision of Pope Sixtus V, has the unenviable distinction of being full of misprints. Barker's edition of the Bible, printed at London in 1632, and notorious in the trade as the Wicked Bible, gives this rendering of the seventh commandment: Thou shalt commit adultery. For this error, undoubtedly made by a malicious compositor, the printer was fined three

thousand pounds, and all obtainable copies of the edition were destroyed.[1] To prevent error, Parliament forbade all unauthorized printing of the Bible.

It was the same spirit of mischief-making that prompted a woman in Germany to steal into her husband's printing-house by night and make an alteration in type that was ready for the press by changing the German word *Herr* to *Narr*, thereby perverting the passage in Genesis iii, 16, from "he shall be thy lord" to "he shall be thy fool." The story goes that she had to atone for this silly joke with her life.

Errors of the press were and are not confined to any nation. Erasmus said that the books printed in Italy were, without exception, full of faults, due largely to the parsimony of publishers who would not pay a proper price for the supervision of the copy. Books were so incorrectly printed in Spain during the sixteenth century that the authorities refused to license their publication before they had been approved by a censor appointed for the duty. He required that all faults noted by him should be corrected in an appended list of errata. Chevillier says that the printers of Geneva during the sixteenth century used execrable paper and made the texts of their books intolerably incorrect. Even the famous Christopher Plantin of Antwerp was not beyond all reproach. One of his eulogists has to admit sorrowfully that he found in Plantin's enormous *Polyglot Bible* many errors of paging which his scholarly proof-readers had overlooked.

The apology of John Froben of Basle for his errata is really pathetic: "I do everything I can to produce correct editions. In this edition of the *New Testament* in Greek I have doubled my care and my vigilance; I have spared neither time nor money. I have engaged with difficulty many correctors of the highest ability, among them John Oecolampadius, a professor of three languages. Erasmus himself has done his best to help me." This book was in press for a year, but after all this care it had errata of one and a half pages.

Erasmus himself charged one of the workmen of Froben with intended malice in perverting (in another book) his tribute of admiration to Queen

---

[1] Sometimes errata have been purposely made to gratify personal malignity. Paul Scarron, the French poet and writer of burlesques, wrote a book of poems in which were verses dedicated to "Guillemette, my sister's dog." Before the book was published, Scarron quarrelled with his sister, and ordered this erratum to be added: "Make 'Guillemette, my sister's dog' read 'Guillemette, my dog of a sister.'"

Elizabeth of Hungary to a passage of unmention-able obscenity. He declared that he would have given three hundred crowns in gold to have prevented the scandalous error.

Examples enough have been presented to show that errors are not always detected by educated printers or by scholarly correctors, but the summing up may be left to earlier writers. Chevillier, writing in 1694, quotes many authors and printers in support of his proposition that a book without an error is impossible,[1] and that early books do not deserve the reputation they have had for superior accuracy. Prosper Marchand, writing in 1738, says that reader is deceived who thinks that old books are more correct than new books; on the contrary, they are much more inaccurate.

Errors of the press often begin with errors of reporters who have misunderstood spoken words. The rule of follow copy compels the compositor to repeat the exact words written by the reporter, and the following blunders are the result of obedience to this rule. A speaker made this statement:

> In these days clergymen are expected to have the wisdom and learning of Jeremy Taylor.

But the reporter wrote, and the compositor repeated:

> . . . the wisdom and learning of a journeyman tailor.

Another speaker quoted these lines:

> O come, thou goddess fair and free,
> In heaven yclept Euphrosyne.

They were printed as written:

> O come, thou goddess fair and free,
> In heaven she crept and froze her knee.

Another orator quoted this line from Tennyson's *Locksley Hall:*

> Better fifty years of Europe than a cycle of Cathay.

[1] Whoever thinks a faultless piece to see,
Thinks what ne'er was, nor is, nor e'er shall be.
Pope.

type for

align

Theodore Low De Vinne
*The Practice of Typography:
Correct Composition*

Oswald Publishing Company
New York 1916

Live copy (to be marked)

[An erroneous] belief has been fostered in the mind of the reader: that printing in its early days was done much better than now; that books were printed more accurately when the methods and machinery of the art were simpler, when printers and publishers were men of high scholarship and had intimate intercourse with the literati of their time. This belief has no basis. The demigods of typograhy are like the demigods of s0-called history: the greatest are those who are at the greatest distance. Not much research is needed to show that demigods of all kinds do not belong to history but to fiction, and that erors of the press were, to say the least, quite as common in the early days of typography as they are now.

With few exceptions, the early printers were foolishly boastful. They bragged of the superior beauty of their types and the greater accuracy of their texts. Gutenberg, first and best of all, seems to have been the only one who refused to magnify himself. Printing had been practised less than twenty years when Peter Schoeffer, the surviving member of the thwe triumverate who developed the art, in his edition on the Institutes of Justinisn of 1468, reminded his readers that he paid great sums to the wise men who corrected his texts, but he adds that there were rival printers who did not take the proper precautions against errors of the press. It may be assumed that Gabriel Petrus of Venice ws one of the growing number of negligent printers, for he published two pages of errata. Before the fifteenth century closed, lists of errata were frequent. Sometimes errors were so numerous that the faulty book had to be reprinted. Robert Gaugin of Paris was so disgusted with the mistakes made by a printer of that city in an edition of french legends (2497) that he ordered a second edition from a printer in Lyons, but the change of printer was not happy: the reprinted book was as faulty as the first.

Cardinal Bellarmine of Rome had a provoking experience in 1581. He cancelled the first edition of his book prpinted at Rome, and sent an amended copy to a printer of Venice, hoping to get acsolutely perfect work, but the new addition was also full of errors.

A book of Picus Miranola, printed at Strasburg in 1507, in the real cradle of typography, contains fifteenpages of errata. The fullest list of errata known is that of a book called The Anatomy of the Mass, printed in 1561. This book of one hundred and seventy-two pages is followed by errata covering fifteen pages. In apology, the writer says the errors were caused by the malice of the devil, who had aloud the manuscript to be drenched with water and made almost illegible before it was placed in the hands of the printers. Not content with this, the devil instigated the printers to commit a surprising number of excusable blunders.

Books of authority and reference made in the sixteen century were quite as full of errors as mpre unpretentious work. Joseph Scalinger said that he would frequently make a bet that he could find an error on any chance-selected page of the Greek Lexicon of Robert Constantine, and that he always won the bet. Chevillier adds that Constantine was responsible for just as many errors as the printer.

The Bible, as a bulky and frequently printed book, presents exceptional opportunity for error. An edition of the Vulgate printed in 1590, and said to have been made under the supervision of Pope Sixtus V, has the unenviable distinction of being full of misprints. Barker's edition of the Bible, printed in London in 1632, and nototious in the trade as the Wicked Bible, gives this rendering of the seventh commandment: Thou shalt commit adultery. For this error, undoubtedly made by a malicious compositor, the printer was fined three thousand dollars, and all obtainable copies of the edition were destroyed.[1] To prevent error, Parliament forbade all unauthorized printing of the Bible.

In his Memoirs, Baron de Grimm tells of a French author who died in a spasm of anger after he had detected more than three hundred typographical errors in a newly printed copy of his work.

It was the same spirit of mischief-making that prompted a woman in Germany to steal into her husband's printing-house by night and make an alteration for the the press by changing the German word Herr to Narr, thereby perverting the passage in Genesis iii, 16, from "he shall be thy lord" to "he shall be thy fool." The story goes that she had to atone for this silly joke with her life.

Errors of the press were and are not confined to any nation. Erasmus said that the books printed in Italy were, without exception. full of faults, due largely to the parsimony of pub-publishers who would not pay a proper price for the supervision of the copy. Books were so incorrectly printed in Spain during the sixteenth century that the authorities refused to license their publication before they had been approved by a censor appointed for the duty. He requirted that all faults noted by him should be corrected in an appended list of errata.

Chevillier says that the printers of Geneva during the sixteenth century used execrable paper and made the texts of their books intolerably incorrect. Even the famous Christopher Plantin of Antwerp was beyond reproach. One of his eulogists has

---

[1]Sometimes errata have been made purposely to gratify personal malignity. Paul Scarron, the FRench poet and writer of burlesque, wrote a book of poems in which verses were dedicated to "Guillemette, my sisters' dog." Before the book was published, Scarron qualrrelled with his sister, and ordered this erratum to be added: "Make 'Guillemette, my sister's dog' read 'Guillemette, my dog of a sister.'"

to admit sorrowfully that he found Plantin's enormous <u>Poylglot</u> <u>Bible</u> many errors of paging which his scholarly proof-<u>readers</u> had overlooked.

The apology of John Froben of Basle for his errata is really pathetic: "I do everything I can to produce correct editions. In this edition of the <u>New Testament</u> in Greek I have doubled my care and my vigilance; I have spared neither time nor money. Erasmus himself has done his best to help me." In this edition of the <u>New Testament</u> in Greek I have doubled my care and my vigilance; I have spared neither time nor money.

This book was in press for a year, but after all this care it had errata of one and a half pages. I have engaged with difficulty many correctors of the highest ability, among them John Oecolampadius, a pofessor of three languages.

Erasmus himself charged one of the workmen of Froben with intended malice in perverting (in another book) his tribute of admiration to Queen Elizabeth of Hungry to apassage of unmentionable obscenity. He declared that he would have given three hundered crowns in gold to have prevented the scandalous error.

Examples enough have been presented to show that errors are not always detected by educated printers or by scholarly co-rrectors, but the summing up may be left to earlier writers. Chevallier, writing in support of his proposition that a book without an error is impossible,[1] and that early books do not deserve the reputation they have had for superior accuracy. Prosper Marchand, writing in 1738, says that the reader is deceived who thinks that old books are more correct that new books; on they contrary, they are mush more inaccurate.

Theodore Low De Vinne
<u>The Practice of Typography:</u>
<u>Correct Composition</u>
<u>Oswald Publishing Company</u>
<u>New York 1916</u>

---

[1]Whoever thinks a faultless piece to see,
    Thinks what ne'er was, nor is, nor e'er shall be.
Pope

Exercise 28. Poetry: The Passionate Printer

Instructions: Proofread the live copy of *The Passionate Printer to His Love* by comparing it with the dead copy. Mark *only* the live copy; do *not* edit the material.

Dead copy

(Clc)

THE PASSIONATE PRINTER TO HIS LOVE*
(Whose name is Amanda)

With Apologies to the Shade of Christopher Marlowe

(Indent & block lines 2-4 of every verse)

Come live with me and be my Dear;
And till that happy bond shall lapse,
I'll set your Poutings in Brevier,
Your Praises in the largest CAPS.
There's Diamond--'tis for your Eyes;
There's Ruby--that will match your Lips;
Pearl, for your Teeth; and Minion-size
To suit your dainty Finger-tips.
In Nonpareil I'll put your Face;
In Rubric shall your Blushes rise;
There is no Bourgeois in your Case;
Your Form can never need "Revise"
Your Cheek seems "Ready for the Press";
Your Laugh as Clarendon is clear;
There's more distinction in your Dress
Than in the oldest Elzevir.
So with me live, and with me die;
And may no "Finis" e'er intrude
To break into mere "Printers' Pie"
The Type of our Beatitude!
(Erratum--If my suit you flout,
And choose some happier Youth to wed,
'Tis but to cross Amanda out,
And read another name instead.)

Macmillan

Austin Dobson in De Libris
McMillan, 1908 || FℓR

(cut off rule)

*Brevier, diamond, ruby, pearl, minion, nonpareil,
and bourgeois are names for type sizes used before
the introduction of the point system of measurement. A rubric is a red initial or line in a manuscript. A case is a drawer in a type cabinet, with
partitions for the different characters. A form is
a block of type locked up for printing. Clarendon is a
highly readable typeface. An elzevir is a small
book printed by the Elzevir press in the 18th (sp)
century. Printer's pie occurs when a form is
dropped and the characters are mixed up (pied).

Live copy

The Passionate Printer to His Love
(Whose name is Amanda)

With apologies to the shade of Christopher
Marlowe

Come live with me and be my Dear;
   And till that happy bond shall lapse,
   I'll set your Poutings in *Brevier*
   Your Praises in the largest CAPS.

There's *Diamond*—'tis for your Eyes:
   There's *Ruby*—that will match your Lips;
   Pearl, for yor teeth; and Minion-size
   To suit your dainty Fingertips.

In Nonpareil I'll put your Face;
   In Rubric shall your Blushes rise;
   Ther is no *Bourgeois* in your *Case*;
   Your Form can never need *"Revise"*.

Your Cheek seems *"Ready for the Press"*;
   Your laugh as *Clarendon* is clear;
   There's more distinction in your Dress
   Than in the oldest *Elzevir*.

So with me live, and with me die;
   And may no "FINIS" e'er intruse
   To break into mere *"Printer's Pie"*
   The Type of our Beautitude!

ERRATUM. If my suit you flout,
   And choose some happier Youth to wed.
   'Tis but to cross AMANDA out,
   And read another name instead.)
             —Austin Dobson
                in *De Libris*
              McMillan, 1908

---

*Brevier, diamond, ruby, pearl, minion, nonpareil, and
bourgeois are names for type sizes used before the introduction of the point system of measurement. A *rubric* is a red
initial or line in a manuscript. A *case* is a drawer in a type
cabinet with partitions for different characters. A form is a
block of type locked up for printing. *Clarendon* is a highly
readable typeface. An *elzevir* is a book printed by the Elzevir press in the eighteenth century. Printer's pie occurs
when a form is dropped and the characters are mixed up
(pied).

Exercise 29. Menu: Bill of Fare

Instructions: Proofread the live copy of *Bill of Fare* by comparing it with the dead copy. Mark *only* the live copy; do *not* edit the material.

Dead copy

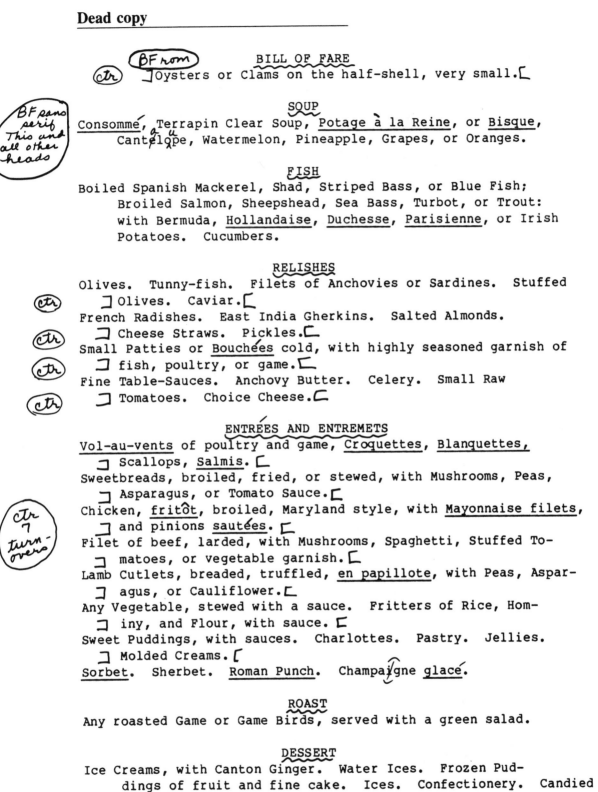

BILL OF FARE

Oysters or Clams on the half-shell, very small.

SOUP

Consommé, Terrapin Clear Soup, Potage à la Reine, or Bisque,
Cantelope, Watermelon, Pineapple, Grapes, or Oranges.

FISH

Boiled Spanish Mackerel, Shad, Striped Bass, or Blue Fish;
Broiled Salmon, Sheepshead, Sea Bass, Turbot, or Trout:
with Bermuda, Hollandaise, Duchesse, Parisienne, or Irish
Potatoes. Cucumbers.

RELISHES

Olives. Tunny-fish. Filets of Anchovies or Sardines. Stuffed
Olives. Caviar.
French Radishes. East India Gherkins. Salted Almonds.
Cheese Straws. Pickles.
Small Patties or Bouchées cold, with highly seasoned garnish of
fish, poultry, or game.
Fine Table-Sauces. Anchovy Butter. Celery. Small Raw
Tomatoes. Choice Cheese.

ENTRÉES AND ENTREMETS

Vol-au-vents of poultry and game, Croquettes, Blanquettes,
Scallops, Salmis.
Sweetbreads, broiled, fried, or stewed, with Mushrooms, Peas,
Asparagus, or Tomato Sauce.
Chicken, fritôt, broiled, Maryland style, with Mayonnaise filets,
and pinions sautées.
Filet of beef, larded, with Mushrooms, Spaghetti, Stuffed To-
matoes, or vegetable garnish.
Lamb Cutlets, breaded, truffled, en papillote, with Peas, Aspar-
agus, or Cauliflower.
Any Vegetable, stewed with a sauce. Fritters of Rice, Hom-
iny, and Flour, with sauce.
Sweet Puddings, with sauces. Charlottes. Pastry. Jellies.
Molded Creams.
Sorbet. Sherbet. Roman Punch. Champaigne glacé.

ROAST

Any roasted Game or Game Birds, served with a green salad.

DESSERT

Ice Creams, with Canton Ginger. Water Ices. Frozen Pud-
dings of fruit and fine cake. Ices. Confectionery. Candied
Fruit. Nuts. Foreign Preserves without syrup. Oriental
Sweetmeats. Coffee.

Live copy

BILL OF FARE

Oysters or Clams on the half-shell, very small.

SOUP

Consommé, Terrapin Clear Soup, *Potage à la Reine*, or *Bisque*, Cantelope, Watermelon, Pineapple, Grape Fruit, or Oranges.

FISH

Broiled Spanish Mackerel, Shad, Striped Bass, or Blue Fish; or, Boiled Salmon, Sheepshead, Sea Bass, Turbot, or Trout: with Bermuda, *Hollandaise*, *Duchesse*, *Parisienne*, or Irish Potatoes. Cucumbers.

RELISHES

Olives. Tunny-fish. Filets of Anchovies or Sardines. Stuffed Olives. Caviare.
French Radishes. East India Gherkins. Salted Almonds. Cheese Straws. Pickles.
Small Patties or *Bouchées* cold, with highly seasoned garnish of fish, poultry, or game.
Fine Table-Sauces. Anchovy Butter. Celery. Small Raw Tomatoes. Choice Cheese.

ENTRÉES AND ENTREMETS.

Vol-au-vents of poultry and game, *Croquettes*, *Blanquettes* Scallops, *Salmis*.
Sweetbreads, broiled, fried, or stewed, with Mushrooms, Peas, Asparagus, or Tomato Sauce.
Chicken, *fritôt*, broiled, Maryland style, with *Mayonnaise filets*, and pinions *sautées*.
Filet of beef, larded, with Mushrooms, Spaghetti, Stuffed Tomatoes, or vegetable garnish.
Lamb Cutlets, breaded, truffled, *en papillote*, with Peas, Asparagus, or Cauliflower.
Any Vegetable, stewed with a sauce. Fritters of Rice, Hominy, and Flour, with sauce.
Sweet Puddings, with sauces. Charlottes. Pastry. Jellies. Moulded Creams.
Sorbet. Sherbet. *Roman Punch*. Champagne *glacé*.

ROAST

Any Game or Game Birds roasted, and served with a green salad.

DESSERT

Ice Creams, with Canton Ginger. Water Ices. Frozen Puddings of fruit and fine cake. Ices. Confectionery. Candied Fruit. Nuts. Foreign Preserves without syrup. Oriental Sweetmeats. Coffee.

Exercise 30. Chemistry: Synthesis of Eudalene

Instructions: Proofread the live copy of *Synthesis of Eudalene* by comparing it with the dead copy. Mark *only* the live copy; do *not* edit the material. Assume that the typesetter is experienced in setting technical material; do not question his use of smaller type.

Dead copy

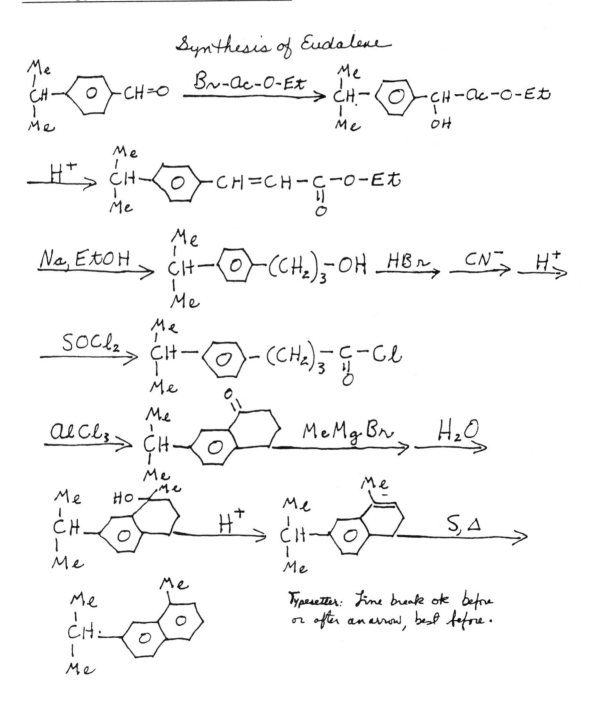

Live copy

SYNTHESIS OF EUDALENE

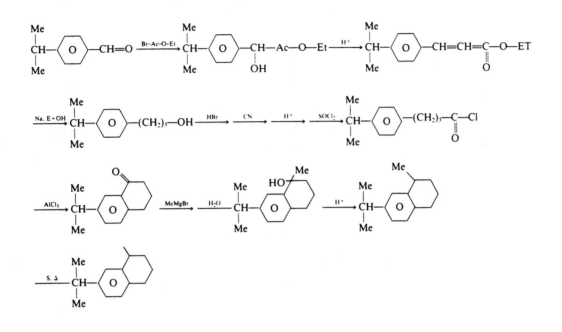

Exercise 31. Table: Market for Nuclear Plants

Instructions: Proofread the live copy of the table in this exercise by comparing it with the dead copy. Mark *only* the live copy; do *not* edit the material.

Dead copy

(handwritten proofreader's marks: "Cor col under heads"; "Bf"; "ital"; "8/9 rom"; "sp")

FIGURE 6.—MARKET FOR NUCLEAR PLANTS BY SIZE OF UNIT (1981–1990)

Capacity, MW	150	200	250	300	400	500	600	800	1000	1200	1500	Total GW
India								4	6	15		27.2
Spain									5	5	6	20.0
Poland					5			2	1	2		7.0
Brazil								2	2	6		10.8
Czechoslovakia					2		3	1	2	2		7.8
Yugoslavia							2	6	4			10.0
Romania					5		2		2			5.2
Mexico							1	4	6	8	1	20.9
Argentina							2	3	3			6.6
Bulgaria					4		4	2				5.6
Iran							3	4	5			10.0
Taiwan							7	4				7.4
Hungary					6		3					4.2
Venezuela							6	1				4.4
Korea							5	2	4			8.5
Turkey							3	4				5.0
Colombia						1	2					1.7
Greece						4	5					5.0
Pakistan							8					4.8
Egypt							7	1				5.0
Israel					6	3						3.9
Thailand		1		1	1	2	3					3.7
Peru					2	1						1.3
Philippines							2	2	2			4.8
Hong Kong				2	4	2						3.2
Chile				3	2							1.7
Cuba			2	4	1							2.1
Singapore			5		6		1					4.3
Malaysia		3	1	3								1.7
Indonesia		4		3								1.7
Republic of Viet Nam	1	4										1.0
Bangladesh		2	2		2	1	3					4.0
Uruguay	1	2	2									1.1
Kuwait	2	4	1									1.4
Iraq	2	4										1.1
Jamaica	5	2		2								1.7
Ghana	2											0.3
Morocco		2										0.4
Nigeria	2	1										0.5
Algeria	3											0.45
Lebanon	0											0.
Syria	3											0.45
Cameroon	0											0.
Costa Rica	2											0.3
Dominican Republic	1											0.15
Ecuador	1											0.15
Panama	1											0.15
Albania	1											0.15

Bf FIGURE 6.--MARKET FOR NUCLEAR PLANTS BY SIZE OF UNIT (1981-1990) (CONTINUED)

Capacity, MW	150	200	250	300	400	500	600	800	1000	1200	1500	Total GW
Uganda.	1											0.15
Tunisia	1											0.15
Bolivia	1											0.15
Zambia.	1											0.15
Saudi Arabia.	1											0.15
Guatemala	1											0.15
Liberia	1											0.15
El Salvador	1											0.15
Sudan	0											0.
Number of Units . . . . .⊐35⊏		⊐29⊏	⊐13⊏	⊐18⊏	46	14	72	42	42	38	7	⊐356⊏
Total Capacity, GW. . .	5.3	5.8	3.3	5.4	18.4	7.0	43.2	34.4	42.0	45.6	10.5	220.0

SOURCE: Market Survey for Nuclear Power in Developing Countries: General Report published September 1973; Update Report published 1974.

Reports available from the International Atomic Energy Agency and its agents.

Live copy

FIGURE 6—MARKET FOR NUCLEAR PLANTS BY SIZE OF UNIT (1981–1990)

Capacity, MW	150	200	250	300	400	500	600	800	1000	1200	1500	Total GW
India								4	6	15		27.2
Spain									5	5	6	20.0
Poland					5			2	1	2		7.0
Brazil								2	2	6		10.8
Czechoslovakia					2		3	1	2	2		7.8
Yugoslavia							2	6	4			10.0
Romania					5		2		2			5.2
Mexico							1	4	6	8		20.9
Argentina							2	3	3			6.6
Bulgaria					4		4	2				5.6
Iran							3	4	5			10.0
Taiwan							7	4				7.4
Hungary					6		3					4.2
Venezuela							6	1				4.4
Korea							5	2	4			8.5
Turkey							3	4				5.0
Columbia						1	2					1.7
Greece						4	5					5.0
Pakistan							8					4.8
Egypt							7	1				5.0
Israel					6	3						3.9
Thailand		1		1	1	2	3					3.7
Peru					2	1						1.3
Philippines							2	2	2			4.8
Hong Kong				2	4	2						3.2
Chile				3	2							1.7
Cuba			2	4	1							2.1
Singapore			5		6		1					4.3
Malaysia		3	1	3								1.7
Indonesia		4		3								1.7
Rep. Viet Nam	1	4										1.0
Bangladesh		2	2		2	1	3					4.0
Uruguay	1	2	2									1.1
Kuwait	2	4	1									1.4
Iraq	2	4										1.1
Jamaica	5	2		2								1.7
Ghana	2											0.3
Morocco		2										0.4
Nigeria	2	1										0.5
Algeria	3											0.45
Lebanon	0											0.
Syria	3											0.45
Cameroon	0											0.
Costa Rica	2											0.3
Dominican Rep	1											0.15
Ecuador	1											0.15
Panama	1											0.15
Albania	1											0.15
Uganda	1											0.15
Tunisia	1											0.15
Bolivia	1											0.15
Zambia	1											0.15
Saudi Arabia	1											0.15
Guatemala	1											0.15
Liberia	1											0.15
El Salvador	1											0.15
Sudan	0											0.
Number of Units	35	29	13	18	46	14	72	42	42	38	7	356
Total Capacity, GW	5.3	5.8	3.3	5.4	18.4	7.0	43.2	34.4	42.0	45.6	10.5	220.0

SOURCE: Market Survey for Nuclear Power in Developing Countries: General Report published September 1973: Update Report published 1974.

Reports available from the International Atomic Energy Agency and its agents.

Exercise 32. Technical copy: Epinephrine Physiology

Instructions: Proofread the live copy of *Epinephrine* by comparing it with the dead copy. Mark *only* the live copy; do *not* edit the material.

Dead copy

(ctr)]EPINEPHRINE PHYSIOLOGY [

The manifold catabolic effects of epinephrine are due, in part, to an amplification cascade of the molecule's signal via a pathway involving 3',5'-monophosphate (cAMP) as a second messenger.

Cyclic AMP is formed by the reaction of adenyl cyclase, a membrane-bound enzyme, on ATP. The reaction is slightly endergonic, driven by the hydrolysis of pyrophosphate.

The hormone's principle site of action is the exterior surface of the plasma membrane. Epinephrine (10^{-10}M to 10^{-8}M) binds to a specific receptor, allosterically activating pro-adenyl cyclase, which then catalyzes the synthesis of cAMP at a maximum concentration of 10^{-6}M. Inactive protein kinase is bound to cAMP, releasing its regulatory subunit, disinhibiting its catalytic subunit. Active protein kinase then catalyzes the phosphorylation of dephospho-phosphorylase kinase, in the presence of Ca^{++}, which, in turn, activates phosphorylase b, yielding phosphorylase a. Finally, phosphorylase a acts on glycogen to yield glucose-1-phosphate, which, after isomerization to glucose-6-phosphate and dephosphorylation, is secreted from the ~~hepatcyte~~ hepatocyte into the blood.

Of course, with the exceptions of the initial binding, the isomerization, and the dephosphorylation, the reactions are endergonic. Since each step in the process is catalytic, the net effect is one of amplification of signal.

Epinephrine and the other catecholamines are bound to ATP and proteins and stored in granules in the medulla. Acetylcholine released from the preganglionic neurons increases the permeability of the secretory cells to Ca^{++} in the extracellular fluid, triggering exocytosis.

Epinephrine physiology thus has a two-fold significance: release is triggered by a nervous impulse, meeting the need for a quick response; and mediation by cAMP amplifies its small quantity to a general metabolic effect.

EPINEPHRINE PHYSIOLOG

The manifold catabolic effects of epinephrine are due in part to an amplification cascade of the molecule's signal via a pathway involving $3',5'$-monophosphate (cAMP) as a second messenger,

Cyclic AMP is formed by the reaction of adynl cyclase, a membrane-bound enzyme, on ATP. The reaction is slightly endergonic, driven by the hydrolysis of pyrophosphate.

The hormone's principle site of action is the exterior surface of the palsma membrane. Epinephrine (10^{-10}M to 10^{-8}M) bind to a specific receptor, allostericalty activating pro-adynl cyclase, which then catalyzes the synthesis of cAMP at a maximum concentration of 10^{-6}M. inactive protein kinase is bound to cAMP, releasing its regulatory subunit, disinhibiting its catalytic subunit. Active protein kinase then catalyzes the phos phorylation of dephosphophosphorylase kinase, in the presence of CA^{++}, which in turn activates phosphorylase b, yielding phosphorylase a. Finally, phosphorylase a acts on glycogen to yoield glucose-1-phosphate, which, after isomerization to glucose-6-phosphate and dephosphorylation, is secreted from the hepatacyte into the blood. Of course, with the exceptions of the initial binding, the isomerization, and the dephosphorylition, the reactions are endergonic. Since each step is catalytic, the net effect is one of amplification of signal.

Epinephrine and the other catecholamines are bound to ATP and the other catecholamines are bound to ATP and proteins and stored in grains in the medulla. Acetylcholine released from the pre-ganglionic neurons increase the permeability of the secretory cells to Ca^{++} in the extracellular fluids, triggering exocytosis.

Epinephrine physiology thus has a two-fold significance. Release is triggered by a nervous impulse, meeting the need for a quick response; and mediation by cAMP amplifies its small quantity to a general metabolic defect.

Exercise 33. Special material

Instructions: Dry read the following material at level 2. Use proofmarks.

A. Financial statement:

Fairfax Sunday College
Income Statement
For Year Ended December 31, 1992

Revenues		
Tuition Fees Earned	$527,000	
Endowment Income	42,200	
		$569,200
Operating Expenses		
Salaries Expense	$231,500	
Rent Expense	90,000	
Office Suppies Expense	1,375	
Utilities expense	1,900	
Miscellaneous Expense	274	
Total Operating Expense		$325,049
Net Income		$244,511

B. Text for a bronze plaque to be placed on a vehicle:

In Fond Memory of
Dr. George Jason Jemiston,
His Friends
Have Donated This Mobile Medical Unit to
Feathersville Area Emergency Services, Inc.
(FACES)
Honoring the Doctor's Lifelong Commitment
To Serve his Community

C. Headlines:

1. BAN ON SOLICITING DEAD IN TROTWOOD
2. BEATING WITNESS PROVIDES NAMES
3. ALL UTAH CONDEMNED TO FACE FIRING SQUAD
4. BABY NAMED AFTER HER COUSIN
5. WOMAN HELD IN FIRE
6. DOCTOR TESTIFIES IN HORSE SUIT
7. POLICE KILL MAN WITH AX
8. POLICE RUN DOWN SPEEDERS

Exercise 34. Sorted material:
Directory and Miscellaneous Publishers

Instructions: For this exercise, you will be comparing dissimilar copy. The dead copy is a list of addresses sorted in alphabetical order. The live copy has been sorted over again according to these instructions:

> Typist: Type address labels on computer. Address each to Managing Editor, and code each S038. Use ZIP code state abbreviations. Remember that the program will accept no more than 25 characters or spaces on a line, that each field must be kept on one line, and that the program won't print commas.

Your job is to see if the typist did everything right and, if not, to mark the live copy for corrections. Because there are no margins and the copy is single spaced, you will need to use a combination of editing and proofreading marks—editing marks where they are clear and proofreading marks, sometimes with a guide line, where there's no room above an error to write.

Dead copy

```
          DIRECTORY AND MISCELLANEOUS PUBLISHERS
Allied Graphic Arts, Inc.
1515 Broadway
New York, N.Y. 10036

American Elsevier Publisher, Inc.
2 Park Ave.
New York, N.Y. 10016

American Printing House for the Blind
1839 Frankfort Ave.
Louisville, Ky.  40206

Aspen Systems Corp.
20010 Century Blvd.
Germantown, Md. 20767

Audio-Digest Foundation
1577 E. Chevy Chase Dr.
Glendale, Calif. 91206

Bureau of Business Practice
24 Rope Ferry Rd.
Waterford, Conn. 06386
```

[handwritten insert:] Brentano's Inc.
545 Fifth Ave.
New York, N.Y. 10017

Bureau of National Affairs, Inc.
1231 25th St. N.W.
Washington, D.C. 20037

Catalogue Service
of Westchester
159 Main St.
New Rochelle, N.Y. 10801

Concord Reference Books Inc.
135 W. 50th St.
New York, N.Y. 10020

General Telephone Directory Co.
2004 Miner St.
Des Plaines, Ill. 60016

Gibson C R Co Inc.
32 Knight St.
Norwalk, Conn. 06856

Grandville Printing Co., Inc.
4520 Spartan Industrial Dr.
Grandville, Mich. 49418

Inter-Collegiate Press, Inc.
6015 Travis Lane
Shawnee Mission, Kansas 66202

Martindale-Hubbell, Inc.
630 Central Ave.
New Providence, N.J. 07974

McCall Publishing Co.
230 Park Ave.
New York, N.Y. 10017

Music Sales Corp.
799 Broadway
New York, N.Y. 10003

New York Graphic Society, Ltd.
140 Greenwich Ave.
Greenwich, Conn. 06830

Official Airlines Guides
20000 Clearwater Dr.
Oak Brook, Ill. 60621

Pace Publication Arts, Inc.
3531 E. Miraloma
Anaheim, Calif. 92806

Packard Press Corp.
10th and Spring Garden Sts.
Philadelphia, Pa. 19123

Real Estate Data, Inc.
2398 N.W. 119th St.
Miami, Fla. 33167

Sidwell Co., Inc.
28 W. 240 North Ave.
West Chicago, Ill. 60185

Simplicity Pattern Co., Inc.
200 Madison Ave.
New York, N.Y. 10016

ThunderGrass Music, Ltd.
3340 Broadway
Riviera Beach, Fla. 33404

Van Dyck Printing Co.
370 State St.
North Haven, Conn. 06473

Wards Natural Science, Inc.
5100 Henrietta Rd.
Rochester, N.Y. 14622

Whitney Communications Corp.
110 W. 51st St.
New York, N.Y. 10020

Ziff-Davis Publishing Co.
One Park Ave.
New York NY 10016

Live copy

```
..........................................................................................
         S038 .              S038 .                        S038
Managing Editor          . Managing Editor        . Managing Editor
Bureau of Bus. Practice  . Van Dyck Printing Co.   . New York Graphic Soc.
24 Rope  Ferry Rd.       . 370 State st.           . 140 Greenwich Ave.
Waterford CT 06386       . North Haven CT 06473    . Greenwich CT 06830
..........................................................................................
         S038 .              S038 .                        S038
Managing Editor          . Managing Editor        . Music Sales Corp.
Gibson C R Co Inc        . Martindale-Hubbell Inc. . 799 Briadway
32 Knight St             . 630 Central Ave.        . New York NY 1ooo3
Norwalk CT 06956         . New Providence NJ 07974 .
..........................................................................................
         S038 .              S038 .                        S0388
Managing Editor          . Managing Editor        . Managing Editor
American Elsevier Publ.  . Simplicity Pattren Co.  . Ziff-Davis Publishing Co
2 Park Ave.              . 200 Madison Ave.        . One Park Ave.
New York NY 10016        . New York NT 10016       . New York NY 100016
..........................................................................................
         S038 .              S038 .                        S038
Managing Editors         . Managing Editor        . Managing Editor
Brentano´s Inc.          . McCall Publishing Co.   . Concord Reference Books
545 Fifth Ave.           . 230 Park Ave.           . 135 W. 50th St.
New York NY 10017        . New York NY 10017       . New York NY 10020
..........................................................................................
         S038 .              S038 .                        S083
Managing Editor          . Managing Editor        . Managing Editor
Whitney Communications   . Allied Graphic Arts Inc . Catalogue Srv Westchester
110 W 51st St.           . 1515 Broadway           . 159 Main St.
New York NY 10020        . New York NY 10036       . New Rochelle NY 10801
..........................................................................................
         S038 .              SO38 .                        S038
Managing Editor          . Managing Editor        . Managing Editor
Wards National Science   . Packard Press Corp.     . Bureau of Natl Affairs
5100 Henrietta Rd.       . 10th & Sring Garden Sts . 1231 25th St. N.W.
Rochester NY 14622       . Philadelphia PA 19132   . Washington DC 20037
..........................................................................................
         S038 .              S038 .                        S038
Managing Editor          . Managing Editor        . Managing Editor
Aspen Systems Corp.      . Real Estate Data Inc.   . ThunderGrass Music Ltd.
20010 Century Blvd.      . 2398 N.W. 119th St.     . 3340 Broadway
Germantown MD 20767      . iami FL 33167           . Riviera Beach FL 33404
..........................................................................................
         S038 .              S038 .                        S038
Managing Editor          . Managing Edtior        . Managing Editor
Am. Printng Hse fr Blind . Grandville Printing Co.  . Sidwell Co., Inc.
1839 Frankfurt Ave.      . 4520 Spartan Industrial . 28 W. 240 North Ave.
Louisville KY. 40206     . Grandville MI 49418     . West Chicago IL 60185
..........................................................................................
         S037 .              S038 .                        S038
Managing Editor          . Managing Editor        . Managing Editor
Official Airlines Guides . Inter-Collegiate Press   . Pace Publication Arts
20000 Clearwater Dr.     . 6015 Travis Lane        . 3531 Miraloma
Oak Brook IL 60621       . Shawnee Mission KS 66202. Anaheim CA 92806
```

Exercise 35. Querying

Instructions: Query the faults you find in the following. Assume that the live copy duplicates the dead and that you have no authority to correct errors other than PEs.

Live copy

1. Other show business personalities who lending their names to good causes are happy—and indeed inwardly content—merely to be listed on the notepaper and to make occasional speeches.

2. With your right hand, take ahold of lever A.

3. A look at the issues and consequences of last fall's prolonged teachers' strike at Levitttown.

4. Application of these methods in stores in San Diego and Houston have resulted in a 30 percent drop in robberies.

5. *Bookkeeping*
   Interested in producing your own honey? Two courses on beekeeping will be offered by the Beekeeper's Association of Northern Virginia in conjunction with the County extension service at

6. Intenational and Unintentional Modification of the Atmosphere

7. *Parishoners Celebrate*

8. A total of forty-seven interviews were conducted with approximate equal coverage of the four countries in the report.

9. In order to elicit specific responses, we selected for each respondent a sub-sample of between five and ten documents that had been sent to the respondents' office.

10. **TABLE 4.1.—PERCEPTION OF ROLE IN FOREIGN POLICY REPORTING SYSTEM**

Role	# of Producers	% of Total Producers
Reporter	20	42.6%
Research Analyst	12	25.5%
Operational-Administrative	7	14.9%
Combination of Two of the Above	8	17.0%
	47	

Exercise 36. AAs and PEs

Instructions: Proofread the following dead copy against the following live copy. Use standard marks to correct PEs (where the live copy fails to follow the dead copy, the specifications, or normal standards) and to correct AAs (blatant errors, including misspellings, that appear in the dead copy and are repeated in the live). Label the AAs as shown in the example.

Remember not to change material from previously printed sources; it must be quoted exactly. (For this exercise, assume that the writer got the quotations right.)

Example:

Dead copy

```
Mary had a little lamb;
It's fleece was white as snow,
And everyone that Mary went
The lamb was sure to go.
```

Live copy

Marie had a little lamb;
It's fleece was white as snow,
And everyone that Mary went
The lamb was sure go.

Dead copy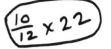

⌐ The rule for marking printer's errors (PEs) only--~~and not~~
to the exclusion (stet) ~~marking even the worst of~~ author's errors (AAs)--was *first* recorded

~~first~~ in 1608 by Jerome Hornisch of the Beyer printing office in

Meiningen, germany. Writing of "a conscientious corrector," he
said,
~~made the following unequivocal statement:~~ "Never should he make

changes in the text, even though he believes it would be improved

there by."

Exactly the same rule applies to a compisotor, of course.
Joseph
As Moxon wrote (in <u>Mechanick Exercises on the Whole Art of</u>

<u>Printing</u>, 1683/84), "By the Laws of Printing, a Compositor is

strictly to follow his Copy, viz. to observe and do just so much

and no more than his Copy will bear him out for; so that his Copy

is to be his Rule and ~~his~~ Authority."
however,
~~But~~ <u>u</u>nlike today, ~~back~~ in Moxon's time and later, the Laws

of Printing required compositors and proofreaders to correct
bad
~~errors in~~ spelling and ~~in~~ puntuation.

To quote *on the compositor's responsibility in*
¶ ~~On this topic,~~ Moxon ~~wrote the following:~~ *the 17th century.*

> The carelessness of some good Authors, and the ig-
> norance of other Authors, has forc'd Printers to in-
> troduce a Custom, which among them is look'd upon as
> a task and duty incumbent on the Compositor, viz. to
> discern and amend the bad Spelling and Pointing of his
> Copy, if it be English; But if it be in any Forrain
> Language, the Author is wholy left to his own Skill
> and Judgement in Spelling and Pointing.

And to quote <u>The Inland Printer</u> of May 1897 on "The

Proofreader's Responsibility" (italics added):

Strictly speaking, the responsibility of a
proofreader should be very narrowly defined. In an
ideal state of affairs it would never go beyond the
close following of copy in every detail....The limit
[of] the proofreader's responsibility...is merely the
exact reproduction of what is written, as to the
wording, but including proper spelling and
punctuation.

separate dots in ellipses: ⓒ # ① # ☉

Print shops today put many more ~~constraints~~ *limits* on

responsibility; they ~~expect~~ *train* compositors and comparison

proofreaders to "follow copy out the window"—even though correct

spelling and punctuation go out the window, too.

As another arcitle, in the September 1897 Inland Printer

~~explains~~ *says*, "You must remember that the customers of printing offices

think they know a thing or two, and nothing is gained by doing

their work in such a manner as to arouse their antagonism...no

matter how much more you may know about how it ought to be done."

A solution to the problem is querying. Says the earlier

Inland Printer: "Even hurried work from manuscript can

generally be referred to the author in cases of real

doubt....Submission of [queries] to the author for his

decision should be an important feature of the

proofreader's responsibility."

Live copy

The rule for making printer's errors (PEs) only—to the exclusion of author's errors (AAs)—was first recorded in 1608 by Jerome Hornisch of the Beyer printing office in Meiningen, germany. Writing of "a con scientious corrector," he said, "Never should he make changes in the text, even though he beleives it would be improved there by."

The same rule applies to a compisotor, of course. As Joseph Moxon wrote (in*Mechanick Exercises on the Whole Art of Print*, 1683–84), "By the Laws of Printing, a Compositor is strictly to follow his Copy, viz. to observe and do just so much and no more than his Copy will bear him out for; so that his Copy is to be his rule and Authority."

Unlike today, however, in Moxon's time and later, the Laws of Printing required compositors and proofreaders to correct bad spelling and puntuation. To quote Moxon on the compositor's responsibility in the 17th century—

> The carelessness of some good Authors, and the ignorance of other Authors, has forced Printers to introduce a Custom, which among them is look'd upon as a task and duty incumbent on the Compositor, viz. to discern and amend the bad Spelling and Pointing of his Copy, if it be English; But if it be in any Forrain Language, the Author is wholy left to his own Skill and Judgment in Spelling and Punctuation.

And to quote *The Inland Printer* of May 1897 on "The Proofreader's Responsibilities":

> Strictly speaking, the responsibility of a proofreader should be narrowly defined. In an ideal state of affairs it would never go beyond the close following of copy in every detail . . . The limit [of the proofreader' responsibility . . . is merely the exact reproduction of what is written, as to wording, but including proper spelling and punctuation.

Print shops today put more limits on responsibillity; they expect compositors and comparison proofreader to "follow copy out the window"—even though correct spelling and punctuation go out the window, too.

As another arcitle in the September 1897 *Inland Printer* says, "You must remember that the customers of printing offices think they know a thing or two, and nothing is gained by doing their work in such a manner as to arouse their antagonism . . . no matter how much more you may know about how it ought to be done."

A solution to the problem is querying. Says the earlier *Inland Printer:* "Even hurried work from manuscript can generally be referred to the author in cases of real doubt . . . Submission of [queries] to the author for his decision should be an unimportant feature of the proofreader's responsibility."

Exercise 37. General proofreading: De Vinne on Errors of the Press

Instructions: Proofread the live copy of *De Vinne on Errors of the Press* by comparing it with the dead copy. Mark *only* the live copy; do not *edit* the material. Note that when footnote numbers in the dead copy start at 1 on every page, the numbers in the live copy usually have to be changed to accommodate to changes in paging (as in this exercise). Note that footnote format may change, too. In this exercise, the footnotes in the dead copy are set off from the text with extra line spacing and small type. The footnotes in the live copy are set off with a short rule.

Dead copy

] De Vinne on Errors of the Press [

Errors of the press often begin with errors of reporters who have misunderstood spoken words. The rule of follow copy compels the compositor to repeat the exact words written by the reporter, and the following blunders are the result of obedience to this rule. A speaker made this statement:

In these days clergymen are expected to have the wisdom and learning of Jeremy Taylor.

But the reporter wrote, and the compositor repeated:

. . . the wisdom and learning of a journeyman tailor.

Another speaker quoted these lines:

O come, thou goddess fair and free,
In heaven yclept Euphrosyne.

They were printed as written:

O come, thou goddess fair and free,
In heaven she crept and froze her knee.

Another orator quoted this line from Tennyson's *Locksley Hall:*

Better fifty years of Europe than a cycle of Cathay.

But the quotation was written and printed:

Better fifty years of Europe than a circus in Bombay.

One of the worst perversions of a hackneyed quotation (incorrectly given by the speaker) is this, which seems to be the joint work of the zealous reporter and the equally reckless printer:

Amicus Plato, amicus Socrates, sed major veritas.
I may cuss Plato, I may cuss Socrates, said Major Veritas.

Here are other illustrations of the great danger of following the sound regardless of the sense:

Those lovely eyes bedimmed.
Those lovely eyes be damned.
Behold the martyr in a sheet of fire!
Behold the martyr in a shirt on fire!
This battle-scarred veteran.
This battle-scared veteran.[1]

A congressman advocated grants of public lands, not to railroad corporations, but to "actual settlers." The tired translator of the telegraphic report of the speech construed the last words as "cattle stealers."

[1] Pendleton, Newspaper Reporting, pp. 172–183.

set in text size

the word platoon, and thought it proper to make this foolish correction. It must have been a raw compositor of this class who set Dogs of the League, and parboiled sceptic for purblind sceptic. These wild guesses at the meaning of the writer had to be hazarded when writing was indistinct.

Many pages could be filled with illustrations of similar blunders—some silly or unmeaning, others frightful or blasphemous—but in most instances it is evident that the blunders were the outcome of careless or illegible writing. The compositor who is told to follow copy learns to do so mechanically, even if his rendering does not "make sense."

A critical reader may ask why the master printer ~~does not avert, or go many errors~~ ~~to a paragraph.~~

¶ • • Even when exceeding care has been taken ~~in the selection of the compositors and readers~~, there is liability to error from oversights and unforeseen accidents. Crapelet[1] tells us of the sore distress of his father in discovering the error of Pelenope for Penelope, in a treatise which he had carefully read three times with intent to make it in all points a faultless book. He had read it too often; he did not have the assistance of a second reader; and his memory failed when most needed. Even the careful reader may pass unobserved the transposition of letters or syllables in a proper name. Looking too intently on one object does not always make that object more distinct; it may produce a temporary obscurity. Proof read and corrected too often by one reader only may have errors in the last proof that did not exist in the first.

[1] Études pratiques et littéraires sur la typographie, p. 233.

An editor closed his leader concerning some municipal abuse that he wished to reform with the quoted Latin lament, *o tempora! o mores!* which the compositor transformed to "O temperance! O Moses!" and it was so printed.

A reporter of a trial tried to write that "the jury disagreed and were discharged," but he wrote indistinctly, and the compositor construed the writing into "the jury disappeared and were disgraced."

A petitioner appealed to a legislature as "individuals" as well as lawmakers. He wrote illegibly, and the clerk read "indian devils" instead of individuals, much to the indignation of the assembly. Drew[1] attributes these blunders to bad writing:

The book Typographical Antiquities was cited as Typographical Ambiguities.

In testimony concerning a compound microscope the witness said that its efficiency would vary with the power of the "eye-piece" employed. Eye-piece was too carelessly written, and the compositor rendered it as lye-juice.

At a public dinner this toast was offered to the President, "May he live to a green old age." But it was printed, "May he live to a grim old age."

The last words of the poorly written sentence, "Alone and isolated, man would become impotent and perish," were not understood by the compositor, and they were printed as "impatient and peevish."

A bloody battle was so described in a newspaper:

It was fearful to see. The men fell in ranks and marched in pantaloons to their final account.

It is probable that the compositor did not know

[1] Pens and Types, pp. 16-24.

379

¶ ... Errors are frequently made by the compositor who corrects a proof: in trying to correct one error he may make another ~~and he may damage adjacent letters~~ ... Whenever he makes any change in type that has not been marked on the proof, he should take another proof and draw a large ring with lead-pencil around the place of change, and the proof-reader should re-read the entire paragraph by copy as if it were new composition. ~~A similar marking should be made by the electrotyper or the pressman who has bruised letters in a plate, so that~~

¶ ... Authors who correct the final proof with a lead-pencil provoke the making of new errors. They note an error in phrasing and write down the correction. After re-reading this correction they see that it does not fully convey the meaning intended. The first pencil markings are rubbed out and other words take their place. Sometimes two or three alterations have to be made, and all are written over markings previously made. Repeated rubbing out makes the writing illegible and liable to perversion. Sometimes an addition is made to a singular nominative which should compel the selection of a plural form of verb or pronoun in the words that precede or follow, but the plural forms may be and often are overlooked. ... ~~When the press is kept waiting for this final proof, it is possible that the errors corrected will be those only that are marked in the proof.~~ It follows that the author as well as the printer has to suffer the stigma of an inexcusable violation of plain grammatical rules.[1]

set in text size

[1] Here is the story of an error not made by a compositor or reader, pressman or mischief-maker. An author, intent on having an immaculate book, and not content with the official reading of the printing-house, had the last proof revised by another expert reader, who certified that the last reading was without fault. The book was printed, bound, and distributed, and bragged of as a book without an error. A year after publication the author, in making a cursory reëxamination of the work, discovered this phrase, "his too nasty steps." Filled with anger and alarm, he went to the printing-house and demanded the reason why this shocking alteration had been made. The last proof was found and it plainly showed that the phrase was "his too hasty steps." It was clear that a change had been made after the final reading, and possibly in the electro-type plate. The plate was sent for, and, when closely examined under a magnifying-glass, revealed the origin of the error. The solder which fastened the copper shell to the lead base had a minute air-bubble under the top of this letter h, which was unseen and unsuspected by the electrotyper. Some copies of the book (how many could not be ascertained) showed this letter h accurately, but after several perfect copies had been printed, a knot in the paper or a grain of sand or plaster had fallen over the top of this letter h, and had crushed or depressed it in the hollow air-bubble below, practically changing it to the letter n. This depression of the letter h was too small a fault to be noticed by the pressman, who could give but a glance at the sheets when the press was printing apparently faultless copies at the rate of fifteen in a minute.

Live copy

J. De Vinne on Errors of the Press

Errors of the press often beginn with errors of reporters who have misunderstood spoken words. The rule of follow copy compels the compositor to repeat trhe exact words written by the reporter, and the following blunders are the result of obedience to this rule. A speaker made this statement:

In these days clergyman are expected to have the wisdom and learning of Jeremey Taylor.

But the reporter wrote, and the compositor repeated:

...the wisdom and learning of a journeyman tailor.

Another speaker quoted these:

O come, thou goddess fair and free,
In heaven yelept Euphrosyne.

They were printed as written:

O come, thou goddess fair and free,
In heaven she cretp and froze her knee.

Another orator quoted this line from Tennyson's *Locksley Hall*:

Better fifty years of Europe than a cycle of Cathy.

But the quotation was written and printed:

Better fifty years of Europe than a circus in Bombay.

One of the worst perversions of a hackneyed quotation (incorrectly given by the speaker) is this, which seems to be the joint work of the zeal reporter and the equally reckless printer:

Amicus Plato, amicus Socrates, sed major v eritas.
I may cuss Plato, I may cuss Socrates, said Major Veritas.

Here are the other illustrations of the danger of the following the sound regardless of the sense:

Those lovely eyes bedimmed,
Those lovely eyes be dammned.
Behold the matry in a sheet of fire,
Behjold the martyr in a shirt on fire.

This battle-scarred veteran.
This battle-scared veteran.1

A congress advocated grants of public lands, not to railroad corporations, but to "actual settlers." The tired translater of the telegraphic report of the speech construed the last words as "cattle stealers."

An editor close his leader concerning some municipal abuse that he wished to reform with the quoted Latin lament, *o tempora. or mores.* which the compositor transformed to "O temporance. O Moses." and it was so printed.

A reporter of a trail tried to write that "the jury

Examples of gross modern blunders 353

disagreed and were discharged," but he wrote indistinctly, and the compositor construed the writing into "the jury disappeared and were disaraced."

A petitioner appealed to a legislature as "individuals" as well as lawmekers. He wrote illegibly, and the clerk read "indian devils" instead of individuals, much toi the indignation of the assembly.

Drew2 attributes these blunders to bad writing:

The book Antiquities was cited as Topographical Ambiguities.

In testimony concerning a compound microscope the witness said its efficiency would vary with the power of the "eye-piece" employed. Eye-piece was to careflessly written, and the compositor rendered it as lye-juice.

At a public dinner this toast was offered to the President, "May he live to a gree old age," But it was printed, "May he live to a grim old age."

1Pendleton, Newspaper Reporting, ppp. 172-183.
2Pens and Types, pp. 16-24.

The last words of the poorly written sentence, "Alone and isolated, man would become impotent and perish," were not understood by the compositor, and they were printed as "impatient and peevish,"

A bloody battle was so describedin a newspaper:

It was fearful to see. The men feel in tanks and marched in pantaloons to their final account.

It is probable that the compoisotr did not know the word platoon, and thought it proper to make this foolish correction. It must have been a raw compositor of this class who set Dogs of the Sein for Days of the Legue, and parboiled sceptic for purblind sceptic. These wild guesses at the meaning of the writer had to be hazarded when writing was indistinct.

Many pages could be filled with illustrations of similar blunders—some silly or unmeaning, other frightful or blasphemous—but in most instances it is evident that the blunders were the outcome of careless or illegible writing. The compositor who is told to follow copy learns to do so mechanically, even if his rendering does not "make sense."

. . . Even when exceeding care has been taken . . . there is liability to error from oversights and unforeseen accidents. Crapelet tell us of the sore distress of his father in discovering the error Pelenope for Penelope, in a treatise which he had carefully read three times with intent to make it in all points a faultless book. He had read it too often; he did not have the assistance of a second reader; and his memory failed when most needed. Even the careful reader may pass unobserved the transposition of letters or syllables in a proper name. :ppking too intently on one object does not always make that object more distinct; it may produce temporary obscurity, Proof read and corredt too often by one reader only may have errors in the last proof that did not exist in the first.

. . . Errors are frequently made by the compositor who correct a proof; in trying to correct one error he may make another. Whenever he makes any change in type that has not been marked on the proof, he should take another proof and draw a large ring with lead-pencil around the place of change, and the proof-reader should re-read the entire paragraph by copy as if it were new composition.

. . . Authors who correct the final proof with a lead-pencil provoke the making of new errors. They note an error in phrasing and write down their correction. After re-reading this correction they see that it does not fully convey the meaning intended. The first pencil markings are rubbed other words take their place. Sometime two or three alterrations have to be made, and all are written over markings previously made. Repeated rubbing out makes the writing illegible and liable to perversion. Sometimes an addition is made to a singular nominative which should compel the selection of a plural form of verb or pronoun in the words that precede or follow, but the plural forms may be and often are overlooked . . . It follows that the author as well as the printer has to suffer the stigma of an inexcusable violation of plain grammatical rules.[1]

---

[1] Here is the study of an error not made by a compisotor or reader, pressman or mischiefmaker. An author, intent on having an immaculate book, and not intent with the official reading of the printing-house, had the last proof revised by another expert reader, who certified that the last reading was without fault. The book was bound and distributed, and bragged of as a book without an error. A year after publication the author, in making a cursory reexamination of the work, discovered the phrase, "his too nasty steps." Filed with anger, and alarm, he went to the printing-house and demanded the reason why this shocking alteration had been made. The last proof was found and it plainly showed that the phrase was "his too hasty steps." It was clear that a change had been made later the final reading, and possibly in the electrotype plate. The plate was sent for, and when closely examined under a magnifying-glass, revealed the origin of the error. The solder which fastened the copper shell to the lead base was unseen and unsuspected by the electro-typer. Some copies of the book (how many could not be ascertained) showed that letter h accurately, but after several perfect copies had been printed, a knot in the paper or a grain of sand or plaster had fallen over the top of this letter h, and had crushed or depressed it in the hollow air-bubble below, practically changing it to the letter n. This depession of the letter h was too small a fault to be noticed by the pressman, who could give but a glance at the sheets when the press was printing apparently faultless copies at the rate of fifteen in a minute.

Exercise 38. Aldus Manutius

Instructions: With this exercise you can test your proofreading speed in relation to the key-boarding speed.

When you've finished reading these instructions, including the note below, and when you're ready to work and have a sharp pencil in your hand and the live and dead copy side by side, set a timer.

First, do a word-by-word, line-by-line solo comparison proofreading. Record the time you took.

Next, set the timer again, and review or check the copy as you normally would. Record the time you took.

The instructions for figuring your speed and accuracy appear at the end of the answer key.

NOTE: Assume that all specs have been met and that there is nothing to query. The text of this exercise is quoted from an old book; ignore such seeming problems as the old-fashioned use of capitals, the strange use of commas, the hyphen in "proof-reading," and the British spellings (utilising, labour, centre, etc.).

Dead copy

ALDUS MANUTIUS

(Excerpted from Books and Their Makers During the Middle Ages
by Geo. Haven Putnam, reprinted from an 1896-1897 edition by
Hillary House Publishers of New York in 1962)

Aldus Manutius was born at Bassiano in the Romagna in
1450, the year in which Gutenberg completed his printing-
press. He studied in Rome and in Ferrara, and after having
mastered Latin, he devoted himself, under the tutorship of
Guarini of Verona, to the study of Greek. Later, he delivered
lectures on the Latin and Greek classics. One of his fellow
students in Ferrara was the precocious young scholar Pico
della Mirandola, whose friendship was afterwards of material
service. In 1482, when Ferrara was being besieged by the
Venetians and scholarly pursuits were interrupted, Aldus was
the guest of Pico at Mirandola, where he met Emanuel
Adramyttenos, one of the many Greek scholars who, when driven
out of Constantinople, had found refuge in the Courts of
Italian princes. Aldus spent two years at Mirandola, and
under the influence and guidance of Adramyttenos, he largely
increased his knowledge of the language and literature of
Greece. His friend had brought from the East a number of manuscripts, many of which found their way into the library of
Pico.

In 1482, Aldus took charge of the education of the sons of
the Princess of Carpi, a sister of Pico, and the zeal and
scholarly capacity which he devoted to the task won for him
the life-long friendship of both mother and sons. It was in
Carpi that Aldus developed the scheme of utilising his scholarly knowledge and connections for the printing of Latin and
Greek classics. The plan was a bold one for a young scholar
without capital. Printing and publishing constituted a prac-

tically untried field of business, not merely for Aldus but
for Italy. Everything had to be created or developed: knowledge of the art of printing and of all the technicalities of
book-manufacturing; fonts of type, Roman and Greek; a force of
type-setters and pressmen and a staff of skilled revisers and
proof-readers; a collection of trustworthy texts to serve as
"copy" for the compositors; and last, but by no means least, a
book-buying public and a book-selling machinery by which such
a public could be reached.

It was the aim of Aldus, as he himself expressed it, to
rescue from oblivion the words of the classic writers, the
monuments of human intellect. He writes in 1490: "I have resolved to devote my life to the cause of scholarship. I have
chosen in place of a life of ease and freedom, an anxious and
toilsome career. A man has higher responsibilities than the
seeking of his own enjoyment; he should devote himself to honourable labour. Living that is a mere existence can be left to
men who are content to be animals. Cato compared human existence to iron. When nothing is done with it, it rusts; it is
only through constant activity that polish or brilliancy is
secured."

The world has probably never produced a publisher who
united with these high ideals and exceptional scholarly attainments, so much practical business ability and persistent
pluck.

The funds required for the undertaking were furnished by
the Princess of Carpi and her sons, probably with some co-
operation from Pico, and in 1494, Aldus organised his printing-
office in Venice. His first publication, issued in 1495, was
the Greek and Latin Grammar of Laskaris, a suitable forerunner
for his great classical series. The second issue from his
Press was an edition of the Works of Aristotle, the first
volume of which was also completed in 1495. This was followed

in 1496 by the Greek Grammar of Gaza, and in 1497 by a
Greek-Latin Dictionary compiled by Aldus himself.

The business cares of those first years of his printing
business were not allowed to prevent him from going on with his
personal studies. In 1502, he published, in a handsome quarto
volume, a comprehensive grammar under the title of _Rudimenta_
Grammatices Linguae Latinae, etc. cum Introductione ad Hebraicam
Linguam, to the preparation of which he had devoted years of
arduous labour. Piratical editions were promptly issued in
Florence, Lyons, and Paris. He also wrote the _Grammaticae_
Institutiones Graecae (a labour of some years), which was not
published until 1515, after the death of the author.

It will be noted that nearly all the undertakings to which
he gave, both as editor and as publisher, his earliest attention,
were the necessary first steps in the great scheme of the complete series of the Greek classics. Before editors or proofreaders could go on with the work of preparing the Greek texts
for the press, dictionaries and grammars had to be created.
Laskaris, whose Grammar initiated the series, was a refugee from
the East, and at the time of the publication of his work, was an
instructor in Messina. No record has been preserved of the ar-
rangement made with him by his Venetian publisher, a deficiency
that is the more to be regretted as his Grammar was probably the
very first work by a living author, printed in Italy. Gaza was a
native of Greece, and was for a time associated with the Aldine
Press as a Greek editor.

In 1500, Aldus married the daughter of the printer Andrea
Torresano of Asola, . . . the successor of the Frenchman Jenson
and the purchaser of Jenson's matrices. In 1507, the two printing concerns were united, and the savings of Torresano were
utilised to strengthen the resources of Aldus, which had become
impaired, probably through his too great optimism and publishing
enterprise.

During the disastrous years of 1509-1511, in which Venice
was harassed by the wars resulting from the League of Cambray,
the business came to a stand-still, partly because the channels

of distribution for the books were practically blocked, but partly also on account of the exhaustion of the available funds. Friends again brought to the publisher the aid of which, on the ground of his public-spirited undertakings, he was so well entitled, and he was enabled, after the peace of 1511, to proceed with the completion of his Greek classics. Before his death in 1515, Aldus had issued in this series the works of Aristotle, Plato, Homer, Pindar, Euripides, Sophocles, Aristophanes, Demosthenes, Lysias, Aeschines, Herodotus, Thucydides, Xenophon, Plutarch, and others, in addition to a companion series of the works of the chief Latin writers. The list of publications included in all some 100 different works, comprised (in their several editions) in about 250 volumes. Considering the special difficulties of the times and the exceptional character of the original and creative labour that was required to secure the texts, to prepare them for the press, to print them correctly, and to bring them to the attention of possible buyers, this list of undertakings is, in my judgment, by far the greatest and the most honourable in the whole history of publishing.

It was a disadvantage for carrying on scholarly publishing undertakings in Venice, that the city possessed no university, a disadvantage that was only partly offset by the proximity of Padua, which early in the fifteenth century had come under Venetian rule. A university would of course have been of service to a publisher like Aldus, not only in supplying a home market for his books, but in placing at his disposal scholarly assistants whose services could be utilised in editing the texts and in supervising their type-setting. The correspondence of members of a university with the scholars of other centres of learning, could be made valuable also in securing information as to available manuscripts and concerning scholarly undertakings generally. In the absence of a university circle, Aldus was obliged to depend upon his personal efforts to bring him into relations, through correspondence, with men of learning throughout Europe, and to gather about the Aldine Press a group of scholarly associates and collaborators.

Live copy

ALDUS MANUTIUS

(Exerpted from <u>Books and Their Makers During the Middle Ages</u> by Geo. Haven Putnam, reprinted from an 1896-1897 edition by Hillary House Publishers of New York in 1962)

Aldus Manutius was born at Bassiano in the Romagna in 1450, the year in which Gutenberg completed his printing-press. He studied in Rome and in Ferrara, and after having mastered Latin, he devoted himself, under the tutorship of Guarini of Verona, to the study of Greek. Later, he delivered lectures on the Latin and Greek classics. One of his fellow students in Ferrara was the precocious young scholar Pico della Mirandola, whose friendship was afterward of material service. In 1482, when Ferrara was being besieged by the Venetians and scholarly pursuits were interrupted, Aldus was the guest of Pico at Mirandola, where he met Emanuel Adramyttenos, one of the many Greek scholars who, when driven out of Constantinople, had found refuge in the Courts of Italian princes. Aldus spent two years at Mirandola, and under the influence and guidance of Adramyttenos, he largely increased his knowledge of the language and literature of Greece. His friend had brought from the East a number of manuscripts, many of which found their way into the library of Pico

In 1482, Aldus took charge of the education of the sons of the Princess of Carpi, a sister of Pico, and the zeal and scholarly capacity which he devoted to the task won for him the life-long friendship of both mother and sons. It was in Carpi that Aldus developed the scheme of utilising his scholarly knowledge and connections for the printing of Latin and Greek classics. The plan was a bold one for a young scholar without capital. Printing and publishing constituted a practically untired field of business, not merely

for Aldus but for Italy. Everything had to be created or developed: knowledge of the art of printing and of all the technicalities of book-manufacturing; fonts of type, Roman and Greek; a force of type-setters and pressmen and a staff of skilled revisers and proof-readers; a collection of trustworthy texts to serve as "copy" for the compositors; and last, but by no means least, a book-buying public and a book-selling machinery by which such a public could be reached.

It was the aim of Aldus, as he himself expressed it, to rescue from oblivion the words of the classic writers, the monuments of human intellect. He writes in 1490: "I have resolved to devote my life to the cause of scholarship. I have chosen in place of a life of ease and freedom, an anxious and toilsome career. A man has higher responsibilities than the seeking of his own enjoyment; he should devote himself to honourable labour. Living that is a mere existence can be left to men who are content to be animals. Cato compared human existence can be left to men who are content to be animals. Cato compared human existence to iron. When nothing is done with it, it rusts; it is only through constant activity that polish or brilliance is secured.

The world has probly never produced a publisher who untied with these high ideals and exceptional scholarly attainments, so much practical business ability and persistent pluck.

The funds required for the undertaking were furnished by the Princess of Carpi and her sons, probably with some co-operation from Pico, and in 1494, Aldus organised his printing-office in Venice. His first publication, issued in 1495, was the Greek and Latin Grammar of Laskaris, a suitable forerunner for his great classical series. The second issue from his Press was an edition of the Works of Aristotle, the first volume of which was also completed in 1495.

This was followed in 1496 by the Greek Grammar of Gaza, and in 1497 by a Greek-Latin Dictionary compiled by Aldus himself.

The business cares of those first years of his printing business were allowed to prevent him from going on with his personal studies. In 1502, he published, in a handsome quarto volume, a comprehensive grammar under the title of Rudiment Grammatices Linguae Latinae, etc. cum Introductione ad Hebraicam Linguam, to the preparation of which he had devoted years of arduous labour. Piratical editions were promptly issued in Florence, Lyons, and Paris. He also wrote the Grammaticae Institutiones Graecae (a labour of some years), which was not published until 1515, after the death of the author.

It will be noted that nearly all the undertakings to which he gave, both as editor and as publisher, his earliest attention, were the necessary first steps in the great scheme of the complete series of the Greek classics. Before editors or proof-readers could go on with the work of preparing the Greek texts for the press, dictionaries and grammars had to be created. Laskaris, whose Grammar inititiated the series, was a refugee from the East, and at the time of the publication of his work, was an instructor in Messina. No record has been preserved of the ar-rangement made with him by his Venetian publisher, a deficiency that is the more to be regretted as his Grammar was probably the very first work by a living author, printed in Italy. Gaza was a native of Greece, and was for a time associated with the Aldine Press as a Greek editor.

In 1500, Aldus married the daughter of the printer Andrea Torresano of Asola, . . . the successor of the Frenchman Jenson and the purchaser of Jenson's matrices. In 1507, the two printing concerns were united, and the savings of Torresano were utilised to strengthen the resources of

Aldus, which had become impaired, probably through his too
great optimism and publishing enterprise.

During the disastrous years of 1509-1511, in which
Venice was harassed by the wars resulting from the League of
Cambray, the business came to a stand-still, partly because
the channels of distribution for the books were practically
blocked, but also partly on accout of the exaustion of the
available funds. Friends again brought to the publisher the
aid of which, on the ground of his public-spirited under
takings, he was so well entitled, and he was enabled, after
the peace of 1511, to proceed with the completion of his
Greek classics. Before his death in 1515, Aldus had issued
in this series the works of Aristotle, Plato, Homer, Pindar,
Euripides, Sophocles, Aristophanes, Demosthenes, Lysias,
Aeschines, Herodotus, Thucydides, Xenophon, Plutarch, and
others, in addition to a companion series of the works of
the chief Latin writers. The list of publications included
in all some 100 different works, comprised (in their several
editions) in about 250 volumes. Considering the special
difficulties of the times and the exceptional character of
the original and creative labour that was required to secure
the texts, to prepare them for the press, to print them
correctly, and to bring them to the attention of possible
buyers, this list of undertakings is, in my judgment, by far
the greatest and the mnost honourable in the whole history
of publishing.

It was a disadvantage for carrying on scholarly publishing undertakings in Venice, that the city possessed no
university, a disadvantage that was only partly offset by
the proximity of Padua, which early in the fifteenth century
had come under Venetian rule. A university would of course
have been of service to a publisher like Aldus, not only
supplying a home market for his books, but in placing at his

disposal scholarly assistants whose services could be utilised in editing the texts and in supervising their typesetting. The correspondence of members of a university with
the scholars of other centres of learning, could be made
valuable also in securing information as to available manuscripts and concerning scholarly undertakings generally. In
the absence of a university circle, Aldus was obliged to depend upon his personal efforts to bring him into relations,
through correspondence with men of learning throughout
Europe, and to gather about the Aldine Press a group of
scholarly associates and collaborators.

Answer Keys

KEY to Proofreading aptitude test

<u>SPELLING</u>

Write <u>G</u> next to any spelling you guess at and would look up in a dictionary if you were proofreading.

A. <u>Recognition</u>: Cross through every misspelled word and write out the entire word with correct spelling in the righthand column.

The occurrence of a misspelled word in print is ~~totaly~~   *totally*

impermissible. The ~~affect~~ is disastrous, an embarrass-   *effect*

ment to the printer, a distraction to the reader, and a   _____

~~slurr~~ on the writer's competence. Misspelling is a sign   *slur*

that the role of the proofreader has been slighted or   _____

misunderstood. Although the proofreader is ~~principly~~   *principally*

committed to see that the proof follows the copy   _____

accurately, there is a further ~~committment~~ to prevent   *commitment*

the author, editor, or printer from looking ~~rediculous~~.   *ridiculous*

A proofreader is never ~~presumtuous~~ in correcting (or--   *presumptuous*

better--querying) an incorrect spelling. Let no   _____

conscientious proofreader ~~wholey~~ acquiesce to the rule   *wholly*

of "follow copy" in regard to spelling.

B. <u>Choosing between letters</u>: Fill in the missing letter, choosing one of the two in parentheses.

1.	comput*e*r	(e;o)	6.	inadvert*e*nt	(a;e)
2.	deduct*i*ble	(a;i)	7.	indispens*a*ble	(a;i)
3.	defend*a*nt	(a;e)	8.	resist*a*nt	(a;e)
4.	depend*e*nt	(a;e)	9.	sep*a*rate	(a;e)
5.	super*s*ede	(c;s)	10.	tox*i*n	(e;i)

C. <u>Choosing among words</u>: Underline the correct spelling.

    1,2. I look foreword/foreward/forword/<u>forward</u> to writing
        the <u>foreword</u>/foreward/forword/forward to your book.
(continued)

3,4,5,6. As <u>principal</u>/principle of this school, my first
principal/<u>principle</u> is to balance the budget.
My <u>principal</u>/principle concern is to avoid reducing
our endowment's principal/<u>principle</u>.

7. <u>accommodate</u>; acommodate; accomodate
8. <u>changeable</u>; changable
9. chrystal; <u>crystal</u>
10. conscensus; concensus; <u>consensus</u>
11. <u>conscience</u>; consience; concience
12. cooly; <u>coolly</u>
13. drunkeness; <u>drunkenness</u>
14. <u>engineering</u>; enginneering
15. <u>harass</u>; harras; harrass
16. hypocracy; <u>hypocrisy</u>
17. irresistable; <u>irresistible</u>
18. liason; <u>liaison</u>; laiason; laison
19. <u>limousine</u>; limosine
20. managable; <u>manageable</u>
21. necesary; <u>necessary</u>; neccessary; neccesary
22. <u>parallel</u>; parralel; paralell
23. preceed; <u>precede</u>
24. prefering; <u>preferring</u>
25. <u>privilege</u>; priviledge
26. <u>proceed</u>; procede
27. <u>publicly</u>; publically
28. questionaire; <u>questionnaire</u>
29. <u>receive</u>; recieve
30. recomendation; <u>recommendation</u>; reccomendation; reccommendation
31. <u>seize</u>; sieze
32. <u>siege</u>; seige
33. vaccum; <u>vacuum</u>; vacumn
34. <u>weird</u>; wierd

D. Assessment of results

If you marked <u>G</u> (for guess) on words you misspelled (or spelled
correctly), they do not count as misspellings in this aptitude test.
However, if you guessed at more than four or five, or if you made more
than two or three misspellings, you must improve your spelling. You
might set up a program of study and memorization based on repetition
and review, beginning with the words you missed in this test and
continuing with self-study books available in libraries and bookstores.

Answer Keys

KEY to Exercise 1. Simple deletion

Dead copy

Some think too little and
write too much.
Some think too little and
write too much.
Some think too little and
write too much.
Some think too little and
write too much.

The proof-reader's position is
not an enviable one. When he
does his best and makes his
book correct he does no more
than his duty. He may correct
ninety-nine errors out of a
hundred, but if he misses the
hundredth he may be sharply
reproved for that negligence.
                    --Theodore De Vinne

Live copy

Some think too little and
write too much.
Some think too little and
write too much.
Some who think too little and
write too much.
Some think too little little and
write too much.

The proof-reader's position is
not at all an enviable one.
When he does his very best and
makes his book correct he does
no more than his duty. He may
correct ninety-nine errors out
off a hundred, but if he misses
the hundred, but if he misses
the hundredth he may be sharply
reproved for that negligence.
                    --Theodore De Vinne

KEY to Exercise 2. Deletion with the close-up mark
(in the middle of words or groups of characters)

Dead copy

Proofreading is essential for
perfection.

The proof-reader's position is
not an enviable one. When he
does his best and makes his
book correct he does no more
than his duty. He may correct
ninety-nine errors out of a
hundred, but if he misses the
hundredth he may be sharply
reproved for that negligence.
                    --Theodore De Vinne

Live copy

Proofreading is essentential
for perfection.

The proof-reader's possition
is not an enviable one. When
he does his beast and makes
his book correct he does no
more than his duty. He may
correct ninety-nine errors out
of a hundred, but if he
misses the hundredth he may be
sharply reproved for that
negegligence.
                    --Theodore De Vinne

415

KEY to Exercise 3. Simple deletion and deletion with the close-up mark

Dead copy	Live copy

The proof-reader's position is not an enviable one. When he does his best and makes his book correct he does no more than his duty. He may correct ninety-nine errors out of a hundred, but if he misses the hundredth he may be sharply reproved for that negligence.
   --Theodore De Vinne
	The proof-reader's position is not an ~~un~~enviable one. When he ~~he~~ does his best and makes his book$ corr∫ect∕ he does no more than his duty. ~~He may correct no more than his duty.~~ He may correct ninety-nine errors out of a hundred, but if he misses the hundredth he may be sharply re∫proved for that negligence.
	   --Theodore De Vinne

KEY to Exercise 4. Simple insertion

Dead copy	Live copy
Patty Piper proofread a perfect page. If Patty Piper proofread a perfect page, where is the perfect page that Patty Piper proofread?	Patty Piper ͜proofread a perfect page. If Patty Piper proofread a perfect page, where is the ^page that Patty Piper proofread? *perfect*

KEY to Exercise 5. Insertion with the close-up mark
(at the beginning or end of a word or group of characters)

Dead copy	Live copy
Patty Piper proofread a perfect page. If Patty Piper proofread a perfect page, where is the perfect page that Patty Piper proofread?	Patty Piper ^roofrea^ a perfect page. If Patty Piper proofread a perfect page, ^here is the perfect page that Patty Pipe^ proofread? *pc/ɔd* *wɔ/* *ɔr*

KEYS to Exercise 6. Long and short outs

KEY to Exercise 6A.

Dead copy	Live copy

Elegance in prose composition is mainly this: a just admission of topics and of words; neither too many nor too few of either; enough of sweetness in the sound to induce us to enter and sit still; [enough of illustration and reflection to change the posture of our minds when they would tire;] and enough of sound matter in the complex to repay us for our attendance.
   --Walter Savage Landor *(det)*
	Elegance in prose composition is mainly this: a just admission of topics and ^words; neither too many nor ^too few of either; enough of sweetness in the sound to induce us to ^sit *enter and* still; ^and enough of sound matter ^in the complex to repay us for our attendance.
	   --Walter Savage Landor *of* (out, see copy, p.A4)

KEY to Exercise 6B.

Dead copy

Elegance in prose composition
is mainly this: a just admis-
sion of topics and of words;
neither too many nor too few of
either; enough of sweetness in
the sound to induce us to enter
and sit still; enough of illustration and reflection to change
the posture of our minds when
they would tire; and enough of
sound matter in the complex to
repay us for our attendance.
--Walter Savage Landor

Live copy

Elegance in prose composition
is mainly this: a just amis-
sion of topics and words; neither too many nor too few of
either; enough of sweetness in
the sound matter in the complex to repay us for our
attendance.
--Walter Savage Landor

d

of

(out, see attached)

(Insert for P. A5)

*to induce us to enter and sit
still; enough of illustration and
reflection to change the posture of
our minds when they would tire;
and enough of sound*

KEY to Exercise 7. Inserting and deleting space

Dead copy

Our transition from barbarism
to civilization can be attributed to the alphabet.--Otto Ege

Live copy

Our transition from barbarism
to civilization can beat trib-
uted tothe alphabet.--Otto Ege

⊃/#

#/⊃

#

KEY to Exercise 8. Deletion and insertion

Dead copy

Bacon cautions writers not "to
hunt more after words than matter, and more after the choiceness of the phrase, and the
round and clean composition of
the sentence, and the sweet
falling of the clauses, and the
varying and illustration of
their works with tropes and
figures, than after the weight
of matter, soundness of argument, life of invention or
depth of judgment."

Live copy

Bacon cautions writers "to hunt
more after words than matter,
and more ~~after words than matter, and more~~ after the ~~choice~~
choiceness of the phase, and
the round and clean composition
of the sentence, and the sweet
falling of the clauses, and the
varying and illustration of
their work with tropes and
figures, than after the weight
of matter, sound ness of argument, life of invention/ or
depth of judgment."

not

ʃ

ʃ //

ʌ

ʃ

c∆/#

⊃

ʃ

417

KEY to Exercise 9. Replacement

Dead copy	Live copy
My Lord, I do here, in the name of all the learned and polite persons of the nation, complain to Your Lordship as First Minister, that our language is extremely imperfect; that its daily improvements are by no means in proportion to its daily corruptions; that the pretenders to polish and refine it have chiefly multiplied abuses and absurdities; and that in many instances it offends against every part of grammar. --Swift	My Lord, I do ~~hear~~, in the name of all the learned and polite ~~people~~ of the nation, complain to Your Lordship as First Minister, that our language is extremely i̸mperfect; that its daily improvements are by no means in pr̸portion to its daily corruptions; that the pretenders to polish and refine it have chiefly multiplied abuses and absurdities; and that in many ~~cases~~ it offends against every part o̸ gramm̸r. --Swift

(Margin marks, Live copy: *here* / *persons* / *m* / *o* / *instances* / *f* / *a*)

KEY to Exercise 10. Transposition

Dead copy	Live copy
ITALIC The italic letter claims an origin quite independent of the roman to which it is an accessory. It is said to be an imitation of the handwriting of Petrarch. Aldus Manutius, seeking a letter that took less space than roman, introduced italic for the printing of the entire text of a series of classics which otherwise would have required bulky volumes. The original font is lowercase only; it was used with roman capitals in the six sizes that Aldus produced. Italic was later used to distinguish front and back matter--such as introductions, prefaces, indexes, and notes--from the roman text itself. Still later it was used in the text for quotations; and finally it served the double purpose of <u>emphasizing</u> words and, in some works, chiefly translations of the Bible, of marking words not properly belonging to the text.	ITALIC The italic letter claims an origin quite indepe(nd)ent of the roman (which it is an accessory) (to). It is said to be an imitation of the handwriting of Petrarch. Aldus Manutius, seeking a letter that took less space than roman, int(ro)duced italic for the printing of the entire text of a series of classics which otherwise would have required bu(lk)y volumes. The ori(gin)al font is lowercase only; it was used with roman capitals in the six sizes that Aldus produced. Italic was (used)(later) to distinguish front and back matter--such as (prefaces,)(introductions,) indexes, and notes--from the roman text itself. Still later it was used in the text for quotations; and finally it served the do(ub)le purpose of <u>emphasizing</u> words and, in some works, chiefly ~~tralanstions~~ of *translations* the Bible, of marking words not (belonging)(properly) to the text.

(Margin marks, Live copy: *tr* / *tr* / *tr* / *tr* / *g/n* / *tr* / *tr* / *tr* / *tr*)

KEY to Exercise 11. Replacement, including special replacement marks

Dead copy

At the mill, a ream--500 sheets--of 17 x 22-inch paper of the heaviest general office bond weighs 24 pounds. When this paper is cut into 8-1/2 x 11-inch sheets, it's called 24-pound bond--but, of course, it takes four reams to weigh 24 pounds. The following chart shows the common weights and uses of business papers:

Weight	Use
9 lb	carbon copies
13 lb	legal documents, court briefs
16 lb	general office reports, second sheets, file copies
20 lb	letterhead
24 lb	heavy letterhead

Live copy

At the mill, a ream--500 sheets--of 17 x 22-inch paper ⊗
of the heaviest general office bond weighs 24 (lbs). When this ⒶⓅ paper is cut into 8-1/2 x 11-inch sheets, it's called 24-pound bond--but, of course, it takes ④ reams to weigh 24 ⒶⓅ pounds. The following chart shows the commo(n) weights and ⊗ uses of business papers:

(Wt)	Use	ⒶⓅ
9 lb	carbon copies	
13 lb	legal documents, court briefs	
16 lb	(genl) office reports, (2nd) sheets, file copies	ⒶⓅ ⒶⓅ
20 lb	letterhead	
24 lb	heavy letterhea(d)	⊗

KEY to Exercise 12. Review

A. Words

Deletion

1. Change "now" to "no."   noẉ   ♂

2. Change "there" to "here."   ∤there   ♀

3. Change "pencil" to "pen."   pen~~cil~~   ♂

4. Change "grandchild" to "child."   ~~grand~~child   ♂

5. Change "friend" to "fiend."   f∤iend   ⦵

6. Change "exist" to "exit."   exi∤t   ⦵

7. Change "adulterate" to "adulate."   adul~~ter~~ate   ⦵

8. Change "proofreading" to "read."   ~~proof~~read~~ing~~   ♂//

9. Change "English" to "is."   ~~Engl~~ish∤   ♂//

10. Change "language" to "an."   l̶a̶n̶guage   ℑ‖

11. Change "complete" to "let."   c̶o̶m̶plet̶e̶   ℑ‖

12. Change "renewal" to "new."   r̶enewa̶l̶   ℑ‖

Insertion

13. Change "no" to "now."   no^   ⌒w

14. Change "here" to "there."   ^here   t⌒

15. Change "pen" to "pencil."   pen^   ⌒cil

16. Change "child" to "grandchild."   ^child   grand⌒

17. Change "fiend" to "friend."   fi^end   r

18. Change "exit" to "exist."   exi^t   s

19. Change "adulate" to "adulterate." adul^ate   ter

20. Change "read" to "proofreading."   ^read^   proof⌒/⌒ing

21. Change "is" to "English."   ^is^   Engl⌒/⌒h

22. Change "an" to "language."   ^an^   l⌒/⌒guage

23. Change "let" to "complete."   ^let^   comp⌒/⌒e

24. Change "new" to "renewal."   ^new^   re⌒/⌒al

Replacement

25. Change "sensible" to "sensibly."   sensibl̶e̶   y

26. Change "unto" to "into."   u̶nto   i

27. Change "type" to "typical."   typ̶e̶   ical

28. Change "borrow" to "tomorrow."   b̶orrow   tom

29. Change "use" to "usage."   us̶e̶   age

30. Change "survey" to "surveillance." surve̶y̶   illance

31. Change "father" to "mother."   f̶a̶ther   m/o

32. Change "near" to "far."   n̶e̶ar   ℑ/f

33. Change "exercise" to "exorcise."   exe̶rcise   o

34. Change "flour" to "flower."   flou/r   *we*

35. Change "example" to "exemplary."   exampl/   *e/ary*

Transposition

36. Change "casual" to "causal."   cas/u/al   (tr)

37. Change "marital" to "martial."   mar/it/al   (tr)

38. Change "trial" to "trail."   tr/ia/l   (tr)

39. Change "united" to "untied."   un/it/ed   (tr)

40. prece/ed/   (tr)

41. proce/de/   (tr)

42. bel/ei/ve   (tr)

43. s/ie/ze   (tr)

44. Feb/ur/ary   (tr)

45. p/er/scription   (tr)

46. Change "sky blue" to "blue sky."   (sky blue)   (tr)

47. Change "human being" to "being human."   (human being)   (tr)

B. Sentences

48. Proofreading ~~and editing are forms of~~   *is*
     quality control ~~in publishing~~.   3̶

49. Proofing is quali~~fied~~ control.   *read/ty*
                       ^

50. Proofread~~ers form the core of our business,~~ *ing is/*
     ~~a business that is known for its~~ quality.   *s/control*

C. Paragraph

Dead copy	**Live copy**

Over the office door of Aldus Manutius (1450-1515), founder of the Aldine Press in Venice, appeared this legend: Whoever you are, you are earnestly requested by Aldus to state your business briefly and to take your departure promptly. In this way you may be of service even as was Hercules to the weary Atlas, for this is a place of work for everyone who enters.

Over the office door of Aldus Manutius (1450-1515), founder of the Aldine Press in ~~Vienna~~, appeared this ~~motto~~: Whosever you are, you are eanestly requested by Aldus to state your business briefly and take your departure promptly. In this ~~this~~ way you may be of service even as Hercules was, for this ~~is a place of Atlas for this~~ is a place of worship for ~~you~~ and everyone who enters ~~here~~.

KEY to Exercise 13. Punctuation: Humpty Dumpty

"When *I* use a word," Humpty Dumpty said in rather a scornful tone, "it means just what I choose it to mean/neither more nor less."

"The question is, said Alice, "whether you *can* make words mean so many different things/"

"The question is," said Humpty Dumpty, "which is to be master/that's all."/

Alice was too much puzzled to say anything/so after a minute Humpty Dumpty began again. "They've a temper, some of them—particularly verbs/they're the proudest—adjectives you can do anything with but not verbs—however, *I* can manage the whole lot of them! Impenetrability! That's what *I* say/"

"Would you tell me please," said Alice, "what that means/"

"Now you talk like a reasonable child," said Humpty Dumpty, looking very much pleased. I meant by impenetrability that we've had enough of that subject, and it would be just as well if youd mention what you mean to do next, as I suppose you don't mean to stop here all the rest of your life/

"That's a great deal to make one word mean," Alice said/in a thoughtful tone.

"When I make a word do a lot of work like that," said Humpty Dumpty, "I always pay it extra/"

KEY to Exercise 14: Punctuation, capitals, and lowercase: Inaugural Address

John stuart Mills inaugural address (as Rector of the University of SAINT Andrew) on february 1, 1867, included the following words:

To question all things;—never to turn away from any difficulty; to accept no doctrine either from ourselves or from other people without a rigid scrutiny by negative criticism; letting no Fallacy, or incoherence, or confusion of thought, step by unperceived/Above all, to insist upon having the meaning of a word clearly understood before using it, and the meaning of a proposition before assenting to it—these are the lessons we learn from Ancient Dialecticians.

KEY to Exercise 15. Proofreading practice:
Eugene Field on Printers' Blunders

EUGENE FIELD ON PRINTER(S) BLUNDERS

The most distressing blunder I ever read in print was made at the time of the burial of the famous antiquary and littéateur, John Payne Collier. In the London newspapers of Sept. 21, 1883, it was reported that "the remains of the late Mr. John Payne Collier were yesterday interred in Bray churchyard, near Maidenhead, in the presence of a large number of spectators." Thereupon the Eastern daily press published the following remarkable perversion: "The Bray Colliery Disasters. The remains of the late John Payne, collier, were interred yesterday afternoon in the Bray churchyard in the presence of a large number of friends and spectators."

Far be it from the book-lover and the book-collector to rail at blunders, for not unfrequently these very blunders make books valuable. . . . The genuine first edition of Hawthorne's "Scarlet Letter" is to be determined by the presence of a certain typograhical slip in the introduction. The first edition of the English Scriptures printed in Ireland (1716) is much desired by collectors, and simply because of an error. Isaiah bids us "sin no more," but the Belfast printer, by some means or another, transposed the letters in such a way as to make the injunction read "sin on more."

The so-called Wicked Bible is a book that is seldom met with, and, therefore, in great demand. It was printed in the the time of Charles I, and it is notorious because it omits the adverb "not" in its version of the seventh commandment; the printers were fined a large sum for this gross error. . . .

Once upon a time the Foulis printing establishment at Glasgow determined to print a perfect Horace; accordingly the proof sheets were hung up at the gates of the university, and a sum of money was paid for every error detected.

Notwithstanding these precautions the edition had six uncorrected errors in it when it was finally published. Disraeli says that the so-called Pearl Bible had six thousand errata. The works of Picus of Mirandula, Strasburg, 1507, gave a list of errata covering fifteen folio pages, and a worse case is that of "Missae ac Missalic Anatomia" (1561), a volume of one hundred and seventy-two pages, fifteen of which are devoted to the errata. The author of the Missea felt so deeply aggrieved by this array of blunders that he made a public explanation to the effect that the devil himself stole the manuscript, tampered with it, and then actually compelled the printer to misread it. . . .

We can fancy Richard Porson's rage (for Porson was of a violent temper) when, having written the statement that "the crowd rent the air with their shouts," his printer made the line

---

*From Eugene Field, *The Love Affairs of a Bibliomaniac*, Charles Scribner's Sons, New York, 1896

read "the crowd rent the air with their snouts." However, this error was a natural one, since it occurs in the "Catechism of the Swinish Multitude."

KEY to Exercise 16A. Changes in space: Letter spacing

These apparently conflicting words from a famous architect and an American president can apply to the nitpicking quality of proofreading. Interpret them as you like:

All the difficulties of this world are in the details.—President Clinton

God is in the details.—Ludwig Mies van der Rohe

KEY to Exercise 16B. Changes in space: Unequal word space

Not just large errors need to be watched for; small ones, too, cause trouble. Fowler's thoughts on the results of the use of wrong words (*insuccess* for *failure*, *deplacement* for *misplacement, unquiet* for *unrest*) can apply to any of the small mistakes to which writing is subject.

These are "mere slips, very likely," he wrote, and "indeed quite unimportant in a writer who allows himself only one such slip in fifty or a hundred pages; but one who is unfortunate enough to make a second before the first has faded from memory becomes at once a suspect. We are uneasily on the watch for his next lapse, wonder whether he is a foreigner or an Englishman not at home in the literary language, and fall into that critical temper which is the last he would choose to be reading."

—H. W. Fowler, *The King's English*

A ligature is a character that contains two or more   9
letters. Ligatures were employed by the medieval   6
scribes since they could be easily constructed with   7
a pen and enabled them to write at a more rapid   8
rate. Gutenberg's movable type included an extensive   6
assortment of ligatures because he wanted to create   10
a printed page that was undistinguishable from the   8
hand drawn manuscript. The number of ligatures   8
decreased as time went on for economic rather than   12
esthetic reasons.   4

Computer-aided photocomposition systems have   7
made possible a different approach to the design of   9
letterforms. We are no longer restricted to the 26-   9
character alphabet since an unlimited number of   8
letters can be stored in the memory of the computer.   13
The use of ligatures in the design of letterforms is the   13
next evolutionary step in the development of modern   9
reading systems.   1

KEY to Exercise 17. Word division

The pro/ *of*

ς ~~of~~ of the prin- ‸ *t*

ς /ing is in the read/- ⌒

i⌃ ‸ng.

"To que- ‸ *ᴅ*

ς /tion all things;—ne- ‸ *ᴠ*

ς /er to turn a/ *way*

ς ~~way~~ from any diff- ⌒

f⌃ ‸iculty; to ac¢- ⌒

c⌃ ‸ept no doc/- ⌒

tr⌃ ‸ine either from our~~selv~~- ⌒

selv⌃ ‸es or from other pe- ‸ *σ*

ς /ple without a rigid scru/- ⌒

t⌃ ‸iny by negative criti¢- ⌒

c⌃ ‸ism; letting no fal/- ⌒

l⌃ ‸acy or inco/- ⌒

h⌃ ‸erence or co- ‸ *ᴎ*

ς /fusion of thought,

step by unper¢- ⌒

c⌃ ‸eived; ab/ *ove*

ς ~~ove~~ all, to in/- ⌒

s⌃ ‸ist upon ha- ‸ *ᴠ*

ς /ing the mea- ‸ *ᴎ*

ς /ing of a word clea- ‸ *ʀ*

ς /ly understood bef/ *ore*

ς ~~ore~~ using it, and t/ *he*

ς ~~he~~ meaning of a pro- ‸ *ᴩ*

ς /position before as/¢- ⌒

se⌃ ‸nting to it;—the/ *se*

ς ~~se~~ are the les/- ⌒

s⌃ ‸ons we learn fr/ *om*

ς ~~om~~ an¢/- ⌒

ci⌃ ‸ent dia/- ⌒

l⌃ ‸ecticians."

KEY to Exercise 18. Spacing and positioning

Practice A

\#
\#
⊃

At onḙside is the author's and editor's work; at
the other̭is the typesetter's work. My work goes
be⌣tween the two. I'm the cheese betweeṋtwo
slices of bread to make a sand⌣wich.

\#
⌢

Practice B

TO THE SCRIBES⌐AT⌐
SAINT MARTIN'S
MONASTERY,
TOURS, FRANCE

⌐

⌐ (circa 782 A.D.) ⌐

⌐L

Here let the scribes beware of making
⌐mistakes through haste. Let them distinguish the proper sense by colons
and commas, and let them set down
the points, each one in its due place,
and let not⌐him⌐who reads the⌐words⌐
to them either read falsely or pause
⌐suddenly.

⌐

⌐

⌐

⊔

Practice C

align

eg \#

straighten

Proofreading is my vocation and my obsession. I search for
errors on cereal boxes and in travel folders, mail order catalogues, and greeting cards. I write proofreader's corrections
on letters from friends and query the instruction sheets that
come with new appliances. Some dark night I will take a
can of red paint and a brush to the nearby street sign
that reads "Greenfied Rd." and paint a caret between the
e and the *d* and an *l* at the side.   —Proofreader

ƽ\#

\#

Practice D

Dead copy

```
MARKING FAULTS
CITED IN
GPO STYLE MANUAL
```

```
    "The manner in which correction
marks are made on a proof is of
considerable importance," says the
U.S. Government Printing Office
Style Manual.
    It goes on to list some faults
in marking, as follows:
    ● straggling, unsymmetrical
characters
    ● disconnected marks placed in
the margin above or below the
lines to which they relate
    ● irregular lines leading from
an incorrect letter or word to a
correction
    ● large marks
    ● marks made with a blunt pen-
cil
    ● indistinct marks
    ● frequent use of the eraser to
obliterate marks hastily or incor-
rectly made.
    Some proofreading supervisors
would add, "not-thorough-enough
use of the eraser."  Obliterated
marks must be infrequent--and
invisible.
```

Live copy

MARKING FAULTS CITED IN GPO STYLE MANUAL

"The manner in which correction marks are made on a proof is of considerable importance," says the U.S. Government Printing Office *Style Manual.* It goes on to list some faults in marking, as follows:

- straggling, unsymmetrical characters
- disconnected marks placed in the margin above or below the lines to which they relate
- irregular lines leading from an incorrect letter or word to a correction large marks
- marks made with a blunt pencil
- indistinct marks
- frequent use of the eraser to obliterate marks hastily or incorrectly made.

Some proofreading supervisors would add, "not-thorough-enough use of the eraser."

Obliterated marks must be infrequent—and invisible.

KEY to Exercise 19. Moving type and space:
Ben Franklin's Complying Temper

⟨tr⟩] Benjamin Franklin's ⟨Complying⟩ [⟨run over⟩
Temper

⟨straighten⟩ In "An Apology to Printers," Benjamin Franklin asked all ⟨run on⟩
who were angry with him "on the account of printing things they don't
like" to consider a list of twelve particulars. Number seven of the
particulars was this:

It is unreasonable to imagine printers approve of
everything they print, and to censure them on any
particular thing accordingly; since in the way of
their business they print such a great variety of

things opposite and contradictory. It is likewise
as unreasonable what some assert, "That printers
ought not to print anything but what they approve";
since if all of that business should make such a
resolution and abide by it, an end would thereby
be put to free writing, and the world would after-
fwards have nothing to read but what happened to
be the opinions of printers.

Franklin went on to tell this story:
A certain well-meaning man and his son were ——— trav-el-ling
travelling towards a market town with an ass which
they had to sell. The road was bad, and the old man
therefore rode, but the son went afoot. The first
[passer by they met asked the father if he was not
ashamed to ride by himself, and suffer the poor lad
to wade along through the mire; this induced him to
take up his son behind him. He had not travelled
far, when he met others, who said, they are two un-
merciful lubbers to get both on the back of that
poor ass in such a deep road. Upon this the old
man got off, and let his son ride alone. The next
they met called the lad a graceless, rascally
young jackanapes, to ride in that manner through
the dirt, while his aged father trudged along on
foot; and they said the old man was a fool for su-
ffering it. He then bid his son come down, and
walk with him, and they travelled on leading the
ass by the halter, till they met with another company, who called them a couple of senseless block-
heads, for going both on foot in such a dirty way,

430

when they had an empty ass with them, which they
might ride upon. The old man could bear it no
longer. 'My son,' said he, 'it grieves me much]
that we cannot please all these people. Let me
throw the ass over the next bridge, and be no further troubled with him.' Franklin concluded:
Though I have a temper almost as complying as [the
old man's] . . . I intend not to imitate him. . . .
I consider the variety of humors among men, and
despair of pleasing everybody; yet I shall not therefore leave off printing. I shall continue my business.
I shall not burn my press and melt my letters.

KEY to Exercise 20. Review of marks

A. In-text and marginal marks

Marks used only in the text

<u>2</u>	delete or replace a word of two or more characters per marginal mark
<u>3</u>	insert character or word per marginal mark
<u>1</u>	fix spacing problem between lines per marginal mark
<u>8</u>	move to center

Marks used in both the text and the margin

<u>11</u>	close up
<u>6</u>	move right
<u>9</u>	move down
<u>10</u>	move left
<u>5</u>	move up
<u>4</u>	*in text*: delete or replace one character per marginal mark *in margin*: separates marginal marks; indicates how many times to make a correction; concludes an inconspicuous mark

Mark used in the margin for deletion

<u>7</u>	delete

(1) sideways caret ⎯⎯⟨

(2) crossbar ⎯⎯⎯

(3) upright caret ⋀

(4) slash /

(5) ⌐

(6) ⌐

(7) ∫

(8) ⌐⌐

(9) ⎵

(10) ⌐

(11) ⊂

Marks used in the margin

26	insert omission longer than one line	(1)	2
24	insert word space	(2)	2
24	insert line space		
1	set superscript 2	(3)	∧
2	set subscript 2	(18)	ℋ
4	apostrophe	(4)	∨
25	colon	(19)	no ℋ
3	comma	(5)	↗
23	opening bracket	(20)	(set) ?
15	hyphen	(6)	←
15	short dash on typewriter	(21)	(set) !
14	en dash	(7)	∨
22	long dash on typewriter	(22)	– – /
13	em dash	(8)	;/
21	exclamation point	(23)	[(bracket)
6	opening parenthesis	(9)	2/M
5	closing parenthesis	(24)	#
16	period	(10)	– – – –/
20	question mark	(25)	:/
11	opening double quotes	(11)	″∨
12	closing double quotes	(26)	(out, see copy, p. X)
7	opening single quote	(12)	″∨
4	closing single quote		
8	semicolon	(13)	1/M
17	slash, shill, virgule		
18	paragraph	(14)	1/N
19	no paragraph		
9	2-em dash	(15)	=/
10	typewritten equivalent of 2-em dash		

(16)	⊙	
(17)	/ (shill)	

433

B. Corresponding marks that differ in the text from in the margin

Meaning of mark	Dead copy	Live copy	
spell out	four feet	(4 ft.)	(sp)
wrong font	proofreading	proofreading)	(wf)
defective character	proofreading	proofreading	(x)
delete and close up	proofreading	proofreading	3
transpose characters	proofreading	proofreading	(tr)
transpose words	proofreading manual	manual proofreading)	(tr)
align horizontally	proofreading	p r o o f r e a d i n g	(straighten)
align vertically	proof- reading manual	proof- reading manual	(align)
run on	proofreading manual	proofreading manual	(run on)
carry back to previous line	Editorial Experts Proofreading Manual	Editorial Experts) Proofreading Manual	(run back)
carry down to next line	Editorial Experts Proofreading Manual	Editorial Experts (Proofreading Manual	(run over)
insert space between lines in typing	Proofreading Manual	Proofreading Manual	#
insert space between lines in typeset copy	Proofreading Manual	Proofreading Manual	#
equalize space	proofreading	proofreading	(eq#)
set in roman	proofreading	(proofreading)	(rom)
set in italic	*proofreading*	proofreading	(ital)
set in lightface	proofreading	(**proofreading**)	(lf)
set in boldface	**proofreading**	proofreading	(bf)
set in caps	PROOFREADING	proofreading	(caps)
set in lowercase	proofreading	PROOFREADING	(lc)
set in caps and lowercase	Proofreading Manual	PROOFREADING MANUAL	(clc)
set small caps	PROOFREADING	**PROOFREADING**	(sc)
set caps & small caps	PROOFREADING MANUAL	Proofreading Manual	(c+sc)
use ligature	**fly off**	**fly off**	(lig) fl/ff

C. Abbreviations

1. sp   spell out

2. wf   wrong font

3. rom   roman type

4. lf   light face

5. tr   transpose, transfer

6. ital   italic type

7. sc   small cap

8. bf   boldface

9. lc   lowercase

10. Clc   caps and lowercase

11. C+sc   caps and small caps

12. eq #   equal space

13. stet   let it stand

14. ctr   center

15. shill   shilling, virgule

16. cap   capital

17. ltr #   letter space

18. lig   ligature

EXCERPTS FROM BENJAMIN DREW

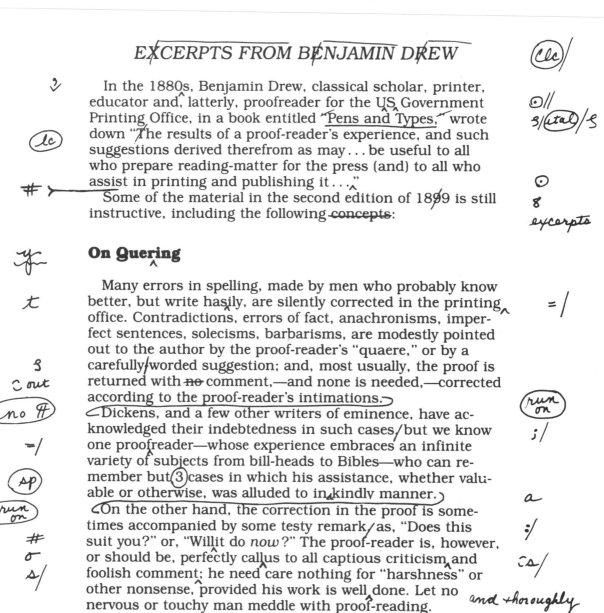

In the 1880s, Benjamin Drew, classical scholar, printer, educator and, latterly, proofreader for the US Government Printing Office, in a book entitled "Pens and Types," wrote down "The results of a proof-reader's experience, and such suggestions derived therefrom as may . . . be useful to all who prepare reading-matter for the press (and) to all who assist in printing and publishing it . . ."

Some of the material in the second edition of 1899 is still instructive, including the following concepts:

On Quering

Many errors in spelling, made by men who probably know better, but write hastily, are silently corrected in the printing office. Contradictions, errors of fact, anachronisms, imperfect sentences, solecisms, barbarisms, are modestly pointed out to the author by the proof-reader's "quaere," or by a carefully worded suggestion; and, most usually, the proof is returned with no comment,—and none is needed,—corrected according to the proof-reader's intimations.

Dickens, and a few other writers of eminence, have acknowledged their indebtedness in such cases, but we know one proofreader—whose experience embraces an infinite variety of subjects from bill-heads to Bibles—who can remember but 3 cases in which his assistance, whether valuable or otherwise, was alluded to in kindly manner.

On the other hand, the correction in the proof is sometimes accompanied by some testy remark, as, "Does this suit you?" or, "Will it do now?" The proof-reader is, however, or should be, perfectly callous to all captious criticism and foolish comment; he need care nothing for "harshness" or other nonsense, provided his work is well done. Let no nervous or touchy man meddle with proof-reading.

On Style

The proof-reader knows, that . . . every printing office has its own style and that, if left to itself, its style would be practical, uniform, and always respectable,—and he soon learns that some writers for the press have very firm opinions about matters of little or no consequence, and are very tenacious, if not pugnacious, in preferring *tweedledee* to *tweedledum*; not because it is written with more *e's*, but because it is more correct—in their opinions . . .

We have known two works to be in hand at the same time, one with directions to "capitalize freely," the other, to "use capitals sparingly." The "Directions" are sometimes quite minute, almost microscopic; still, it is the duty of the proof-reader to follow them into the very extremities of their small-ness. One writer says, "Put up 'eastern,' 'western,' etc. in such cases as this: 'The purple finch sometimes passes the cold season in Eastern Massachusetts, and even in Northern Nevada'"; another directs, 'Put compass points down, as 'In northern New Hampshire." If the office style is "Hudson and Connecticut Rivers," a direction will be sent in thus: "In all my works, print 'Weber and Severn rivers,' 'Phalan's and Johannah lakes'—not Lakes." One author wants "VII-inch gun and 64-pounder"; another looks upon this as numerically and typographically erroneous, and insists on "8-inch gun and LXIV-pounder"; still another prefers Arabic figures throughout, and prints an "8-inch gun and 64-pounder"; yet another likes best the first of the above styles but wishes a period placed after the Roman numerals, so it shall read, an "VIII. in gun"; one more dislikes double pointing," and would retain the period, but strike out the hyphen. "In my novel, spell 'Marquis De Gabriac' with a big D, and 'Madame de Sparre' with a small 'd,'"/ . . .

Suppose half a dozen works going through the press at the same time, embracing three styles of orthography, and four or five styles in capitalization; one style which requires turned commas at the beginning only of a quotation, and one which requires them at the beginning of every line of an extract,— you see at once that a proof-reader, so beset, must needs have his wits about him . . . .

The publishers of the "Life of John" desire to have it in uniform style with their "watch-pocket series," in which names of ships were put between quotation-marks; the author of the "Life of James" insists, that, in his work, names of ships shall not be quoted, and shall be set in roman; the "Life of William," being in office style, requires names of ships to be in italics . . .

Among these literary foolishnesses and idle discriminations, are inter-readings of pamphlets on the leather trade; the Swamtown Directory, the copy being the pages of an old edition, pasted on broadsides of paper, half the names stricken out, and new ones inserted haphazardly on the wide margin, their places in the text indicated by lines crossing and recrossing each other, and occasionally lost in a plexus organglion; reports of the Panjandrum Grand Slum Mining Co, the Glenmuchkin Railroad Company, and the new and improved Brown Paper Roofing Company; Preceedings of the National Wool-Pulling Association, and of the Society for Promoting the Introduction of Water-Gas for Culinary and illuminatory Purposes; likewise auction-bills, calendars, ball-cards, dunning-letters (some of these to be returned through the post-office, the proof-reader's own

⊙

e

ratio

feathers winging the shaft), glowing descriptions of Dyes, Blackings, Polishes, and Varnishes; in short, proofs of the endless variety of matters which constitute the daily pabulum of a book and job office,—and, in all these style has its requirements, ... We have known more than (40) special directions to be sent to a printing-office with the manuscript copy of one book. An author may fancy that numerous minute rulings will insure uniformity and beauty to his book; but the chances of discrepancy and mistakes are increased in direct ~~proportion~~ to the number of such rulings as run counter to the office style. His "more requires less," but produces "more."

⌃ sp

s of his

KEY to Exercise 22A. Specifications: Type specimens

Not only alphabets (including figures, punctuation, and other special characters) are used as type specimens; many specimens are text, and many of these texts can be informative or amusing.

The following specimen of Century Schoolbook type provides information on how typefaces may be compared. This text is repeated in 48 different typefaces with each one's name introducing the information (in *Type and Typefaces* by J. Ben Lieberman, The Myriade Press, New Rochelle, NY, 2nd edition, 1978).

CENTURY SCHOOLBOOK MAY BE COMPARED with other typefaces in many ways. First is readability: some faces help the eye more than others. Second is color: letters in mass can appear light or dark, dull or sparkling. Third is tone: faces suggest authority, richness, modernity, simplicity, etc. Fourth is efficiency for a given job—fitness for the size of type and sheet required, the kind of paper, *the printing process to be used. Since no one typeface is likely to be best in every respect, these matters have*

The following specimen of Helvetica carries a message extolling photocomposition. The same message also appears in specimens of 26 other typefaces in a book on typeface recognition (*Primer of Typeface Identification,* by A.S. Lawson and Archie Provan, National Composition Association, 1976).

Helvetica ^

Photocomposition offers the advantages of razor sharp crispness, proportional spacing, a wider selection of type styles in a greater variety of sizes, better type alignment and an unequalled uniformity of density.

Typesetting itself offers a number of advantages: typeset copy is more legible, thus it increases comprehension; reading speed and retention of the message are improved; typeset copy lends authority and professionalism to the written word/ typestyles contribute to the spirit of the message—from serious to humorous; typeset copy is more compact, reducing printing and distribution costs; and, finally, typeset copy is more inviting, encouraging wider readership.

(reset 9/12)

Some specimens keep the word spacing even by continuing from line to line without regard to hyphens or the rules of word division. (The following example is from _The TypEncyclopedia_ by Frank J. Romano, R.R. Bowker Company, New York and London, 1984.)

ORACLE
The history of writing is, in a way, the hist
ory of the human race, since in it are bou
nd, severally and together, the developm
ent of thought, of expression, of art, of int
ercommunication, and of mechanical inv
ention. Indeed, it has been said that the in
vention of writing is more important than

The previous example also shows how many specimens break off in the middle of a word or sentence. Different typefaces set at the same measure will break at different words or sentences, even though the type is the same size. For example, here's almost the same text as that above in a different face:

ENGLISH TIMES

The history of writing is in a way the history of the human race, since in it are bound, sev erally and together, the development of tho ught, of expression, of art, of intercommun ication, and of mechanical invention. It has been said that the invention of writing is of more importance than all the victories ever

In 18th-century issues of _The Inland Printer_ are type specimens conveying some flights of fancy and some expressions of the continuous enmity between typesetters and editors (the typefaces used aren't the same as those in the original):

A hat is the canopy of thought, the roof of imagination. A high hat is a proper loft for lofty ideas
and things to skip around in. A soft hat often covers
hard thoughts.

DOES THE EDITOR SIT IN HIS SANCTUM GRIM
NOT MUCH, MY SON, NOT ANY FOR HIM, AMID SYLVAN GROVES AND
PASTURES GREEN, WHERE HILLS RISE UP THE VISTAS BETWEEN

THE EDITOR SITS BENEATH THE SKIES,
DOTH FISH AND WISH DEATH UNTO THE FLIES; TO-MORROW HIS PAPER
WILL SWARM WITH—NOT LIES, BUT FISH STORIES

A WASP CAME BUZZING TO HIS WORK
AND VARIOUS THINGS DID TACKLE: HE STUNG A BOY AND
THEN A DOG, THEN MADE A ROOSTER CACKLE

AT LAST UPON AN EDITOR'S CHEEK HE
SETTLED DOWN TO DRILL: HE PRODDED THERE FOR
HALF-AN-HOUR AND THEN HE BROKE HIS BILL

INJUNCTION THAT SHOULD
BE GENERALLY HEEDED

The Chicago Society of Proofreaders recommends the abrogation of
the diphthongs in words which have
been incorporated in our language,
including legal and medical terms,
and the substitution of *e* for them;
hence, spell archeological, diarrhea,
subpena, eolian, etc.; also in proper
names, thus: Cesar, Etna, Esculapius, Linnean, etc.

Waiting for Purchasers: One male and eight
female unicorns; seven ~~area~~ serpents; three
griffins, fully developed; four mermaids,
extremely beautiful; seven dragons,
descendants of the one slain by St. George;
one hippogriff, just weaned; four salamanders, basking in the glow of an anthracite furnace; eleven sphynxes, very docile
and amiable; three centaurs, lately domesticated; with many other interesting curiosities.

Open for inspection on Monday, April
6, 1894

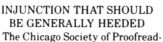

KEY to Exercise 22B. Specifications: Marks for type style

A Writer's Goals

Maugham on Fiction
It seems to me that I must aim at lucidity, simplicity, euphony.
I have put these three qualities in the order of the importance I

assigned to them.——SOMERSET MAUGHAM, *THE SUMMING UP*

SHIPLEY ON NONFICTION
Ha
had he been speaking of nonfiction, Maugham might have replaced
euphony with verity.——Joseph T. Shipley, O*R*igins of English Words

KEY to Exercise 22C. Specifications: Wrong font

If I do not clearly express what I mean, it is either for the reason that,
having no conversational powers, I cannot express what I mean, or
that having no meaning, I do not mean what I fail to express.
——Mr. Grewgious, in Dickens' *The Mystery of* Edwin Drood

441

The Continuing Need
for Proofreading

just

tickets ⌃
e

t⌃

e⌃

Words in type, printed materials, are every
where, not ~~only~~ in books, pamphlets, magazines,
catalogues, and newspapers, but in the products
of job printing—handbills, calendars, greeting cards, checkbooks, office forms, and business stationary; on display at the roadside—posters, billboards, road signs; on our pantry shelves—boxes, tin cans, and bottles; in
decorative and novelty printing on paper, cloth,
and plastic—napkins, towels, playing cards, basball cards, game boards, yard goods, shower curtains, shopping bags, tee shirts; and in music,
maps, and stamps. Type and printing are everywhere, from our birth certficates to our death
notices. And very word is subject to the gaucheries of misspelling, typographic errors, and care
less printing.

=/

#

(break up)

e
3

⌘
i

3/=

𝓅

(tr)
ℓ

⊙

t
⌗

Even the best writers suffer a loss of word
sense now and then; even the best help technology offers fails to "prove" a work's quality in
all typograhic and linguistic respects. As a
scholar-proofreader wrote in 1889, "So long as
authors the most accomplished are liable to err,
so long as compositors the most careful make
occasional mistakes, so pong must there be individuals trained and training too detect er-
rors/..proofreaders."

Failure to catch problems can ruim a well written, well edited, well desinged job. But goood
proofreading can preserve quality and can even
turn a bad job into an acceable one and a good
job into an excellent one. Proofreading is true
quality control.

3

n
(tr)/#/3

g/ Don't slight it ⊙

as dictionaries authorize various
spellings, just so long

KEYS to Exercise 24. Modified marking techniques

KEY to Exercise 24A. Writing out instructions

add i
add em

take out
par

He, whose busness it is to offer this unusual
apology, very well rembers to have been sitting
with Dr. Johnson, when an agent from a neigh-
boring press brought in a proof sheet of a re-
publication, requesting to know whether a par-
particular word in it was not corrupted.

"So far from it, sir," (replied the doctor with
some harshness), "that the word you suspect,
and would displace, is conspicuously beautiful
where it stands, and is the only one that would
do the duty expected of it by Mr. Pope"

—From an apology for errors
in a book published in 1793

less space

cap D

change w to c
add period

align 3

KEY to Exercise 24B. Marking in the margins only

business
remembers

particular

He, whose busness it is to offer this unusual
apology, very well rembers to have been sitting
with Dr. Johnson, when an agent from a neigh-
boring press brought in a proof sheet of a re-
publication, requesting to know whether a par-
particular word in it was not corrupted.

"So far from it, sir," (replied the doctor with
some harshness), "that the word you suspect,
and would displace, is conspicuously beautiful
where it stands, and is the only one that would
do the duty expected of it by Mr. Pope"

—From an apology for errors
in a book published in 1793

less #
in ^ a

Doctor

would
Pope.

179³

KEY to Exercise 24C. Making a handwritten correction list

Corrections for "Apology for errors"

Dead copy			Live copy			Error	Cxn
P	#	line	P	#	line		
1	1	1	1	1	1	business	i
		2			2	rembers	em
		4			4	in ∧ a	(less #)
		5			5,6	....par ~~particular~~	⌒
	2	1	2		1	doctor	D̲̲
		4			4	would	c
		5			5	Pope∧	⊙
		last			last	179|³	⨆

KEY to Exercise 24D. Making a typed correction list

Dead copy			Live copy			Corrected errors	Cxn to make
p	para	line	p	para	line		
1	1	1	1	1	1	business	add i
		2			2	remembers	add ēm
		4			4	in a	less word #
		5			5,6	.......par-ticular	take out extra "par"
	2	1	2		1	Doctor	cap D
		4			4	could	change w̄ to c̲
		5			5	Pope.	add perīod
		last			last	1793	align 3̲

KEY to Exercise 24E. Making corrections yourself

He, whose busⁱness it is to offer this unusual

apology, very well rem*em*bers to have been sitting

with Dr. Johnson, when an agent from a neigh-

boring press brought in a proof sheet of a re-

publication, requesting to know whether a par-

~~par~~ticular word in it was not corrupted.

"So far from it, sir," (replied the *D*doctor with

some harshness), "that the word you suspect,

and would displace, is conspicuously beautiful

where it stands, and is the only one that *c*would

do the duty expected of it by Mr. Pope."

—From an apology for errors

in a book published in 1793

KEY to Exercise 24F. Using editing marks with checkmarks in the margin

He, whose busⁱness it is to offer this unusual   ✓

apology, very well rem*em*bers to have been sitting   ✓

with Dr. Johnson, when an agent from a neigh-

boring press brought in⁀*less#* a proof sheet of a re-   ✓

publication, requesting to know whether a par-

✓   ~~par~~ticular word in it was not corrupted.

"So far from it, sir," (replied the *D*doctor with   ✓

some harshness), "that the word you suspect,

and would displace, is conspicuously beautiful

where it stands, and is the only one that *c*would   ✓

do the duty expected of it by Mr. Pope⊙."   ✓

—From an apology for errors

in a book published in 1793   ✓

445

This step involves transferring or integrating the new system into an operational status. New system operating instructions are∧ ~~pre~~pared, and the completed system documentation is turned over to appropriate personnel. The system is then considered operational, and control passes from the system-development function to the Department.

pre =

KEY to Exercise 25B. Dry reading: The Mississippi

Key (1). Minimum corrections

The Route Øf the Mississippi River

From Minnesota, the Mississippi river flows southward along the borders of Wisconsin, Illinois, and
seven other states, past Dubuque, St. Louis and Memphis, past the State that bears the river's name towards
its ~~source~~ at New Orleans, La.

lc
cap
3
^ mouth ?

Key (2). Style choices (see Notes below)

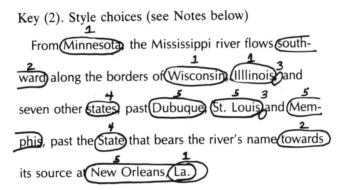

EXPLANATIONS OF CORRECTIONS

Key (1) shows straightforward corrections. Rings and numbers in Key (2) show corrections for which you have a style choice.

1. Inconsistency: three state names are spelled out and one is abbreviated. Solution: if
it's sensible, choose the style that requires the least number of changes—here, that would
be the spelled-out state names.

2. Inconsistency: two forms of the same suffix appear in *southward* and *toward*. Solution: chose *-ward* or *-wards* (*-ward* is the common American usage).

3. Inconsistency: a comma is used in the series "Wisconsin, Illinois, and seven other
states" but no comma is used in the series "Dubuque, St. Louis and Memphis." Solution:
use the serial comma consistently or omit it consistently. Technical writers and followers
of academic style guides generally use a serial comma; journalists generally omit it.

4. Inconsistency: "states" is lowercased; "State" is capitalized. Solution: use cap or
lowercase (lowercase is the common usage except in government documents).

5. Inconsistency: Dubuque, St. Louis, and Memphis are not identified by state, but
New Orleans is. Solution: You might add state names (either spelled out or abbreviated)
to three cities; you might take out the one state name; or you might leave the copy as it is
because you decide that this isn't really a problem.

KEY to Exercise 25C. Dry reading: Renaissance printing

Printing in the Renaissance

Stimulated to reaction against ecclesiastical and feudal tyranny and responding to influences possibly brought to life by the influx of scholars from Byzantium, Italy had already done much toward rehabilitating the classical products of antiquity when the balance of Europe began to throw off the shackles of intellectual despotism and to succumb to those mighty spiritual energies that ended in the emancipation of reason, the freedom of thought, and the recognition of natural rights.

The course of the Renaissance, determined by the revival of learning, vitalized the Italian scholarship of the fifteenth century, afforded tremendous impetus to the rise of Greek and the accumulation of its classical documents, and encouraged the new art of typography that gave to Italy an Aldus Manutius and to France the Estiennes.

The awakening that came to mankind first entered the Italian mind first as the arts of Italy reflected the humanistic spirit of her letters and as science and philosophy bridged the chasm between the ancient and the 15th-century worlds. The Turkish threat against Constantinople more and more influenced the emigration of learned Greeks into Italy, and with them came the literature of Greece—the writings of Pindar, Plato, and Aristotle. As scholars sought to evolve a new critical apparatus to express the renascent culture, a classical education became a necessity, and the knowledge of antiquity was indefatigably explored.

From Italy the tidal wave swept across the Alps into Germany, where where modifications akin to the nature of the sturdy Teutonic inhabitants effected a liberty of religious conviction and a license in expressing it that were powerfully enlarged by the agency of the printing press.

The achievements and aims of Froben, at Basle, reflect the position of printing in Germany at the time. As the power of the press spread through out Europe, the pulpit began to lose its claim to be the supreme center from which all knowledge emanated. France, however, was effected differently.

In fifteen-century France, the terror of classical learning, of the Oriental, Hebrew, and Greek studies that encourage Biblical criticism, held sway the longest. Only to art was liberty accorded: in architecture, the fine arts, and, to a limited extent, literature, through the patronage of Francis I, shone forth a genius that was wanting in the domain of biblical study. But the press, that is, the printing industry, was governed by the ecclesiastical body of the time, the college of the Sorbonne.

On the one hand, the patronage of the sovereign developed the material beauty and splendor of books: Grolier was encouraged to bind; Robert Stephens was encouraged to print; a magnificent Greek type was cast at the expense of the royal treasury; and, when a sumptuary law prohibited gilding houses and furniture, book binding was, by a special clause, exempted. The enrichment of the physical aspects of books—the expanse of margin, the thick-wove paper, and the brilliant type—all that came from the idea that Rosso and Cellini formed of their royal master's patronage of letters. The king's taste had a materialistic direction, expressed in his oft-quoted saying to Cellini, *Je l'etoufferai dans l'or* (I'll smother it in gold). So it is that the magnificence of the revival left it's mark in the Greek editions from the press of Robert Stevens, printer to the king.

On the other hand, the spirit of curiosity that had arisen among the public made other demands on the press. The public wanted to learn. The people desired books, not to place in a cabinet but to read in order to know—first and foremost, to know the truth in the matter of religion; next to know the causes and remedies of the evils, moral and material, by which they felt themselves crushed; and finally, to know how to struggle with nature, how to rest from her more comforts and more enjoyment.

But the press as a medi*um* of knowledge—as an arena for debating spiritual and social problems—was not the press that Francis I would encourage. This is the explanation of the apparent inconsistency in the public acts of that monarch, the acts that have caused him to be represented in such different lights.

While Francis I is invoked by some historians as the Father of Letters, others brand him as a bigot and persecutor whose zealous despotism would not tolerate the least dissent or the gentlest criticism. The truth is that Francis I ~~the First~~ was both at once.

KEY to Exercise 25D. Dry reading: Reading ease and comfort

How to Foster Ease and Comfort in Reading

Douglas McMurtrie, a well known typographer and book designer, tells us (in *The Book,* Dorset Press, 1943) that the average reader demands a book easy and comfortable to read, easy and comfortable to handle, and easy and comfortable to purchase.

The following list, based on his prescriptions for ease and comfort in reading, apply to many kinds of publication besides books.

Design Elements

- A typeface "free of affectation or labored drawing."
- Type size "large enough to read with ease under average lighting, or worse, by readers of average acuity of eyesight, or worse."
- Line spacing enough "to direct the eye back from the end of one line to the beginning of the next without possibility of confusion."
- Spacing that is "reasonably snug" between words & sentences.
- Lowercase rather than capitals so far as possible in chapter heads, subheads, and so on.
- Margins with traditional proportions, especially when specified by "designers of modest ability." Tradition calls for the gutter margine to be the narrowest, and the margins at the top, outer edge, and bottom of the page to increase progressively.

Editorial Elements

- Frequent paragraph ~~brakes~~ breaks to give the eye of the reader a "pause that refreshes."
- Books for study or reference "as liberally provided with sign posts in the way of subheads, and so forth, as the well-marked highway."

Production Elements

- Pages printed "sharply and clearly in good black ink, and uniform color and strength of impression maintained."
- Pages that line up accurately.
- pages that back up accurately.

Bag It at Householder's Hardware—

Shop with this discount bag

and get 10 % off everything in it!

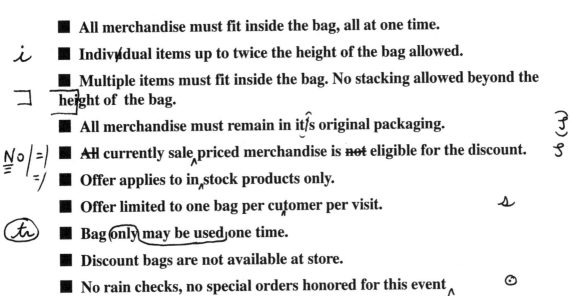

■ All merchandise must fit inside the bag, all at one time.

i ■ Individual items up to twice the height of the bag allowed.

⊐ ■ Multiple items must fit inside the bag. No stacking allowed beyond the height of the bag.

■ All merchandise must remain in it/s original packaging. 𝔷 (s

No /=| ■ All currently sale priced merchandise is not eligible for the discount.

=/ ■ Offer applies to in stock products only.

■ Offer limited to one bag per cutomer per visit. ꜱ

ⓣᵣ ■ Bag only may be used one time.

■ Discount bags are not available at store.

■ No rain checks, no special orders honored for this event ∧ ☺

EXPLANATIONS OF CORRECTIONS

Line	Problem
5, 8, 11	Typos or misspellings
7	Inconsistent spacing
9	You may prefer to query: Which do you mean—"Not all currently sale-priced merchandise is eligible ..." ⑦ Or "No currently sale-priced merchandise is eligible ..." ⑦ Or mark the change and query: OK ⑦
9, 10	Hyphens missing in unit modifiers

Line	Problem
3 up	Misplaced modifier. "Only" is said to be the most frequently misplaced word in the language; its position can determine what a sentence means, as these examples show:

> Only I challenged him to try proofreading.
> I only challenged him to try proofreading.
> I challenged only him to try proofreading.
> I challenged him only to only try proofreading.
> I challenged him to try proofreading only.

Line	Problem
last	Missing period

KEY to Exercise 25F. Dry reading: Editorial problems to catch

Fifteen

~~A dozen~~ kinds of editorial problems to catch

1. Typos:
   - typos

2. Misspellings:
   - misspellings

3. Wrong word use;
   - Every day I ~~lay~~ down and take a nap.
   - Bee especially careful of homophones.

4. Faulty thinking:
   - The price of coffee dropped 100 percent.

   ok ? 100% would make coffee free

5. Factual inaccuracy:
   - In 1492, Columbus sailed the ocean blue.
   - "Beauty is truth, truth beauty"
     —Ode to a Grecian Urn, John Keats

6. Mismatch of references to what they refer to;
   - Descriptions should fit what they describe (for example, in headings, captions, and tables).
   - Labels should match what they label in words, editorial style, and alphabetical or numerical sequence (for example, footnotes should match their callouts; tables of contents and lists of illustrations should match the heads and captions they list).
   - Cross-references should be accurate (for example, see the related items, 4 and 5, ~~below~~ *above*, on illogic and factual inaccuracy).

7. Errors in alphabetical order or numerical sequence.

8. Punctuation faults, including the following:
   - misleading punctuation, including "needless" quotation marks
   - excessive punctuation!!!
   - too little punctuation, for example, missing commas
   - marks of punctuation used incorrectly

9. Substandard grammar and usage:
   - Not every proofreader writes ~~good~~ *well*.

10. Disagreement between a singular subject and a plural verb:
   - Knowledge about grammar and spelling are a big part of successful editing.

10. Disagreement between a plural verb and a singular subject:
    - With the job of an editor comes a need for sensitivity and an absolute requirement for courtesy to the writer.
11. Pronoun problems, including problems of case, agreement, and indefinite antecedents:
    - To whom do I give the correct answer?
    - Who do I give the correct answer to?
    - Every editor should be able to cite an appropriate authority for every error they correct. *[he or she]*
    - Margaret told the editor that one of her sentences was brilliant. *[Margaret or editor?]*
12. Modifier problems:
    - Using an adjective when an adverb is the proper form looks badly.
    - The comparative, not the superlative, degree is the correct choice when two things are being compared, as in "He is the tallest of her two sons." *[taller]*
    - Modifiers that could have two possible meanings are called "squinting." Modifiers that squint *can* confuse the reader.
13. *[Lack of]* Parallel construction.
14. Inconsistent Editorial Style.

KEY to Exercise 25G. Dry reading: Pronouns

PERSONNEL PRONOUNS

(arranged by ~~case,~~ number, person, and case)

	Singular			Plural		
	1st	2nd	3rd	1st	2nd	3rd
Nominative	I	you / thou	he / she / it	we	you / ye	they
objective	me	you / thee / ye[2]	him / her / it	us	you / you-all[1] / ye[2]	them
Possessive[3]	my	your / thy	his / her	our	your / thy	~~them~~ *their*
	mine	yours / ~~thy~~ / thine	his / hers / it's	ours / ~~thy~~ / thine	yours	theirs

[1] (or "y'all") Acceptable colloquialism in the southern United States.
[2] Nominative ye is used sometimes in literature also as objective, as in Shakespeare and others.
[3] Some grammarians classify these possessives as adjectives, not pronouns; some only classify the first two rows (my-their, thy-the) as adjectives and consider the rest to be pronouns.

KEYS to Exercise 26. Excerpts from the
U.S. Government Printing Office Style Manual

KEY to Exercise 26A. Early Correctors of the Press

Live copy

It does not appear that the earliest printers had any method of correcting errors before the form was on the press. ~~The learned correctors of errors before the form was on the press.~~ The learned correctors of the first ~~twenty~~ two centuries of printing were not proofreaders in our ~~cents~~; they were rather what we would term office editors. There labors were chiefly to see that the proof corresponded to the copy, but that the printed page was correct in it's Latinity—that the words were there, and that they sense was right? They care little about orthography, bad letters, or purely printer's errors, and ~~where~~ the text seem to them wrong/ they consulted fresh authority or altar it on their ~~one~~ responsibility. Good proofs, in the modern sense, were possible until professional readers where employed—men who first had a printers education and than spent many ~~months~~ in the correction of ~~proof.~~ ~~—U.S. Government Printing Office Style Manual~~

KEY to Exercise 26B. Standardized Spelling

Live copy

The orthography of English, which for the past century has undergone little change, was very fluctuating until after the publication of ~~Webster's~~ Dictionary, and capitals, which have been used with some regularity for the past 90 years, were previously used on the hit or miss plan. The approach to regularity, so far as we have it, may be attributed to the growth of modern printing.

Johnson's

out, see copy, p. E67

KEY to Exercise 26C. The Printer's Wife

Live copy

The story is related that a certain woman in Germany, the wife of a printer/who had become disgusted with the continual assertion of the superiority of man over woman which she had heard,/hurried into the composing room while her husband was at supper and altered a sence in the Bible, which he was printing, so that it read "Narr" instead of ~~of~~ "Herr" thus making the vers read "And he shall be thy fool" instead of "And he shall be thy lord."

ten
ce

KEY to Exercise 27. Standard marks

Live copy

<u>Live copy</u>

caps / _ctr_ ⟧ERRORS IN EARLY PRINTED WORK⟦

[An erroneous] belief has been fostered in the mind of the
reader: that printing in its early days was done much better than‸ _it is_
now; that books were printed more accurately when the methods and
machinery of the art were simpler, when printers and publishers
were men of high scholarship and had‸intimate intercourse with   _more_
the literati of their time. This belief has no‸basis. The demi- _good_
_p_   gods of typograhy are like the demigods of sø-called history: the _lc_
greatest are those who are at the greatest distance. Not much
research is needed to show that demigods of all kinds do‸not
belong to history but to fiction, and that erors of the press   _r_
were, to say the least, quite as common in the early days of
typography as they are now.

_a_   With‸few exceptions, the early printers were foolishly
boastful. They bragged of the superior beauty of their types and
the greater accuracy of their texts. Gutenberg, first and best
of all, seems to have been the only one who refused to magnify
himself. Printing had been practised less than twenty years
when Peter Schoeffer, the surviving member of the ~~three~~ triumvɢrate _ʒ/i_
who developed the art, in his edition oɟ the <u>Institutes of</u>   _ɟ_
_a_   <u>Justiniꞵn</u> of 1468, reminded his readers that he paid great sums
to the wise men who corrected his texts, but he adds that there   _ʃ_
even then were‸rival printers who did not take ~~the~~ proper precautions
against errors of the press. It may be assumed that Gabriel
_a_   Petrus of Venice wꞵs one of the growing number of negligent
a book in 1478 with printers, for he published‸two pages of errata. Before the fifteenth century closed, lists of errata were frequent. Sometimes
errors were so numerous that the faulty book had to be reprinted.
_g/u_ Robert Gaꝗin of Paris was so disgusted with the mistakes made by _F/l_
a printer of that city in an edition of ₣rench legends (⌀497)   _of_
that he ordered a second edition from a printer ~~in~~ Lyons, but the
change of printer was not happy: the reprinted book was as faulty
as the first.

Cardinal Bellarmine of Rome had a provoking experience in
1581. He cancelled the first edition of his book prꝑinted at   ③
Rome, and sent an amended copy to a printer of Venicĕ, hoping to
_ʄ_   get aꜿsolutely perfect work, but the new ~~addition~~ was also full   _e_
of errors.
_d_   A book of Picus Miranꝺola, printed at Strasburg in 1507, in   _#_
the real cradle of typography, contains fifteenꝑages of errata.
_₵_   ‸The fullest list of errata known is that of a book called <u>The</u>
<u>Anatomy of the Mass</u>, printed in 1561. This book of one hundred
and seventy-two pages is followed by errata covering fifteen
pages. In apology, the writer says the errors were caused by the
malice of the devil, who had ~~aloud~~ the manuscript to be drenched _allowed_
with waꞇter and made almost illegible before it was placed in the
hands of the printers. Not content with this, the devil instigated the printers to commit a surprising number of‸excusable   _in⌣_
blunders.

align
¶

Books of authority and reference made in the sixteen century were quite as full of errors as more unpretentious work.
Joseph Scalinger said that he would frequently make a bet that he
could find an error on any chance-selected page of the Greek
Lexicon of Robert Constantine, and that he always won the bet.
Chevillier adds that Constantine was responsible for ~~just~~ as many
errors as the printer.

tr
r

The Bible, as a bulky and frequently printed book, presents
exceptional opportunity for error. An edition of the Vulgate
printed in 1590, and said to have been made under the supervision
of Pope Sixtus V, has the unenviable distinction of being full of
misprints. Barker's edition of the Bible, printed ~~in~~ London in
1632, and notorious in the trade as the Wicked Bible, gives this
rendering of the seventh commandment: Thou shalt commit adultery.
For this error, undoubtedly made by a malicious compositor, the
printer was fined three thousand ~~dollars~~, and all obtainable
copies of the edition were destroyed.[1] To prevent error, Parliament forbade all unauthorized printing of the Bible.

run on

In his Memoirs, Baron de Grimm tells of a French author who
died in a spasm of anger after he had detected more than three hundred typographical errors in a newly printed copy of his work.

It was the same spirit of mischief-making that prompted a
woman in Germany to steal into her husband's printing-house by
night and make an alteration for the ~~the~~ press by changing the
German word Herr to Narr, thereby perverting the passage in
Genesis iii, 16, from "he shall be thy lord" to "he shall be thy
fool." The story goes that she had to atone for this silly joke
with her life.

⁂
⁊
#

Errors of the press were and are not confined to any nation.
Erasmus said that the books printed in Italy were, without
exception, full of faults, due largely to the parsimony of pub-
~~pub~~lishers who would not pay a proper price for the supervision
of the copy. Books were so incorrectly printed in Spain during
the sixteenth century that the authorities refused to license
their publication before they had been approved by a censor
appointed for the duty. He required that all faults noted by
him should be corrected in an appended list of errata.

no ¶

not/all

Chevillier says that the printers of Geneva during the
sixteenth century used execrable paper and made the texts of
their books intolerably incorrect. Even the famous Christopher
Plantin of Antwerp was beyond reproach. One of his eulogists has

for overprint

[1] Sometimes errata have been made purposely to gratify personal
malignity. Paul Scarron, the French poet and writer of burlesque, wrote a book of poems in which verses were dedicated to
"Guillemette, my sisters/ dog." Before the book was published,
Scarron quarrelled with his sister, and ordered this erratum to
be added: "Make 'Guillemette, my sister's dog' read 'Guillemette,
my dog of a sister.'"

tr
lc
tr

to admit sorrowfully that he found Plantin's enormous Po/glot Bible many errors of paging which his scholarly proof-readers had overlooked.

The apology of John Froben of Basle for his errata is really pathetic: "I do everything I can to produce correct editions. In this edition of the New Testament in Greek I have doubled my care and my vigilance; I have spared neither time nor money. Erasmus himself has done his best to help me." In this edition of the New Testament in Greek I have doubled my care and my vigilance; I have spared neither time nor money.

This book was in press for a year, but after all this care it had errata of one and a half pages. I have engaged with difficulty many correctors of the highest ability, among them John Oecolampadius, a professor of three languages.

Erasmus himself charged one of the workmen of Froben with intended malice in perverting (in another book) his tribute of admiration to Queen Elizabeth of Hungry to a passage of unmentionable obscenity. He declared that he would have given three hundred crowns in gold to have prevented the scandalous error.

Examples enough have been presented to show that errors are not always detected by educated printers or by scholarly correctors, but the summing up may be left to earlier writers. Chevallier, writing in support of his proposition that a book without an error is impossible,[1] and that early books do not deserve the reputation they have had for superior accuracy. Prosper Marchand, writing in 1738, says that the reader is deceived who thinks that old books are more correct that new books; on the contrary, they are mush more inaccurate.

Theodore Low De Vinne
The Practice of Typography:
Correct Composition
Oswald Publishing Company
New York 1916

Whoever thinks a faultless piece to see,
Thinks what ne'er was, nor is, nor e'er shall be.

Pope

457

The Passionate Printer to His Love
(Whose name is Amanda)

With apologies to the shade of Christopher
Marlowe

Come live with me and be my Dear;
   And till that happy bond shall lapse,
   I'll set your Poutings in *Brevier*,
   Your Praises in the largest CAPS.

There's *Diamond*—'tis for your Eyes;
   There's *Ruby*—that will match your Lips;
   Pearl, for yor teeth; and Minion-size
   To suit your dainty Fingertips.

In Nonpareil I'll put your Face;
   In Rubric shall your Blushes rise;
   Ther is no *Bourgeois* in your Case,
   Your Form can never need "Revise,"

Your Cheek seems *"Ready for the Press"*;
   Your laugh as *Clarendon* is clear;
   There's more distinction in your Dress
   Than in the oldest *Elzevir*.

So with me live, and with me die;
   And may no "FINIS" e'er intrude
   To break into mere *"Printers Pie"*
   The Type of our Beautitude!

ERRATUM/ If my suit you flout,
   And choose some happier Youth to wed,
   'Tis but to cross AMANDA out,
   And read another name instead.)

          —Austin Dobson
          in *De Libris*
          McMillan, 1908

*Brevier, diamond, ruby, pearl, minion, nonpareil, and
bourgeois are names for type sizes used before the introduction of the point system of measurement. A *rubric* is a red
initial or line in a manuscript. A *case* is a drawer in a type
cabinet with partitions for different characters. A form is a
block of type locked up for printing. *Clarendon* is a highly
readable typeface. An *elzevir* is a book printed by the Elzevir press in the eighteenth century. Printers pie occurs
when a form is dropped and the characters are mixed up
(pied).

BILL OF FARE

Oysters or Clams on the half-shell, very small.

SOUP

a/u

s/ $\frac{3}{2}$

Consommé, Terrapin Clear Soup, *Potage à la Reine*, or *Bisque*,
Cantelope, Watermelon, Pineapple, Grape Fruit, or Oranges.

FISH

Broiled Spanish Mackerel, Shad, Striped Bass, or Blue Fish;
or, Boiled Salmon, Sheepshead, Sea Bass, Turbot, or Trout:
with Bermuda, *Hollandaise*, *Duchesse*, *Parisienne*, or Irish
Potatoes. Cucumbers.

RELISHES

Olives. Tunny-fish. Filets of Anchovies or Sardines. Stuffed
Olives. Caviare.
French Radishes. East India Gherkins. Salted Almonds.
Cheese Straws. Pickles.
Small Patties or *Bouchées* cold, with highly seasoned garnish of
fish, poultry, or game.
Fine Table-Sauces. Anchovy Butter. Celery. Small Raw
Tomatoes. Choice Cheese.

ENTRÉES AND ENTREMETS

Vol-au-vents of poultry and game, *Croquettes*, *Blanquettes*,
Scallops, *Salmis*.
Sweetbreads, broiled, fried, or stewed, with Mushrooms, Peas,
Asparagus, or Tomato Sauce.
Chicken, *fritôt*, broiled, Maryland style, with *Mayonnaise filets*,
and pinions *sautées*.

Filet of beef, larded, with Mushrooms, Spaghetti, Stuffed To-
matoes, or vegetable garnish.
Lamb Cutlets, breaded, truffled, *en papillote*, with Peas, Aspar-
agus, or Cauliflower.
Any Vegetable, stewed with a sauce. Fritters of Rice, Hom-
iny, and Flour, with sauce.
Sweet Puddings, with sauces. Charlottes. Pastry. Jellies.
Moulded Creams.
Sorbet. Sherbet. *Roman Punch*. Champagne *glacé*.

ROAST

Any Game or Game Birds roasted, and served with a green salad.

DESSERT

Ice Creams, with Canton Ginger. Water Ices. Frozen Pud-
dings of fruit and fine cake. Ices. Confectionery. Candied
Fruit. Nuts. Foreign Preserves without syrup. Oriental
Sweetmeats. Coffee.

KEY to Exercise 30. Chemistry: Synthesis of Eudalene

SYNTHESIS OF EUDALENE

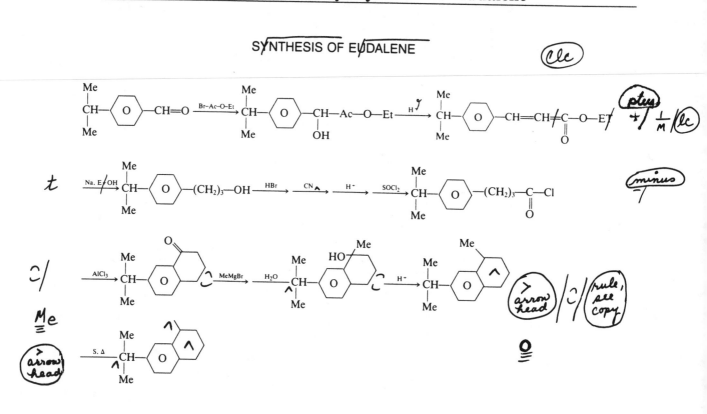

KEY to Exercise 31. Table: Market for Nuclear Plants

FIGURE 6—MARKET FOR NUCLEAR PLANTS BY SIZE OF UNIT (1981–1990)

Capacity, MW	150	200	250	300	400	500	600	800	1000	1200	1500	Total GW
India								4	6	15		27.2
Spain									5	5	6	20.0
Poland				5				2	1	2		7.0
Brazil								2	2	6		10.8
Czechoslovakia				2			3	1	2	2		7.8
Yugoslavia							2	6	4			10.0
Romania				5			2		2			5.2
Mexico							1	4	6	8	^	20.9
Argentina							2	3	3			6.6
Bulgaria					4		4	2				5.6
Iran							3	4	5			10.0
Taiwan							7	4				7.4
Hungary					6		3					4.2
Venezuela							6	1				4.4
Korea							5	2	4			8.5
Turkey							3	4				5.0
Colombia						1	2					1.7
Greece						4	5					5.0
Pakistan							8					4.8
Egypt							7	1				5.0
Israel					6	3						3.9
Thailand		1		1	1	2	3					3.7
Peru					2	1						1.3
Philippines							2	2	2			4.8
Hong Kong				2	4	2						3.2
Chile				3	2							1.7
Cuba			2	4	1							2.1
Singapore			5		6		1					4.3
Malaysia		3	1	3								1.7
Indonesia		4		3								1.7
Rep. Viet Nam	1	4										1.0
Bangladesh		2	2		2	1	3					4.0
Uruguay	1	2	2									1.1
Kuwait	2	4	1									1.4
Iraq	2	4										1.1
Jamaica	5	2		2								1.7
Ghana	2											0.3
Morocco		2										0.4
Nigeria	2	1										0.5
Algeria	3											0.45
Lebanon	0											0.
Syria	3											0.45
Cameroon	0											0
Costa Rica	2											0.3
Dominican Rep	1											0.15
Ecuador	1											0.15
Panama	1											0.15
Albania	1											0.15
Uganda	1											0.15
Tunisia	1											0.15
Bolivia	1											0.15
Zambia	1											0.15
Saudi Arabia	1											0.15
Guatemala	1											0.15
Liberia	1											0.15
El Salvador	1											0.15
Sudan	0											0.
Number of Units	35	29	13	18	46	14	72	42	42	38	7	356
Total Capacity, GW	5.3	5.8	3.3	5.4	18.4	7.0	43.2	34.4	42.0	45.6	10.5	220.0

SOURCE: Market Survey for Nuclear Power in Developing Countries: General Report published September 1973/ Update Report published 1974.

Reports available from the International Atomic Energy Agency and its agents.

EPINEPHRINE PHYSIOLOG

[marginal marks: ꞓ y]

The manifold catabolic effects of epinephrine are due in part to an amplification cascade of the molecule's signal via a pathway involving 3′,5′-monophosphate (cAMP) as a second messenger.

[margin: ⌢ / / ⊙]

Cyclic AMP is formed by the reaction of adynl cyclase, a membrane-bound enzyme, on ATP. The reaction is slightly endergonic, driven by the hydrolysis of pyrophosphate.

[margin: adenyl]

The hormone's principle site of action is the exterior surface of the plasma membrane. Epinephrine (10^{-10}M to 10^{-8}M) bind to a specific receptor, allosterically activating pro-adynl cyclase, which then catalyzes the synthesis of cAMP at a maximum concentration of 10^{-6}M. inactive protein kinase is bound to cAMP, releasing its regulatory subunit, disinhibiting its catalytic subunit. Active protein kinase then catalyzes the phosphorylation of dephosphophosphorylase kinase, in the presence of CA^{++}, which in turn activates phosphorylase b, yielding phosphorylase a. Finally, phosphorylase a acts on glycogen to yield glucose-1-phosphate, which, after isomerization to glucose-6-phosphate and dephosphorylation, is secreted from the hepatacyte into the blood. Of course, with the exceptions of the initial binding, the isomerization, and the dephosphoryltion, the reactions are endergonic. Since each step is catalytic, the net effect is one of amplification of signal.

[margin: principal (?) ne⌢ ℓ/ ꞓ/ ⓛⲥ ꞕ/₃ a in the process]
[margin right: ⒯ₛ/₃ cs adenyl ꞓ =/ ⌢// m σ]

Epinephrine and the other catecholamines are bound to ATP and the other catecholamines are bound to ATP and proteins and stored in grains in the medulla. Acetylcholine released from the pre/ganglionic neurons increase the permeability of the secretory cells to Ca^{++} in the extracellular fluids, triggering exocytosis.

[margin: ꞓ ꞕ granules ꞓ⌂]

Epinephrine physiology thus has a two-fold significance/ Release is triggered by a nervous impulse, meeting the need for a quick response; and mediation by cAMP amplifies its small quantity to a general metabolic defect.

[margin: :/ ⓛⲥ ef]

KEY to Exercise 33. Special material

A. Financial statement:

Fairfax Sunday College
Income Statement
For Year Ended December 31, 1992

Revenues
Tuition Fees Earned	$527,000	
Endowment Income	42,200	
		$569,200

Operating Expenses
Salaries Expense	$231,500	
Rent Expense	90,000	
Office Suppies Expense	1,375	
Utilities expense	1,900	
Miscellaneous Expense	274	
Total Operating Expense		$325,049
Net Income		$244,511

[handwritten margin notes: l, Cap?, add #?, align?, tr ?]

[handwritten notes: Office Suppies — ^, Utilities expense — caret/underline, $244,511 — struck/corrected]

B. Text for a bronze plaque to be placed on a vehicle:

In Fond Memory of
Dr. George Jason Jemiston,
His Friends
Have Donated This Mobile Medical Unit to
Feathersville Area Emergency Services, Inc.
(FACES)
Honoring the Doctor's Lifelong Commitment
To Serve his Community

[handwritten margin notes: add word ?, what does c stand for ?, #]

C. Headlines:

1. BAN ON SOLICITING ~~DEAD~~ IN TROTWOOD   STOPPED (?)
2. BEATING WITNESS PROVIDES NAMES
3. ALL UTAH CONDEMNED TO FACE FIRING SQUAD   FELONS (?)
4. BABY ~~NAMED AFTER~~ HER COUSIN   GIVEN/CS NAME (?)
5. WOMAN HELD IN FIRE   AS WITNESS (?)
6. DOCTOR TESTIFIES IN HORSE ~~SUIT~~   CASE (?)
7. ~~POLICE KILL~~ MAN WITH AX   KILLED BY POLICE (?)
8. POLICE ~~RUN DOWN~~ SPEEDERS   CATCH (?)

=/

KEY to Exercise 34. Sorted material: Directory and Miscellaneous Publishers

S038 .
S038 .
S038

Managing Editor
. Managing Editor
. Managing Editor
Bureau of Bus. Practice
. Van Dyck Printing Co.
. New York Graphic Soc *Ltd*
24 Rope ^ Ferry Rd.
. 370 State st.
. 140 Greenwich Ave.
Waterford CT 06386
. North Haven CT 06473
. Greenwich CT 06830

(less #)

S038 .
S038 .
S038

Managing Editor
. Managing Editor
. *Managing Editor*
Gibson C R Co Inc
. Martindale-Hubbell Inc.
Music Sales Corp.
32 Knight St
. 630 Central Ave.
799 Broadway
Norwalk CT 06956
. New Providence NJ 07974 .
New York NY 10003 000 *(zeros)*

S038 .
S038 .
S0388 *3*

Managing Editor
. Managing Editor
. Managing Editor
American Elsevier Publ.
. Simplicity Pattern Co.
. Ziff-Davis Publishing Co
2 Park Ave.
. 200 Madison Ave.
. One Park Ave.
New York NY 10016
. New York NY 10016
. New York NY 100016

S038 .
S038 .
Managing Editor

Managing Editors
. Managing Editor
. Managing Editor
Brentano's Inc.
. McCall Publishing Co.
. Concord Reference Books
545 Fifth Ave.
. 230 Park Ave.
. 135 W. 50th St.
New York NY 10017
. New York NY 10017
. New York NY 10020

S038 .
S038 .
S038

Managing Editor
. Managing Editor
. Managing Editor
Whitney Communications
. Allied Graphic Arts Inc
. Catalogue Srv Westchester
110 W 51st St.
. 1515 Broadway
. 159 Main St.
New York NY 10020
. New York NY 10036
. New Rochelle NY 10801

S038 .
S038 .
S038

Managing Editor *Natural*
. Managing Editor
. Managing Editor
Wards ~~National~~ Science
. Packard Press Corp. *P*
. Bureau of Natl Affairs
5100 Henrietta Rd.
. 10th & Spring Garden Sts .
1231 25th St. N.W.
Rochester NY 14622
. Philadelphia PA 19122
. Washington DC 20037

S038 .
S038 .
S038

Managing Editor
. Managing Editor
. Managing Editor
Aspen Systems Corp.
. Real Estate Data Inc.
. ThunderGrass Music Ltd.
20010 Century Blvd.
. 2398 N.W. 119th St.
. 3340 Broadway
Germantown MD 20767
. Miami FL 33167
. Riviera Beach FL 33404

S038 .
S038 .
S038

Managing Editor
. Managing Editor
. Managing Editor
Am. Printng Hse fr Blind
. Grandville Printing Co.
. Sidwell Co. Inc.
1839 Frankfurt Ave.
. 4520 Spartan Industrial
. 28 W. 240 North Ave.
Louisville KY 40206
. Grandville MI 49418
. West Chicago IL 60185

S0378 .
S038 .
S038

Managing Editor
. Managing Editor
. Managing Editor
Official Airlines Guides
. Inter-Collegiate Press
. Pace Publication Arts
20000 Clearwater Dr.
. 6015 Travis Lane
. 3531 Miraloma *E*
Oak Brook IL 60621
. Shawnee Mission KS 66202.
Anaheim CA 92806

out, see copy
audio-Digest
General Telephone Directory

1.   Other show business personalities who lending their names to
good causes are happy—and indeed inwardly content—merely to
be listed on the notepaper and to
make occasional speeches.

lend /(?)

2.   With your right hand,
take ahold of lever A.

hold /(?)

3.   A look at the issues
and consequences of
last fall's prolonged
teachers' strike at
Levitttown.

Levitttown /(?) (3 t's)

4.   Application of these methods in stores in San Diego and
Houston have resulted in a 30
percent drop in robberies.

has /(?)
(application ... has)

5. *Bookkeeping*
Interested in pro-
ducing your own
honey? Two courses
on beekeeping will
be offered by the
Beekeeper's Associ-
ation of Northern
Virginia in conjunc-
tion with the
County extension
service at

Beekeeping /(?)

6. Intenational and Unintentional Modification of
the Atmosphere

Intenational /(?)

7. Parishóners Celebrate

Parishoners / ?

8. A total of forty-seven interviews were conducted with approximate equal coverage of the four countries in the report.

was / ?

total ... was

9. In order to elicit specific responses, we selected for each respondent a sub-sample of between five and ten documents that had been sent to the respondents' office.

respondent(s)' / ?

singular

10. TABLE 4.1.—PERCEPTION OF ROLE IN FOREIGN POLICY REPORTING SYSTEM

Role	# of Producers	% of Total Producers
Reporter	20	42.6%
Research Analyst	12	25.5%
Operational-Administrative	7	14.9%
Combination of Two of the Above	8	17.0%
	47	100.0

ctr head over col

align

% already in col. head

∫ ?

add rules

add ld above foot rule

set total ?

KEY to Exercise 36. AAs and PEs

Live copy

The rule for making printer's errors (PEs) only—to the exclusion of author's errors (AAs)—was first recorded in 1608 by Jerome Hornisch of the Beyer printing office in Meiningen, germany. Writing of "a conscientious corrector," he said, "Never should he make changes in the text, even though he believes it would be improved thereby." The same rule applies to a compositor, of course. As Joseph Moxon wrote (in Mechanick Exercises on the Whole Art of Print, 1683–84), "By the Laws of Printing, a Compositor is strictly to follow his Copy, viz. to observe and do just so much and no more than his Copy will bear him out for; so that his Copy is to be his rule and Authority."

Unlike today, however, in Moxon's time and later, the Laws of Printing required compositors and proofreaders to correct bad spelling and punctuation. To quote Moxon on the compositor's responsibility in the 17th century—

> The carelessness of some good Authors, and the ignorance of other Authors, has forced Printers to introduce a Custom, which among them is look'd upon as a task and duty incumbent on the Compositor, viz. to discern and amend the bad Spelling and Pointing of his Copy, if it be English; But if it be in any Forrain Language, the Author is wholy left to his own Skill and Judgment in Spelling and Punctuation.

And to quote *The Inland Printer* of May 1897 on "The Proofreader's Responsibilities":

> Strictly speaking, the responsibility of a proofreader should be narrowly defined. In an ideal state of affairs it would never go beyond the close following of copy in every detail . . . The limit [of the proofreader' responsibility . . . is merely the exact reproduction of what is written, as to wording, but including proper spelling and punctuation.

Print shops today put more limits on responsibility; they expect compositors and comparison proofreader to "follow copy out the window"—even though correct spelling and punctuation go out the window, too.

As another article in the September 1897 *Inland Printer* says, "You must remember that the customers of printing offices think they know a thing or two, and nothing is gained by doing their work in such a manner as to arouse their antagonism . . . no matter how much more you may know about how it ought to be done."

A solution to the problem is querying. Says the earlier *Inland Printer*: "Even hurried work from manuscript can generally be referred to the author in cases of real doubt . . . Submission of [queries] to the author for his decision should be an unimportant feature of the proofreader's responsibility."

Live copy

S ‖   *¶* / **De Vinne on Errors of the Press**

Errors of the press often begin with errors of
reporters who have misunderstood spoken words.
The rule of follow copy compels the compositor to
repeat the exact words written by the reporter, and
the following blunders are the result of obedience
to this rule. A speaker made this statement:

S

   In these days clergyman are expected to have the
   wisdom and learning of Jeremey Taylor.

e   *S*

But the reporter wrote, and the compositor
repeated:

   ...the wisdom and learning of a journeyman tailor.

Another speaker quoted these: *lines*

   O come, thou goddess fair and free,
   In heaven yclept Euphrosyne.

c

They were printed as written:

   O come, thou goddess fair and free,
tr   In heaven she crept and froze her knee.

Another orator quoted this line from Tennyson's
Locksley Hall:

   Better fifty years of Europe than a cycle of Cathy.   *a*

But the quotation was written and printed:

   Better fifty years of Europe than a circus in
   Bombay.

One of the worst perversions of a hackneyed quotation (incorrectly given by the speaker) is this, which
seems to be the joint work of the zeal reporter and   *ous*
the equally reckless printer:

   Amicus Plato, amicus Socrates, sed major veritas.   *⊃/*
   I may cuss Plato, I may cuss Socrates, said Major
   Veritas.

Here are the other illustrations of the danger of the following the sound regardless of the sense:

> Those lovely eyes bedimmed
> Those lovely eyes be damned.
> Behold the matry in a sheet of fire
> Behold the martyr in a shirt on fire
> This battle-scarred veteran.
> This battle-scared veteran.

A congress advocated grants of public lands, not to railroad corporations, but to "actual settlers." The tired translater of the telegraphic report of the speech construed the last words as "cattle stealers."

An editor close his leader concerning some municipal abuse that he wished to reform with the quoted Latin lament, o tempora of mores which the compositor transformed to "O temporance O Moses," and it was so printed.

A reporter of a trial tried to write that "the jury

~~Examples of gross modern blunders 353~~

disagreed and were discharged," but he wrote indistinctly, and the compositor construed the writing into "the jury disappeared and were disgraced."

A petitioner appealed to a legislature as "individuals" as well as lawmakers. He wrote illegibly, and the clerk read "indian devils" instead of individuals, much to the indignation of the assembly.

Drew attributes these blunders to bad writing:

The book Antiquities was cited as Topographical Ambiguities.

In testimony concerning a compound microscope the witness said its efficiency would vary with the power of the "eye-piece" employed. Eye-piece was to carelessly written, and the compositor rendered it as lye-juice.

At a public dinner this toast was offered to the President, "May he live to a gree old age." But it was printed, "May he live to a grim old age."

---

[1] Pendleton, Newspaper Reporting, pp. 172-183.
[2] Pens and Types, pp. 16-24.

The last words of the poorly written sentence, "Alone and isolated, man would become impotent and perish," were not understood by the compositor, and they were printed as "impatient and peevish|"

A bloody battle was so described in a newspaper:

It was fearful to see. The men feel in ranks and marched in pantaloons to their final account.

It is probable that the compoisotr did not know the word platoon, and thought it proper to make this foolish correction. It must have been a raw compositor of this class who set Dogs of the Sein for Days of the Legue, and parboiled sceptic for purblind sceptic. These wild guesses at the meaning of the writer had to be hazarded when writing was indistinct.

Many pages could be filled with illustrations of similar blunders—some silly or unmeaning, other frightful or blasphemous—but in most instances it is evident that the blunders were the outcome of careless or illegible writing. The compositor who is told to follow copy learns to do so mechanically, even if his rendering does not "make sense."

. . . Even when exceeding care has been taken . . . there is liability to error from oversights and unforeseen accidents. Crapelet tell us of the sore distress of his father in discovering the error, Pelenope for Penelope, in a treatise which he had carefully read three times with intent to make it in all points a faultless book. He had read it too often; he did not have the assistance of a second reader; and his memory failed when most needed. Even the careful reader may pass unobserved the transposition of letters or syllables in a proper name. ippking too intently on one object does not always make that object more distinct; it may produce temporary obscurity| Proof read and correct too often by one reader only may have errors in the last proof that did not exist in the first.

. . . Errors are frequently made by the compositor who correct a proof in trying to correct one error he may make another. Whenever he makes any change in type that has not been marked on the proof, he should take another proof and draw a large ring with lead-pencil around the place of change, and the proof-reader should re-read the entire paragraph by copy as if it were new composition.

Études pratiques et litteraires sur la typographie

po 233

... Authors who correct the final proof with a lead-pencil provoke the making of new errors. They note an error in phrasing and write down their correction. After re-reading this correction they see that it does not fully convey the meaning intended. The first pencil markings are rubbed, other words take their place. Sometime two or three alterations have to be made, and all are written over markings previously made. Repeated rubbing out makes the writing illegible and liable to perversion. Sometimes an addition is made to a singular nominative which should compel the selection of a plural form of verb or pronoun in the words that precede or follow, but the plural forms may be and often are overlooked... It follows that the author as well as the printer has to suffer the stigma of an inexcusable violation of plain grammatical rules.[1]

---

[1] Here is the study of an error not made by a compisetor or reader, pressman or mischiefmaker. An author, intent on having an immaculate book, and not intent with the official reading of the printing-house, had the last proof revised by another expert reader, who certified that the last reading was without fault. The book was bound and distributed, and bragged of as a book without an error. A year after publication the author, in making a cursory reexamination of the work, discovered the phrase, "his too nasty steps." Filed with anger and alarm, he went to the printing-house and demanded the reason why this shocking alteration had been made. The last proof was found and it plainly showed that the phrase was "his too hasty steps." It was clear that a change had been made later the final reading, and possibly in the electrotype plate. The plate was sent for, and when closely examined under a magnifying-glass, revealed the origin of the error. The solder which fastened the copper shell to the lead base, was unseen and unsuspected by the electrotyper. Some copies of the book (how many could not be ascertained) showed that letter h accurately, but after several perfect copies had been printed, a knot in the paper or a grain of sand or plaster had fallen over the top of this letter h, and had crushed or depressed it in the hollow air-bubble below, practically changing it to the letter n. This depession of the letter h was too small a fault to be noticed by the pressman, who could give but a glance at the sheets when the press was printing apparently faultless copies at the rate of fifteen in a minute.

KEY to Exercise 38. Aldus Manutius

ALDUS MANUTIUS

error 1

c

(Exerpted from <u>Books and Their Makers During the Middle Ages</u> by
Geo. Haven Putnam, reprinted from an 1896-1897 edition by
Hillary House Publishers of New York in 1962)

Aldus Manutius was born at Bassiano in the Romagna in
1450, the year in which Gutenberg completed his printing-
press. He studied in Rome and in Ferrara, and after having
mastered Latin, he devoted himself, under the tutorship of
Guarini of Verona, to the study of Greek. Later, he delivered lectures on the Latin and Greek classics. One of his
fellow students in Ferrara was the precocious young scholar
Pico della Mirandola, whose friendship was afterward of material service. In 1482, when Ferrara was being besieged by
the Venetians and scholarly pursuits were interrupted, Aldus
was the guest of Pico at Mirandola, where he met Emanuel
Adramyttenos, one of the many Greek scholars who, when
driven out of Constantinople, had found refuge in the Courts
of Italian princes. Aldus spent two years at Mirandola, and
under the influence and guidance of Adramyttenos, he largely
increased his knowledge of the language and literature of
Greece. His friend had brought from the East a number of
manuscripts, many of which found their way into the library
of Pico.

error 2

cs

(3) o

In 1482, Aldus took charge of the education of the sons
of the Princess of Carpi, a sister of Pico, and the zeal and
scholarly capacity which he devoted to the task won for him
the life-long friendship of both mother and sons. It was in
Carpi that Aldus developed the scheme of utilising his
scholarly knowledge and connections for the printing of
Latin and Greek classics. The plan was a bold one for a
young scholar without capital. Printing and publishing constituted a practically untilled field of business, not merely

(4)

(tr)

for Aldus but for Italy. Everything had to be created or developed: knowledge of the art of printing and of all the technicalities of book-manufacturing; fonts of type, Roman and Greek; a force of type-setters and pressmen and a staff of skilled revisers and proof-readers; a collection of trustworthy texts to serve as "copy" for the compositors; and last, but by no means least, a book-buying public and a book-selling machinery by which such a public could be reached.

It was the aim of Aldus, as he himself expressed it, to rescue from oblivion the words of the classic writers, the monuments of human intellect. He writes in 1490: "I have resolved to devote my life to the cause of scholarship. I have chosen in place of a life of ease and freedom, an anxious and toilsome career. A man has higher responsibilities than the seeking of his own enjoyment; he should devote himself to honourable labour. Living that is a mere existence can be left to men who are content to be animals. Cato compared human existence ~~can be left to men who are content to be animals. Cato compared human existence~~ to iron. When nothing is done with it, it rusts; it is only through constant activity that polish or brilliance is secured.

The world has probly never produced a publisher who ~~un-tied~~ with these high ideals and exceptional scholarly attainments, so much practical business ability and persistent pluck.

The funds required for the undertaking were furnished by the Princess of Carpi and her sons, probably with some co-operation from Pico, and in 1494, Aldus organised his printing-office in Venice. His first publication, issued in 1495, was the Greek and Latin Grammar of Laskaris, a suitable forerunner for his great classical series. The second issue from his Press was an edition of the Works of Aristotle, the first volume of which was also completed in 1495.

This was followed in 1496 by the Greek Grammar of Gaza, and in 1497 by a Greek-Latin Dictionary compiled by Aldus himself.)

run back

11 not

The business cares of those first years of his printing business were allowed to prevent him from going on with his personal studies. In 1502, he published, in a handsome quarto volume, a comprehensive grammar under the title of

12 a

Rudiment Grammatices Linguae Latinae, etc. cum Introductione ad Hebraicam Linguam, to the preparation of which he had devoted years of arduous labour. Piratical editions were promptly issued in Florence, Lyons, and Paris. He also wrote the Grammaticae Institutiones Graecae (a labour of some years), which was not published until 1515, after the death of the author.

It will be noted that nearly all the undertakings to which he gave, both as editor and as publisher, his earliest attention, were the necessary first steps in the great scheme of the complete series of the Greek classics. Before editors or proof-readers could go on with the work of pre-paring the Greek texts for the press, dictionaries and gram-mars had to be created. Laskaris, whose Grammar initiiated the series, was a refugee from the East, and at the time of the publication of his work, was an instructor in Messina. No record has been preserved of the arrangement made with him by his Venetian publisher, a deficiency that is the more to be regretted as his Grammar was probably the very first work by a living author, printed in Italy. Gaza was a native of Greece, and was for a time associated with the Aldine Press as a Greek editor.

13

14

In 1500, Aldus married the daughter of the printer Andrea Torresano of Asola, . . . the successor of the Frenchman Jenson and the purchaser of Jenson's matrices. In 1507, the two printing concerns were united, and the savings of Torresano were utilised to strengthen the resources of

Aldus, which had become impaired, probably through his too
great optimism and publishing enterprise.

During the disastrous years of 1509-1511, in which
Venice was harassed by the wars resulting from the League of
Cambray, the business came to a stand-still, partly because
the channels of distribution for the books were practically
blocked, but (also partly) on accout of the exaustion of the
available funds. Friends again brought to the publisher the
aid of which, on the ground of his public-spirited under
takings, he was so well entitled, and he was enabled, after
the peace of 1511, to proceed with the completion of his
Greek classics. Before his death in 1515, Aldus had issued
in this series the works of Aristotle, Plato, Homer, Pindar,
Euripides, Sophocles, Aristophanes, Demosthenes, Lysias,
Aeschines, Herodotus, Thucydides, Xenophon, Plutarch, and
others, in addition to a companion series of the works of
the chief Latin writers. The list of publications included
in all some 100 different works, comprised (in their several
editions) in about 250 volumes. Considering the special
difficulties of the times and the exceptional character of
the original and creative labour that was required to secure
the texts, to prepare them for the press, to print them
correctly, and to bring them to the attention of possible
buyers, this list of undertakings is, in my judgment, by far
the greatest and the most honourable in the whole history
of publishing.

It was a disadvantage for carrying on scholarly publishing undertakings in Venice, that the city possessed no
university, a disadvantage that was only partly offset by
the proximity of Padua, which early in the fifteenth century
had come under Venetian rule. A university would of course
have been of service to a publisher like Aldus, not only
supplying a home market for his books, but in placing at his

disposal scholarly assistants whose services could be utilised in editing the texts and in supervising their typesetting. The correspondence of members of a university with
the scholars of other centres of learning, could be made
valuable also in securing information as to available manuscripts and concerning scholarly undertakings generally. In
the absence of a university circle, Aldus was obliged to depend upon his personal efforts to bring him into relations,
through correspondence, with men of learning throughout
Europe, and to gather about the Aldine Press a group of
scholarly associates and collaborators.

Scoring

Speed

The keyboarder took 20 minutes. To figure how your proofreading speed relates to the keyboarding speed (in terms of percentage), divide the number of minutes it took you to proofread this exercise by 20, and multiply the answer by 100.

You may want to do the computation twice: first, for comparison proofreading excluding reviewing and checking; second, for the total time including reviewing and checking.

The formula is:

$$\frac{\text{proofreading time}}{\text{keyboarding time}} \times 100 = \begin{array}{l}\text{proofreading speed} \\ \text{as \% of keyboarding speed}\end{array}$$

Accuracy

Compare your proofreading marks with the answer key. Count the number of errors you marked (one *out* or one *repeater,* no matter how long, counts as one error, as does one wrong word division).

There are 22 errors to be caught. To figure your percentage of accuracy, divide the number of errors you caught by 22, and multiply the answer by 100.

This is the formula:

$$\frac{\text{number of errors marked}}{\text{number of existing errors}} \times 100 = \% \text{ accuracy}$$

Index